SELECTIONS FROM

HOUSEHOLD HINTS & HANDY TIPS

SELECTIONS FROM

HOUSEHOLD HINTS & HANDY TIPS

Reader's Digest

THE READER'S DIGEST ASSOCIATION, INC.

PLEASANTVILLE, NEW YORK • MONTREAL

SELECTIONS FROM
HOUSEHOLD
HINTS &
HANDY TIPS

The acknowledgments that appear on pages 231–232 and the
Contents page are hereby made a part of this copyright page.

This book consists of selected chapters from *Household Hints & Handy Tips*,
originally published in 1988.

ISBN 0-89577-683-9

Third Printing, October 1996
Printed in the United States of America

STAFF

Project Editor
Sally French

Project Art Director
Joel Musler

Associate Editors
Ben Etheridge
Suzanne E. Weiss
Gerald Williams

Assistant Editor
Thomas A. Ranieri

Art Associate
Perri DeFino

Research Editor
Mary Jane Hodges

Editorial Assistant
James Beran

Reader's Digest General Books

Editor in Chief
John A. Pope, Jr.

Managing Editor
Jane Polley

Art Director
David Trooper

Group Editors
Norman B. Mack
Joel Musler (Art)
Susan J. Wernert

Chief of Research
Monica Borrowman

Copy Chief
Edward W. Atkinson

Picture Editor
Robert J. Woodward

Rights and Permissions
Dorothy M. Harris

Head Librarian
Jo Manning

CONTRIBUTORS

Editors
Virginia Colton
Don Earnest

Writers
Therese Hoehlein Cerbie
Michael Chotiner
Thomas Christopher
Anne Falivena
William E. Hague
Lorna B. Harris
Sherwood Harris
Susan C. Hoe
Lilla Pennant
Mort Schultz
Elizabeth Tener
Karen Theroux
John Warde
Daniel E. Weiss

Copy Editor
Elaine Andrews

Artists
Janice Belove
Joe Dyas
John Gist
Linda Gist
David Hurley
Ed Lipinski
Max Menikoff
Angel Pellegrino
Ken Rice
John Saporito
Bill Shortridge
Ray Skibinski
Vladimir Art Studio

Researcher
Mary Lyn Maiscott

Indexer
Sydney Wolfe Cohen

Testers
Ann Rafferty
Virginia Taylor

Consultants
Jean Anderson
Sherri Austin
Jennifer Birckmayer
John L. Costa, M.D., F.A.A.P.
Sheila Danko
Clark E. Garner
Michael Garvey, D.V.M.,
  Dip. A.C.V.I.M.
Mark Gasper
Leon Grabowski
Walter A. Grub, Jr.
George E. Harlow, Ph.D.
Sara M. Hunt, Ph.D., R.D.
Elliot Justin, M.D.
Carolyn Klass
Joseph Laquatra, Ph.D.
Walter LeStrange
Jim McCann
Jean McLean
Norman Oehlke
Mary E. Purchase, Ph.D.
Peter G. Rose
Gertrude Rowland
Victor J. Selmanowitz, M.D.
Stanley H. Smith, Ph.D.
Janis Stone, Ph.D.
Marco Polo Stufano
Michael Paul Wein, CPA
Paul Weissler, SAE
Thomas A. Wilson, D.D.S.
Gabriel S. Zatlin, M.D.

The editors thank the following for their assistance:
Herb Barndt, Ph.D.
Ted R. Peck
David M. Kopec, Ph.D.
Jack E. Masingale
Julie Pryme
Damon Sgobbo
Louis Sorkin, Ph.D.

About this book

Here is a book packed with thousands of useful hints and expert tips. You can count on it to make your life easier—whether you are an on-the-go career person, a harried homemaker, a neophyte do-it-yourselfer, or someone experienced at juggling job, home, family, and friends.

Some sections of this book—such as Keeping Records, Managing Money (p.21)—suggest blueprints for turning routine chores into easy procedures.

In all sections you'll find help in dealing with specific problems, even crises. For example, what if the kitchen sink won't drain when you're expecting dinner guests? Turn to the opening page of Chapter 2 (p.70), and there, under All Around the House, you'll see listed "Unclogging drains." Then flip through the pages and scan the bold headings; you'll soon discover an illustrated step-by-step description of what to do.

But suppose you don't find the answer right away. Then look in the index under Drains (or under Plumbing) to locate the correct page. You'll find similar help for a host of other problems, including lost or stolen credit cards (p.30), a burn on your carpet (p.96), and a flooded basement (p.119).

In a real emergency you won't have time to look in a book, or the book may not be handy. So it's best to know in advance how to handle a situation. Right now is a good time to learn what to do if

Fat catches fire on the stove   p.106
You smell the odor of gas   p.139
Your brakes fail   p.198

It's also a good idea to read how you can make your home safer, and thus *prevent* emergencies. Burglarproof your home (p.128); prevent accidents in the bathroom (p.113) and the workshop (p.183); know how to turn off electric power (p.163) and how to use a ladder properly (p.171). A little organization goes a long way in helping you deal with the unexpected too. Most common road emergencies, for instance, can be handled with a simple tool kit (p.200).

But this book has a purpose well beyond helping you handle or prevent drastic events. You'll find an enormous variety of hints that you'll turn to again and again for help with all the vexing and perplexing difficulties of daily life.

—*The Editors*

Contents

The editors are grateful to the following for information and guidance:

American Apparel
  Manufacturers Association
American Council for an Energy
  Efficient Economy
American Ladder Institute
American Textile Manufacturers
  Institute
American Wool Council
APC Corporation
Armour-Dial Company
Association of Home Appliance
  Manufacturers
Borden Chemical, Borden, Inc.
Broan Mfg. Co., Inc.
The Carpet and Rug Institute
Clorox Co.
Con Edison
Cooperative Extension Service,
  New York State, Cornell
  University
Cooperative Extension Service,
  Washington State University
General Electric Company

Georgia-Pacific Corporation
Gold Seal Co.
Good Housekeeping Institute
The Handy Hint Journal
Hill's Pet Products Inc.
Home Center Institute/National
  Retail Hardware Association
International Fabricare
  Institute
International Linen Promotion
  Commission
International Silk
  Association-U.S.A.
Johnson Wax, Consumer
  Services Center
Lever Brothers Company
The Maytag Company
National Broiler Council
National Paint & Coatings
  Association
National Turkey Federation
Neckwear Association of
  America

Neighborhood Cleaners
  Association
New York State Energy Office
Porcelain Enamel Institute
The Procter & Gamble Company
Sears Roebuck and Co.
The Soap and Detergent
  Association
Texize, Division of Morton
  Norwich
U. S. Department of Agriculture,
  Science and Education
  Administration
The Wallcovering Information
  Bureau
Western Wood Products
  Association
Whirlpool Corporation
The Wool Bureau Inc.,
  U.S. Branch of International
  Wool Secretariat

CHAPTER ONE

GETTING ORGANIZED

Take a look at these great ideas for organizing your household, keeping personal records, and managing money. Find out how to get the most out of storage space, and the best ways to install shelves and other storage systems.

Keeping Records, Managing Money
Page 21

Your personal records; what to keep in permanent files; developing a filing system; taking an inventory of your home; what to keep in a safe-deposit box; setting up a home business office; writing checks and reconciling bank statements; budgeting; paying bills and dealing with incorrect bills; lost or stolen credit cards; establishing credit; your credit rights; choosing a doctor, lawyer, and other professionals; calculating your net worth; life insurance; financial investments; tips on Social Security and retirement; wills.

Storing It All Away
Page 35

Storage guidelines; how to find new storage space; solving entryway, living room, and kitchen clutter; getting the most use out of your bedroom closets; remodeling a closet; ideas for storage in children's rooms, bathrooms, halls, and attics; how to build rollaway storage units; how to locate wall studs and fasten storage to them; fasteners for hollow walls and masonry; hooks and hangers and how to install them; working with pegboard; buying lumber, plywood, and other shelf materials and hardware; planning and installing shelves and their supports; wire wall systems; how to build cabinets and cases; buying nails and screws; drawer organizers and slides; rollouts and pullouts.

Organizing Your Household
Page 9

The value of making lists; a self-test of how organized you are; making an organizer with a loose-leaf binder; saving time on the telephone; simplifying errands; chores you can accomplish in a matter of minutes; handling your mail efficiently; organizing housework; what to do when company is coming; hiring outside help; how to motivate the kids to pitch in; running a successful garage sale; ways to avoid clutter and massive cleanups.

Organizing Your Household

THE FIRST STEP IS YOU

Getting organized is not an end in itself. There is no "right" way to do things—unless it's right for you. It must fit your style, your energy, and your schedule. Whatever system helps you to function most effectively is the best one for you.

Beware of the tail wagging the dog situation—in which the appointment book, the budget and expenditures records, the filing system, and the master list take more time to maintain than working out the problems they're supposed to solve.

Are you a morning person or a night person? Your efficiency may increase if you arrange your tasks as much as possible around the rhythms of your body. Try scheduling top-priority projects during your peak hours, routine work during your "low" time.

The key is to start now, no matter what! If you have a call to make, start dialing. A letter to write? Start typing.

Use the salami method to reach your goal. If the size of your project overwhelms you, tackle it a piece at a time. You wouldn't eat a salami whole, would you? You'd cut it into slices. Do the same thing with your big projects.

THE MASTER LIST

To organize your family's activities and to keep track of everyone's schedule, put up a large poster-sized master calendar that displays a full year. Enter all important family dates—birthdays, anniversaries, holidays—at the beginning of the year. Also enter appointments, as they are made, for everyone in your family.

Buy a notebook small enough to carry with you at all times. This notebook becomes your master list—a single continuous list that replaces those little scraps of paper. In the notebook, keep track of errands, appointments, things to do or buy, and items that will require action. As they approach, transfer dates from your master calendar to the notebook.

Shop around in stationery and office-supply stores for the notebook that best suits you. You'll probably be pleasantly surprised at the variety available these days.

9

HOW ORGANIZED ARE YOU?

1. Does it often take you more than 10 minutes to unearth a particular letter, bill, report, or other paper from your files or the top of your desk?

2. Are there loose papers on your desk, other than reference materials, that you haven't looked at for a month or more?

3. Has your electricity, gas, or telephone ever been turned off because you forgot to pay the bill?

4. Within the last 2 months, have you overlooked a scheduled appointment, an anniversary, or some other date that you wanted to acknowledge?

5. Do magazines pile up unread?

6. Do you frequently put off a work assignment for so long that it becomes an emergency or a panic situation?

7. Do you frequently misplace your keys, eyeglasses, gloves, handbag, briefcase, or other commonly carried items?

8. Do belongings gather in corners of closets, or on the floor, because you can't decide where to put them?

9. Would your storage problems be solved if only you had more space?

10. Do you want to get organized but everything is in such a mess that you don't know where to start?

11. Do your children have household jobs that they carry out willingly?

12. By the end of the average day, have you accomplished at least the most important tasks you set for yourself?

13. Are the kitchen items you use most often in the most convenient place?

14. Is your living room arranged so that family and guests can speak comfortably without raising their voices? Are there places for drinks and snacks?

Score: 1 point for each yes to questions 1–10.
1 point for each no to questions 11–14.

If your score is

1–3. Systems are under control. Some of the innovative tips in this section might make things even better.

4–7. Disorganization is troublesome. Hints in "Organizing Your Household" could help considerably.

8–10. Life must be very difficult.

11 and up. Disorganized to the point of chaos. Use the hints and ideas to change your life—and get to work immediately.

Include in your notebook all telephone numbers and details needed to accomplish a job. For example: "Call Acme customer service, 374-5000, ext. 295, re $5 overcharge on bill dated 2/4/88, acct. no. 483-456-7899."

Don't overcomplicate your notebook by listing items that are a part of your daily or weekly routine. Save the notebook for reminders and special projects.

Make a "list of lists" section in your notebook—a file of ideas. For example, set aside individual pages to list books to read, movies to rent, current movies to see, places to go when people visit, recommended restaurants, and so on.

At the start of each week—or, better yet, at the end of the previous week—plan several days ahead. It gives you perspective on the week, enables you to spread out the musts, and prevents a frantic rush at week's end.

Set aside a time for fun—treat it like an important appointment. If you don't set aside a specific time for relaxation, your work and other commitments will soon take over your life.

MAKE YOUR OWN ORGANIZER

There's no need to spend a lot of money on a fancy organizer with expensive inserts that may be suited to other people's lives, not yours. Instead, make one to suit your own personal needs.

Simply buy a small loose-leaf binder in a stationery store. Choose one with the pockets in the front and/or back to hold a small calculator and business cards. At the same time, get loose-leaf paper and dividers to fit.

Identify the categories you wish to include in your organizer—addresses and telephone numbers, errands, long-term projects, appointments, expenses, or whatever you wish. Fill in the tabs on the dividers and insert them in the binder along with an adequate amount of paper for each section.

For the appointments section, get a small calendar—perhaps the kind you get free from banks or greeting-card companies. Remove its outer cover and punch holes along the inside crease to fit the rings of the binder. Now you're ready to get organized.

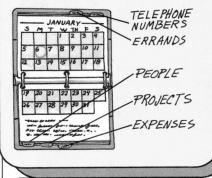

THE VALUE OF MAKING LISTS

1. Writing down activities makes them more concrete.
2. Lists enable you to consider items carefully and to give them their proper priorities.
3. Writing down activities prevents you from forgetting them; on the other hand, once they're written down, you don't have to continue relying on your memory.
4. It feels good to cross items off a list once they've been accomplished.

Keep your list with you at all times. A list is worse than useless if you can't refer to it because you may think that you've disposed of a matter when in fact you haven't.

Set a goal to do one necessary chore each day that you really dislike. You'll have a sense of satisfaction each time you succeed.

Keep a second, separate notebook to cope with complex, special situations—for example, enrolling a child in college, moving to a new home, or organizing a big family holiday.

Don't be in a hurry to throw away notebook pages that have been completed. That stove part you ordered 2 months ago may be all wrong when it arrives, and you may have to call the same people all over again.

THE FAMILY MESSAGE CENTER

Establish a message center in your home. It needn't be elaborate—it can be on the refrigerator or on a bulletin board or a door. Encourage everyone in the household to use the message center to list plans, needs for the next trip to the store, and—especially important—all telephone messages.

Keep the message center current; throw away outdated notes. Take care of as many items as you can each day—or enter them in your notebook for action later.

TELEPHONE TIMESAVERS

Install telephone jacks all around the house or get a cordless phone so that you can talk wherever you are in and around your home.

Get long extension cords for your telephones so that you can move around freely while talking. Often, you can do a chore while talking on the telephone—cooking, tending plants, for example.

To save time—and frustration—whenever possible use the telephone instead of making a trip. Phone to confirm appointments, to check if a store has the item you want, to learn business hours, and so on.

Learn how to cut off time-consuming calls without hurting people's feelings. For example, it's quite all right to say, "This is a terrible time for me, may I call you back?" (Of course, do call back later.)

Sometimes a phone call is more timesaving and effective than a letter. Even a long-distance call may be cheaper, especially when you consider how long it takes to write a letter and how much your time is worth.

Resist the temptation to remove the receiver from its cradle during times when you don't want interruptions. Instead, turn down the bell. Leaving the receiver off the cradle may interrupt phone service even after you've replaced the receiver.

ERRANDS

Keep a running list of groceries and household supplies that you need. By the time you go shopping, there'll be little to add.

Group your errands so that you can accomplish several in a single trip. Try to find a convenient shopping center that has all or most of the stores, offices, and services that you need.

Try to patronize stores and offices near your home, your work, or on the route between the two. Always try to accomplish an errand on the way to something else instead of making a special trip.

Whenever possible, do errands when traffic is light and lines are short—usually between 10 and 3 on weekdays, in the evenings, and all day Sunday.

If you have appointments or errands at several locations, schedule them so that you can go from one to the next with a minimum of wasted time and travel.

Eliminate additional trips by making back-to-back doctor or dentist appointments for family members (or at least for all the kids).

Try to get the first appointment in the morning so that you won't be delayed by someone ahead of you and you'll still have most of the day left when you finish.

Take your weekly list with you whenever you go out on errands. You may be able to fit in something that you scheduled for later in the week.

Get your family to help out with errands. If a shirt has to be returned, leave it in clear sight so that anyone going to or near that particular store can return it. To make it easy, attach a note with instructions—credit to charge account, exchange for a different size or color, or whatever.

USING BITS OF TIME

Most small chores can be accomplished in bits and pieces of time. For instance, while you're waiting in a doctor's office, you can pay bills; while riding the bus, write out your shopping list. The following lists may give you some ideas of what you can do in odd chunks of time.

What you can do in 5 minutes:
Make an appointment.
File your nails.
Water houseplants.
Make out a party guest list.
Order tickets for a concert or a ball game.
Sew back a button.

What you can do in 10 minutes:
Write a short letter or note.
Pick out a birthday card.
Repot a plant.
Hand-wash some clothes.
Straighten up your desktop.
Exercise.

What you can do in 30 minutes:
Go through backed-up magazines
   and newspapers.
Work on a crafts project.
Polish silver and brass.
Vacuum three or four rooms.
Weed a flower bed.

YOU AND YOUR MAIL

Handle most of your mail only once. Immediately discard anything that needs no action, doesn't interest you, or doesn't merit saving—a subscription request for a magazine you're already getting, for example.

If you receive an unsolicited credit card that you don't want, cut it up so that it can't be used and throw it away immediately. Do the same whenever you discard out-of-date credit cards or those you don't intend to use again.

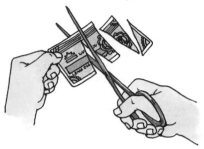

When you need a copy of your reply, make a carbon copy on the back of the original letter. This way you have only one sheet to file, and the chances of mislaying the copy are greatly reduced. No need to type to get a carbon copy either. A handwritten reply done with a ball-point pen makes a perfectly legible carbon.

So that you always have greeting cards for any occasion, buy extras and file them in appropriately labeled folders (birthday, anniversary, get well).

Include on your weekly list of things to do letters that must be written, cards to be mailed, and other kinds of paperwork with deadlines—taxes, auto registrations, and so on.

ORGANIZING HOUSEWORK

Make it a habit to return everything to its proper place and remind others to do so. If you do this daily, it takes less time than waiting until the situation is out of control. An even bigger bonus is that you needn't spend time looking for out-of-place objects.

Do small chores as their need occurs so that they occupy little time. For example, laundry left until the weekend can consume the weekend; instead, start a load before breakfast, put it in the dryer after breakfast, and it's done.

In planning the week's chores, try to set aside a free day (or at least a few hours) for yourself to do whatever you want—whether it's a day out of the house or time alone to finish that book you started several months ago.

Use labor-saving gadgets or appliances whenever they'll *really* save time. But don't overdo it—chopping an onion with a knife may take no longer than using a food processor and then having to take the machine apart and wash and dry it.

Leave some slack in your day for surprises, interruptions, or emergencies. Some activities will take longer than expected, no matter how carefully you plan or allow for delays.

Think before you act—even before you do routine jobs. The way you perform simple, basic tasks is usually the result of habit, not logic. There *may* be a better way.

Why does a half-hour job often take twice as long as you thought it would? Probably because you estimated only the actual working time and didn't take into account the preparation—getting out and putting away tools, for instance.

Tackle big tasks a bit at a time. Straightening every closet in the house might take days; one closet, especially one that hasn't gotten too cluttered, may take no longer than 15 or 20 minutes.

NINETEENTH-CENTURY THOUGHTS ON HOUSEWORK

As society gradually shakes off the remnants of barbarism...a truer estimate is formed of woman's duties, and of the measure of intellect requisite for the proper discharge of them. Let any man of sense and discernment become the member of a large household, in which a well-educated and pious woman is endeavoring systematically to discharge her multiform duties; let him fully comprehend all her cares, difficulties, and perplexities; and it is probable he would coincide in the opinion that no statesman, at the head of a nation's affairs, had more frequent calls for wisdom, firmness, tact, discrimination, prudence, and versatility of talent, than such a woman.

An excerpt from *The American Woman's Home,* by Catherine E. Beecher and Harriet Beecher Stowe, published in 1869.

COMPANY'S COMING

Save time and concentrate on high-payoff cleaning—work on the most conspicuous areas, such as entrance halls and living-room rugs. Have you ever noticed how much cleaning you can do in the hour before company comes?

If company's coming and things aren't quite up to par, bring out the candles, dim the lights, and serve up good food and conversation. As long as soil and disorder don't force themselves on one's attention, no normal person will seek them out.

Once you've attended to basics, such as cleaning the bathroom, concentrate on what shows the most. Any home will pass muster if the clutter is contained, the surfaces are clean, and your best possessions are polished.

Practice cosmetic strategies that fool the eye. Keep the white chair clean, and people will assume that the black one is also clean. If you have fringed rugs, vacuum the fringe so that it lies straight and neat. Guests will assume everything else is equally orderly.

For a last-minute cleanup of the bathroom after the family has used it, go quickly over all surfaces with a spray window cleaner and a paper towel.

THE NIGHT BEFORE

Cut down the morning chaos by doing as much as you can the night before. Write absence notes, bus notes, trip permissions. Lay out clothes, fix lunches, distribute lunch money, book-order money. It doesn't take long.

While you are cleaning up the kitchen after dinner, set the table for breakfast, put out jams, cereals, and any other nonrefrigerated items; you'll have that much less to do in the morning.

MAKING LIFE EASIER

Allow time for making up the beds and tidying the kitchen before leaving the house in the morning. It makes coming home much more pleasant—and sets an example for others in the household.

Keep a bookcase near the back door. Assign each child a shelf on which to assemble lunch, homework, gym clothes, and so on. In the morning, they can pick up everything quickly as they depart; in the afternoon, they can drop their belongings there.

Set up a "way station" for the consolidation in one place of schoolbooks, laundered clothes, toys, mail, and other odds and ends. Once a day, have your kids pick up their belongings from the way station and take them to their rooms. Designate a chair, box, or basket for this purpose and locate it where they can't ignore it.

Designate one bookshelf specifically for library books and make sure your children return all such books to this shelf. This saves a lot of searching for library books that might get scattered around the house or mixed in with your own.

Keep a money dish handy for your small change so that you won't be caught short when someone going out the door suddenly needs last-minute funds.

SHARING THE BURDEN

Try discussing the chores each member of the family likes least and work around them accordingly. One person may hate to scrape the dishes but may not mind taking them out of the dishwasher. Rather than arguing, find something each person enjoys doing instead.

Design a revolving circular chore chart to assign mealtime chores such as setting the table and washing the dishes.

Avoid the "boss" syndrome. As soon as youngsters become proficient at a job, back away and let them be responsible for the results. Resist the temptation to keep checking up.

VARYING STANDARDS

Let family group pressure maintain standards as much as possible. When a chore isn't properly done, hold back for awhile and give others a chance to gripe and solve the problem themselves.

Be sure that you're not imposing too high a standard. When work is honestly shared, all partners are entitled to a say in how well it has to be done. If you're the only one who wants a job done better, reexamine your expectations and perhaps make some adjustments.

If your family is uncooperative, consider whether your standards are too high. If you lower your expectations somewhat, it may be easier to get chores done.

OUTSIDE HELP

If you can't get all your housework done in a reasonable amount of time, hire someone to help you. You'll be surprised at how much more you can accomplish with someone helping out just 3 hours every week!

If you can't afford professional help, be creative. Possible sources of assistance include schoolchildren, college students, and neighbors who might be willing to take over one or two jobs, such as housecleaning, ironing, or grocery shopping—and for considerably less than it costs to hire a professional.

MOTIVATING KIDS TO HELP

Include your youngest child in the housework; it may slow progress, but it's an essential first step in helping that child feel part of the home work force.

Have your young child dust and sweep along with you at first. The youngster will feel grown up, and you'll get more work done.

SOME HOUSEHOLD JOBS A 5-YEAR-OLD CAN DO

1. Make her own bed every day. It may be a little sloppy at first, but it'll improve in the course of time.
2. Put clothes back in the closet or proper dresser drawer.
3. Put toys back in the toy chest.
4. Water houseplants.
5. Feed the dog, cat, or goldfish (if she's reminded).
6. Set the table.
7. Clear the table, one thing at a time.

Teach your child step by step how to do whatever job you ask of her. Don't assume that the task will be completely learned by watching. Show, teach, train.

Once you've given your child certain definite jobs with clear-cut responsibilities, let him work without constant supervision. Check the result when he's finished and compliment him.

Clearly define the time of day when a child's job is to be completed—either before school, right after school, or by dinner. Don't let tasks hang over into the evening.

On weekends, make up a list of chores and negotiate assignments over a leisurely breakfast. Break a big job down into steps and be sure the kids' ages and abilities are equal to their assignments.

Assume that boys and girls will do the housework in equal amounts and without sex designations. Assign their chores accordingly.

Don't redo a chore that a child has just completed. If you insist that a task be done only your way, then do it and be done with it. Redoing is destructive to a child's ego. Just think back to a time when someone redid something you had just completed!

17

Don't expect a youngster to put in a full day's work. An hour is about all that can reasonably be expected of an 8-year-old. A 14-year-old can probably achieve almost as much as an adult, but this depends on the responsibility level of the teenager.

SOME HOUSEHOLD JOBS A TEENAGER CAN DO

In addition to the chores of a younger child (p.17):
1. Empty wastebaskets and ashtrays.
2. Carry out trash cans.
3. Vacuum rugs and floors.
4. Clean and sweep the kitchen floor.
5. Iron his own clothes and the family napkins and tablecloths.
6. Polish silver, brass, copper.
7. Carry in wood and lay fires.
8. Vacuum the inside of the car.
9. Wash the car.

YOUR CHILD'S ROOM

Remind your kids that 5 or 10 minutes of effort a day will keep their rooms in pretty good shape. If they save all their straightening up for Saturday, it will take an hour or two and will surely be met with groans and complaints.

Modify children's rooms so that they can help maintain them. Supply child-sized features, such as a low dresser with nonstick drawers and a closet with hangers and hooks at a child's height.

Once you've helped put a child's room together, the room and the objects in it "belong" to the child. If you take over too much responsibility for keeping it neat, the child will feel the room belongs to you and not to her, and she may not take care of it.

A child as young as 6 can at least "spread up" a bed—it doesn't have to be perfect! Using comforters or quilts on beds will make the job a lot easier.

Ideally, older children's rooms (especially those belonging to adolescents) should be off-limits to any adult interference. Unless the room has reached a level of messiness that threatens to infect the rest of the house, the best policy is hands-off.

WHERE TO PUT THINGS

It all comes down to a place for everything and everything in its place—just as soon as it comes into the house! Otherwise, you'll put it somewhere "for now," but it will really be forever.

Before you buy something, ask yourself, "Where am I going to put it?" and make sure that you have a clearly defined place in mind.

An "I-don't-know-what-it-is" box can be a tremendous help. This is for orphan socks and gloves and all those important-looking but unidentifiable machinery parts, nuts, and bolts you find lying about. From time to time, sort the contents and dump whatever appears useless into the trash.

Keep items used together near one another—for example, tennis rackets, balls, sneakers, and other tennis equipment. Store these related items at or near the place where you use them.

FIGHTING THE "PACK RAT" SYNDROME

Go through your house periodically, eliminating items you no longer want. One possible criterion: when you no longer notice a decorative object (such as a picture), it may be time to get rid of it.

You might consider a trade-off system. Whenever you add a new item to the household inventory, discard an old one.

Caution! Do not throw out someone else's things unless they ask you to do so. Suggest and encourage, but don't take over. This applies to your parents, spouse, and any children over 4 years old.

Be ruthless with your own possessions. Discard all unused junk. When in doubt, throw it out. It takes up space, and you'll just wind up cleaning it and moving it around.

ATTACKING A MESSY CLOSET

When the enthusiasm strikes to clean, start from the outside in. Take care of the clutter scattered around the room before digging into the closet. Starting with the closet first makes a double mess.

If you're faced with an overcrowded closet, schedule an hour to work on it. Write it on your weekly list as a project. But don't try to finish the closet in one session. When the hour is up, quit. Schedule another hour and then another until the closet is done.

To keep mess to a minimum, before you begin cleaning a closet, arrange four boxes nearby to categorize those things that shouldn't go back in. Label them for "charity," "trash," "belongs elsewhere," and "decision pending."

Work on one small section of a closet at a time. Do not empty an entire cluttered closet at once. The resulting chaos is sure to set you back or put you off entirely.

If you absolutely can't bear the thought of throwing something away, take it to Good Will Industries, the Salvation Army, a thrift shop, or a rummage sale.

KEY QUESTIONS WHEN CLEANING A CLOSET

As you weed out a closet, consider each item individually and ask yourself:

1. Have I used this item in the past year? If the answer is yes, it's worth keeping another year. If no, discard it.
2. Does it have either sentimental or monetary value to me? Yes? Then keep it.
3. Might it come in handy someday? If you answer yes but have nothing specific in mind, better put the article into a "throwaway" or "giveaway" box unless you have ample attic or basement storage space. A yes answer usually means that you're hanging onto clutter.

Have a garage or tag sale—it's a terrific way to dispose of a lot of discardable items. If you've never had one before, consider hiring a professional to help you.

SEVEN STEPS TO A SUCCESSFUL GARAGE SALE

1. Check with your local government to see whether you need a permit.
2. Assemble items to be sold. If you don't have enough, ask friends and neighbors to participate in the sale.
3. Run an ad giving time, place, date, and rain date. Post notices at supermarkets, bus stops, and on trees and poles if permitted by authorities.
4. Price goods with tags or tape (use different colors for different owners). When in doubt, price lower.
5. Group similar items together: put clothes on racks, books in boxes, miscellaneous items on card tables.

6. Be prepared to bargain; after all, you're trying to get rid of everything. Reduce prices during the last 2 hours of the sale.
7. Give any leftovers from the sale to your favorite charity. Take down all posters.

A move to a new home is an ideal time to sort and throw out. As you do so, organize the possessions you're taking with you in cartons according to their new storage locations—attic, garage, coat closet, and so on. Using a large marker, write where they are to go on the outside of the box.

"AN OUNCE OF PREVENTION..."

Instead of spending hours a year trying to remove felt-tip marker writing and drawing from walls, spend a couple of minutes putting the markers out of reach of small children. It's also a good idea to restrict potential troublemakers, such as crayons, paints, and clay, to a specified play area.

To avoid frequent cleanups of your oven or your range top, choose large enough pots and pans for your recipes so that the food doesn't boil or slop over.

Confine eating and drinking to certain specified areas in your home. Supply coasters for drinks and small plates for snacks. Don't fill glasses or cups to the rim. When you're entertaining guests, try not to serve crumbly or drippy finger food.

ODDS AND ENDS

To help keep clutter under control, set aside one bowl or basket in a central location to temporarily house small objects that have no current home.

Assign convenient permanent locations for small restless items that would otherwise end up on a tabletop or be mislaid: a hook near the door for keys that you always take when you go out; a small dish on the bureau top to collect loose change or earrings; a mug on the desk to hold pens and pencils.

If messy housemates are a problem, toss their out-of-place belongings into a big cardboard box. When asked where you put an item, indicate the box.

Keeping Records, Managing Money

YOUR PERSONAL RECORDS

Some of the most valued "records" that you have are probably personal letters, photographs, and such mementos as newspaper clippings, diplomas, and graduation programs. Don't feel guilty about saving these, but don't be overly sentimental either—throw out the scraps that will mean little as time passes.

To protect these mementos from fire or flood—and to keep them all in one place as well—store them in a metal strongbox or a small footlocker.

Make sure that you have copies of all birth, marriage, divorce, and death certificates. These records are filed permanently either in a state vital statistics office or in a city, county, or other local office.

To get copies of a birth certificate, write to the appropriate office of the capital of the state where the birth took place. The office may be listed in the phone book under "Vital Statistics" or "Health Depart-

ment." It may even be listed under "Birth Certificates" in a quick-reference list of state or local government offices.

YOUR PERMANENT FILE

Keep the deed to your home, your mortgage agreement, and other papers from the closing—such as surveys and title guarantees—in a permanent file or safe-deposit box.

Maintain a permanent file of the costs of all major improvements, additions, and alterations to your home. These documented costs can help reduce your taxes if you sell the house at a profit later on.

Wills, powers of attorney, and life insurance policies should also be in your permanent file. Be sure to discard expired life insurance policies and superseded wills and powers of attorney.

Save all your children's report cards and school and college records in a permanent file. The kids will appreciate these later in life.

A FILING CHECKLIST

With this procedure, you can develop a filing system from scratch or revise an existing one that isn't working well.

1. Gather together in one place all items to be filed.
2. Have a wastebasket for trash handy, along with file folders, labels, and pens.
3. Pick up the item on the top of the pile (or the first folder if you're revising an existing file) and decide whether it has any value to you. If it doesn't, throw it away. If it does, go on to the next step.
4. If it's worth retaining, choose a folder heading for it, label the folder, and slip in the piece of paper. Some sample headings for a home file: finances, household repairs, personal letters, medical records, taxes, warranties and guarantees.
5. Pick up the next item in the stack and go through the same procedure, the only variation being that this may fit into an existing folder, rather than one with a new heading. Consolidate whenever possible.
6. Assemble your pile of folders and put them in alphabetical order.
7. Put your alphabetized folders into a file drawer or a carton that you have specially set aside for files.
8. Each time you consult a folder, riffle through it quickly and pick out and discard the deadwood. That way, your files won't become crowded.

OTHER FILES

Set up a separate file for each savings account, mutual fund, and other investments. Review their performance from time to time—at least every 3 to 6 months.

Keep canceled checks (if your bank still returns them) in case you have a dispute about whether or not a bill has been paid.

Store bills of sale, warranties, and guarantees in a separate file so that you can quickly locate exactly what you need when equipment requires repair or replacement.

Save all receipts and sales slips so that you're able to check the accuracy of your monthly bills and in case you need to return an item or get it repaired sometime during a warranty period.

Store all your owner's manuals in a file folder or punch holes in them and put them in a ring binder.

If you have accumulated a lot of owner's manuals, installation diagrams, and the like, store them in a box or in a special drawer, perhaps in the kitchen.

You can dispose of your personal tax records after 6 years. Tax returns are only subject to audit for up to 3 years after filing under normal circumstances, for up to 6 years if income has been understated by more than 25 percent.

MEDICAL RECORDS

Keep all the material that you need to process medical and dental insurance claims in one file or folder—instructions, blank forms, eligible bills, birth dates and Social Security numbers of all covered persons, and so on.

If you're moving or changing doctors or dentists, ask for a summary of your medical or dental records to take with you.

When an offspring leaves home for college, to live on his own, or to get married, provide him with a list of his vaccinations, X-rays, childhood illnesses, and the like. This information can come in very handy when medical attention is required.

HOME INVENTORY

For insurance purposes, take photographs of all your possessions and keep them in a metal box or in a safe-deposit box. Then, if any are lost, stolen, or destroyed, you'll have proof of having had them.

Another method of taking inventory is to have someone videotape you while you walk through your house describing and pricing (as best you can) your belongings.

HOW TO KEEP RECORDS

Tired of crossing out and erasing in your address book? Use index cards instead and store them in a file box. Write in your friends' red-letter days and the names of their children—so that you'll be reminded when you call or visit. When there are changes, you can make out a new card in a snap.

Write emergency telephone numbers on a red card and put it in the front of your card file where it will be available with a minimum of fumbling.

Likewise, use blue cards (or some other distinctive color) for plumbers, electricians, babysitters, and all the other household services you use frequently.

WHERE TO KEEP RECORDS

Valuables stored in bank safe-deposit boxes are not automatically protected against loss by burglary, flood, or fire. Some banks may offer insurance on the contents for an extra fee. If your bank doesn't, perhaps your insurance company can provide this kind of protection.

Don't put life insurance policies (or wills) in a safe-deposit box. Safe-deposit boxes are often sealed by court order when the box holder dies. This may cause a substantial delay in obtaining payment on those policies.

WHAT TO STORE IN A SAFE-DEPOSIT BOX

Because of rising crime and insurance rates, many people rent safe-deposit boxes from a bank or from a private safe-deposit company. You should put all your valuable, hard-to-replace, or irreplaceable items in one. Then keep a list of what is in your box in a safe place at home. The following are suggestions of what should be kept in the box.

A *photocopy* of your will, but *not* the original.

All stock or bond certificates or bank savings certificates (but not passbooks) that you have in your possession.

All insurance policies—*except* for life insurance policies.

Property records, such as mortgages, deeds, and titles, but *not* the deeds of burial plots.

Personal documents, such as birth certificates, marriage licenses, divorce papers, military discharge papers, passports.

An inventory of valuable items in your home, such as furs, jewelry, electronic equipment, and collectibles. List the cost and purchase date of each. If possible, include photographs of each item.

Small valuables, such as coins, jewelry, and silver.

Airline tickets bought a long time before departure.

Some files can be stored permanently out of the way on a shelf in the attic, basement, or utility room. After you've finished your taxes for the year, put away all that year's records in a single large envelope or box. At the same time, throw away the contents of the oldest envelope—if it's more than 6 years old.

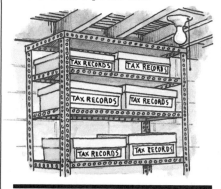

CONDUCTING BUSINESS AT HOME

Buy supplies in double quantities so that you won't have to dash out in the middle of a project to buy an item you've run out of.

To distinguish between your business and personal life, "dress" for work. Don't sit around in your bathrobe all day.

"Walk to work." Walk around the block and back home. You'll get a little morning exercise, and you'll arrive at your "office" in a more businesslike frame of mind, refreshed and ready for work.

Maybe no one will see your office, but clutter can draw on your energy. Throw out dead plants, close closet doors, banish the cat from your desktop.

Be firm with people who interrupt. Because you're at home, others may not take your work as seriously as if you went to an office.

Handle interruptions just as you would at an office—tell others when you'll be free. If friends call during working hours, resist the temptation to socialize. Arrange to call them back later.

SETTING UP AN OFFICE AT HOME

Ideally, your home office should be a separate room, but if one isn't available, choose a corner that will belong to you and you alone. If necessary, invest in partitions to separate yourself psychologically from the rest of the house.

In selecting an area, consider whether there is enough space for a desk and other equipment. Is there a convenient electrical outlet and telephone jack? (If not, they can be installed.)

Your desk needn't be a "desk" at all. All you really need is a surface to write on. Whatever you choose, it should be sturdy and a comfortable height. A hollow door resting on two file cabinets provides plenty of drawer space and a good-sized desktop at just the right height.

BANKING AND BANK ACCOUNTS

Budgeting is easier if you have one bank account solely for paying bills. For couples, make it a joint account. Even if one person usually handles the finances, the other should be able to write the checks if circumstances require it.

If your checking account doesn't pay interest, it might pay to convert to one that does. Shop around for the best deal. Even if the interest is small, it probably beats paying service charges.

HOW LONG DOES IT TAKE TO DOUBLE YOUR MONEY?

How many years will it take for your money to double at a given rate of interest? A simple method for calculating this is called the Rule of 72. By dividing the rate of interest into 72, you will obtain the number of years required to double your money at that rate of interest.

Rate of interest:	Years to double:
5%	72 divided by 5 = 14.4
6	72 divided by 6 = 12
7	72 divided by 7 = 10.3
8	72 divided by 8 = 9
9	72 divided by 9 = 8
10	72 divided by 10 = 7.2
11	72 divided by 11 = 6.5
12	72 divided by 12 = 6

Note: These figures are based on interest compounded annually. On interest compounded semiannually, quarterly, monthly, or daily, your money will double in a somewhat shorter time. Also, these figures do not take taxes into consideration.

It may *not* be worth the effort to hunt down the bank that compounds most frequently. At a 7-percent interest rate, a $10,000 investment will be worth $10,700 at the end of a year if the bank compounds annually, $10,725 if the bank compounds daily.

Don't let a banker's hand be quicker than your eye. A checking or savings account may have a lower monthly fee, but some other service, such as writing a check or using an automatic teller machine, may cost more.

Consider centralizing your bank accounts. Many institutions give you a break on fees if you keep all your money there.

Check the status of any small savings account under $500. Close it if it's earning no interest or if it might be subject to maintenance fees.

Disbelieve every high-rate ad until you have carefully studied all the terms. What the big black type giveth, the spidery type may taketh away.

In choosing a bank, look for one with such extra services as direct deposit of payroll checks, direct deduction of utility payments, bill paying by phone, 24-hour teller machines, drive-up windows, extended banking hours.

WRITING CHECKS

Writing a bad check can cost you a service charge, and writing many can hurt your credit rating.

Checks can bounce even when there seem to be sufficient funds in the account because the funds are in the form of deposited checks that haven't yet cleared at their own banks. Ask your bank to tell you when a deposited check will be credited to your account.

BANK STATEMENTS

Reconcile your bank statement with your checkbook as soon as possible after you receive it. This will help you spot a large mistake and will prevent you from writing checks that your balance won't cover.

A little shaky about reconciling bank statements? Ask your banker for help or use the instructions on the back of your statement. If yours doesn't have any, here's a simplified form to copy and use.

RECONCILING YOUR CHECKING ACCOUNT

STEPS   **YOUR FIGURES**

Checkbook

1. List your checkbook balance .... _____
2. Add earned interest (if any) .... _____
3. Subtract any service charges .... _____
4. Your new balance .... _____

Statement

1. List your statement balance .... _____
2. List checks outstanding .... _____

   Check number   **Amount**

   _____   _____
   _____   _____
   _____   _____

   Subtract checks outstanding .... _____
3. Subtotal .... _____
4. Add deposits not credited on statement .... _____
5. Your checkbook should show this balance .... _____

Spare yourself the frustration of tracking down a few cents' worth of arithmetical errors. Simply add or subtract the small discrepancy and enter the correct figure in your checkbook.

BUDGETING

Review and adjust your budget at least once a year (perhaps at tax time, when you've done a financial review) so as to take into consideration increases or decreases in income, completion of installment debts, a change in priorities. As the needs of living change, so should the budget.

Set up a separate money market or savings account in which you accumulate funds to pay the big bills—for example, quarterly income taxes, property taxes, college tuition, vacation expenses. Total the amount needed, divide by 12, and deposit this amount every month.

Setting spending limits that are too low is a sure way to torpedo a budget. First keep track of your expenditures for a few months; then set limits you can realistically live with, allowing for inflation and overoptimism.

STEP BY STEP TO MANAGING YOUR FINANCES

1. Total your household's yearly income—family salaries, bonuses, dividends, interest, child support.
2. List expenses under two major headings: fixed expenses, such as rent or mortgage payments, taxes, or debt repayments; and flexible expenses—those over which you have some degree of control, such as food and utilities.
3. Add up amounts paid out yearly under the fixed-expenses category.
4. Add up all the flexible expenses.
5. Total the two categories of expenses. If they amount to a sum no more than the household income, congratulations—you're living within your income.
6. To arrive at a monthly spending plan, divide each category of expenses by 12.

A Monthly Budget

INCOME

Total salary	_____
Interest	_____
Dividends	_____
Other	_____
Total income	_____

EXPENSES
Major fixed expenses

Taxes	
Federal	_____
State	_____
Property	_____
Automobile	_____
Rent or mortgage payment	_____
College tuition	_____
Insurance	
Medical	_____
Dental	_____
Life	_____
Property	_____
Automobile	_____
Debt payments	
Automobile	_____
Other	_____
Savings	_____
Total fixed expenses	_____

Flexible expenses

Food and beverages	_____
Utilities	_____
Home maintenance	_____
Furnishings and equipment	_____
Clothing	_____
Personal care	_____
Automobile upkeep, gas, oil	_____
Fares, tolls, other	_____
Medical care (not reimbursed)	_____
Dental care (not reimbursed)	_____
Recreation	_____
Gifts and contributions	_____
Total flexible expenses	_____
Total expenses	_____

SUMMARY

Total income	_____
Minus total expenses	_____
Balance	_____

Budget a contingency amount for unexpected expenses. These are bound to arise, and it's impossible to predict what they'll be. They may range from a wedding gift to replacing an appliance or having dental work done.

Since you won't be making regular withdrawals from your contingency fund, consider putting it in a separate account—such as a money market account—that will pay a higher rate of interest than your checking or savings account.

LIVING WITHIN A BUDGET

Be alert for certain seasonal bargains. The best time to get a bargain on Christmas decorations and wrappings is the day after Christmas!

Seasonal sales usually offer substantial savings on merchandise that's in season. Clearance sales, held after peak demand periods, offer even larger savings.

The best shopping days of a sale are the first and the last. The first because there's usually a better selection, the last because the prices are often lowered.

Shopping from mail-order catalogs prevents the impulse purchases you might make in a store. At home you can choose thoughtfully the products that best suit your needs and budget.

Use catalogs to do research. Read up on what's available so that you'll be equipped to make comparisons as you shop around.

Make impulse purchases difficult—don't carry your checkbook and credit cards with you *all* the time.

WHEN SALES OCCUR

Although seasonal sales still occur, it's now possible to buy almost anything at almost any time of the year. Because of the prevalence of discount stores, there are day-in and day-out sales. Increased competition among department stores has also led to more frequent discounting. It used to be predictable that linens went on sale only in January and August. But such is not the case anymore. If you're shopping for towels or sheets, you can almost always find something on sale. Should you prefer a particular model or brand, you may have to wait—but not for long. Different models and brands go on sale different months.

PAYING BILLS

Check your bills carefully for their payment-due date. To avoid a penalty, pay several days before they're due. If you pay the bills as soon as they arrive, you'll lose the use of your money and any interest that could accrue.

Instead of keeping track of a number of payment-due dates, some people find it easier to set aside two specific days of the month, a couple of weeks apart—usually near payday—to pay bills.

Pay all fixed charges, such as mortgage payments. Then check all monthly bills by matching the charges on the statement with the receipts and sales slips that you have saved.

If you can't pay a bill when it's due, telephone the credit card company before the due date and before it's referred to a collection agency. Explain your problem and state when you're likely to be able to pay at least part of the bill.

If you itemize deductions on your income tax, now's the time to sort and file receipts and statements according to their deduction categories—for example, medical expenses, charitable contributions, mortgage interest, income taxes.

After paying bills and before discarding receipts and sales checks, double-check for any that establish the purchase date for items under warranty. Put these in a separate file.

HOW TO GET ACTION ON AN INCORRECT BILL

Question: What's the best way to handle an incorrect bill?

Answer: Most questions and disputes involving credit can be handled over the phone. Usually there is a toll-free customer-service number provided on your monthly statement. Because credit-card-company telephone lines tend to be busiest on Monday mornings, try calling in the afternoon, preferably toward the end of the week. Write down the date of the call, the name of the person to whom you spoke, and what you and he agreed to do.

Question: What other steps should I take to preserve my legal rights?

Answer: Calling in your problem does *not* preserve your legal rights—only a letter does that. Under the Fair Credit Billing Act, you must write the company within 60 days from the time the first bill containing the error was mailed. Give your name, address, and account number; state the nature and amount of the error; and briefly explain why you think a mistake has been made. Enclose a *photocopy* of the bill or sales slip.

Send the letter to the address given on your bill for billing-error notices. It's wise to send the letter by certified or registered mail with a return receipt requested so that you have proof of the date it was mailed and received.

Once you have sent this letter, you don't have to pay the amount in dispute, make any minimum payments, or pay any finance charges connected with it until the matter is resolved.

Question: Under the law, what must the creditor do?

Answer: The creditor has 30 days to let you know that he has received your letter and two billing cycles (not more than 90 days) to resolve the dispute. Once your letter is received, the creditor cannot do any of the following: close your account; send collection letters or turn the matter over to a collection agency or an attorney; threaten to damage your credit rating or sue you; report the disputed amount as delinquent to a credit bureau.

If the creditor fails to follow these procedures, he may not collect the amount indicated by the customer to be a billing error, up to $50, or finance charges on the amount, even if the bill turns out to be correct.

Question: What if I don't agree with the creditor's decision?

Answer: If you find the creditor's decision unacceptable, the law gives you at least 10 days to write again. But it also gives the creditor the right to report you as delinquent and to take action to collect. At this point, you also have the right to disagree in writing to any firm to whom your credit status has been reported. When the issue is finally resolved, these firms must be notified of the decision.

Question: What if the creditor is wrong?

Answer: If it turns out that the creditor—or his computer—is wrong, you won't have to pay any finance charges on the disputed amount. You also have the right to sue for actual damages, twice the amount of any finance charges (not less than $100 or more than $1,000), plus legal fees.

Question: What if I made the error?

Answer: You'll have to pay the bill; in addition, you may have to pay finance charges on the amount in question.

Nondeductible bills and checks, and receipts that have no warranty value, can be filed every month along with your reconciled bank statements. The simplest way is to tuck everything for the month back into the envelope your bank statement came in; then, for ready reference, write the date of the statement on the outside.

Paying credit card charges before interest and service charges are tacked on saves money and disciplines purchasing.

LOST OR STOLEN CREDIT CARDS

Make two photocopies of all your credit cards. Leave one at home; carry the other with you when traveling. If you lose a card, you'll know the number to report.

Notify the card issuer *immediately* when you discover you've lost a credit card. A toll-free number or some other means of contacting the company is usually printed on your monthly statement. After you have notified the company, you are no longer liable for charges made with your card.

Don't delay! You are liable for up to $50 in charges per card until you notify the card issuer.

If you use a bank's automatic teller machines, your liability is $50 if you notify the bank within 2 business days after the theft or loss of a card; it jumps to $500 if you take 3 to 60 days. After that, liability is unlimited.

Sign up with a credit card protection service offered through banks and credit card firms. For a small charge each year, a service will contact all of your credit card issuers after you notify the service of a theft or loss. Also it pays any liabilities incurred after notification.

USING CREDIT WISELY

After you've finished paying off a loan, continue paying out the same amount to your savings account each month. You probably won't miss the money since you're used to paying it out anyway.

In the long run, you'll save money by making the largest possible down payment and repaying in the shortest possible time.

ESTABLISHING CREDIT

If a woman marries and takes her husband's surname, she should write to her creditors and tell them she wants to keep her own separate accounts.

A married woman can choose to use her maiden name (Smith); her husband's last name (Jones); or a combined last name (Smith-Jones). Just be consistent and use the same form on all accounts.

Establishing your own accounts provides you with your own history of debt management to rely on if circumstances change because of widowhood or divorce.

If you are creditworthy—that is, you pay bills and repay loans on time—a creditor may not require your spouse to cosign your account, with certain exceptions if property rights are involved.

Creditors cannot ask for information about your spouse or former spouse when you apply for your own credit based on your own income—unless that income is alimony, child support, or separate maintenance payments.

Creditors cannot require you to reapply for credit just because you marry or become widowed or divorced. Nor can they close your account or change the terms of your account on these grounds.

YOUR CREDIT RIGHTS

By law, within 30 days of your application, you must be notified whether or not a loan has been approved. If credit is denied, you must be told the reasons, or you must be informed of your right to request an explanation. You have the same rights if an existing account is closed.

A creditor cannot discriminate against you on any of the following grounds: age, sex, marital status, race, color, religion, national origin, or because you receive public income such as veterans' benefits, welfare, or Social Security, or because you exercise your rights under federal credit laws.

If you believe you have been discriminated against, cite the law to the lender. If the lender still says no without a satisfactory explanation, contact a federal enforcement agency. It's a good idea to ask an attorney to help you too.

EXPERTS TO THE RESCUE

It's wise to choose a doctor before you need one. It's equally wise to choose a lawyer at leisure—before a crisis occurs.

To choose a lawyer, check your local bar association's referral service. Or ask an officer at your bank to provide you with a list of several names. You can also consult with friends and associates whose judgment you trust.

If your legal affairs are simple, you might investigate using a legal clinic, a special type of law firm that handles routine cases at a relatively moderate cost.

If you need an accountant, call your local association of accountants for a list of referrals. Or ask your lawyer, bank, or employer for information about certified public accountants (CPA's) or accounting firms with whom they have had favorable dealings.

Consult your friends or business people in your community for the names of insurance brokers from whom they have gotten good service. When you interview these people, ask them for additional references with whom you can check. It's a bad sign if they refuse to provide references.

There is really only one factor in choosing a stockbroker—will that person make money for you? Always ask for references before making a final selection. When checking them, try to get people to speak openly and specifically about the moneymaking ability of the broker. Remember, it's your money that's at risk. All the broker loses is your business.

Don't stay with any adviser you don't like. If you feel that you're not getting adequate service, take time to find someone with whom you feel secure. The relationship between client and professional should be one of compatibility and mutual respect.

NET WORTH

Calculating your net worth can be enlightening. You'll probably be amazed to find out that you're worth a lot more than you thought.

Probably the best way to get an accurate picture of how you're doing financially is to prepare a net-worth statement every year on the same date. Many advisers suggest doing this immediately before starting holiday shopping.

LIFE INSURANCE

Do you need life insurance? Its main purpose—and nothing does it better—is to create an instant estate for your family in the event of your death.

Does a single person need life insurance? Only if someone depends on you for financial support. That someone could be a child, an elderly parent, or any other family member.

HOW MUCH ARE YOU WORTH?

Net worth of (fill in name) ‾‾‾‾‾

As of (fill in date) ‾‾‾‾‾

Liquid assets
Cash and coins on hand ‾‾‾‾‾

Checking account ‾‾‾‾‾

Savings account ‾‾‾‾‾

Money market account ‾‾‾‾‾

Certificates of deposit ‾‾‾‾‾

Life insurance (cash value) ‾‾‾‾‾

Government bonds (current value) ‾‾‾‾‾

Municipal bonds (current value) ‾‾‾‾‾

Corporate bonds (current value) ‾‾‾‾‾

Stocks (current value) ‾‾‾‾‾

Mutual funds (current value) ‾‾‾‾‾

Prepaid taxes ‾‾‾‾‾

Prepaid insurance (current value) ‾‾‾‾‾

Other ‾‾‾‾‾

Other assets
Private pension plan ‾‾‾‾‾

Profit-sharing plan ‾‾‾‾‾

Individual Retirement Account ‾‾‾‾‾

Keogh plan ‾‾‾‾‾

Salary-reduction plan ‾‾‾‾‾

Home (current value) ‾‾‾‾‾

Other real estate (current value) ‾‾‾‾‾

Vehicles (current value) ‾‾‾‾‾

Personal property (value of silver, jewelry, furniture, large appliances) ‾‾‾‾‾

Other personal property (current value of stamp collection, coin collection, etc.) ‾‾‾‾‾

Investment in antiques, art (current value) ‾‾‾‾‾

Loans others owe you ‾‾‾‾‾

Other ‾‾‾‾‾
Total assets ‾‾‾‾‾

Liabilities
Taxes due ‾‾‾‾‾

Unpaid bills ‾‾‾‾‾

Installment debts (balance due) on furniture, TV, appliances, car, etc. ‾‾‾‾‾

Mortgage debts (home and other real estate) ‾‾‾‾‾

Personal loans ‾‾‾‾‾

Other ‾‾‾‾‾
Total liabilities ‾‾‾‾‾

NET WORTH (total assets minus total liabilities) ‾‾‾‾‾

How much insurance should you have? One industry rule of thumb is that a family needs at least enough life insurance to cover four or five times its yearly income.

But that is the rule of thumb from the industry that sells life insurance. You might be better advised to think in terms of how much money you need for how long a period of time in the event of the death of the person who is being considered for insurance.

INVESTMENTS

Before you invest in anything that has the slightest risk, be sure that you have enough insurance and savings to protect yourself against an emergency. Your savings should equal about 3 months of your after-tax income.

Put aside a fixed amount of money each month and invest it regularly.

Diversify. Even if your savings are modest, spread them among several kinds of investments: savings certificates, U.S. Treasury securities, annuities, widely diversified mutual funds.

Don't wait to buy in at the very bottom of a market and don't try to sell out at the very top. *Nobody* is smart enough to do that.

SOCIAL SECURITY

Don't take your Social Security for granted. Check your record every 3 years to make sure that your earnings are being correctly reported. You can get a free "Request for Earnings and Benefit Estimate Statement" form at any Social Security office.

Applications for Medicare should be made 3 months before your sixty-fifth birthday. Otherwise, you will have to wait until the next open enrollment period (January 1 to March 1).

If you plan to retire before you reach 65, you should apply for benefits 3 months before the date you want your benefits to start. You can collect benefits even though you continue to work. However, the Social Security Administration limits the amount you may earn.

RETIREMENT

It's too late to start preparing for your retirement on the day that you pick up your gold watch. Find out right now what your pension plan benefits will be; otherwise you may be in for a shock when you retire.

To enjoy a comfortable retirement, you should figure on needing at least 55–75 percent of your preretirement salary. To meet this goal, you'll need your pension plan benefits, Social Security, and your own savings.

If you don't understand the provisions of your pension, discuss them with your company's employee-benefits managers. They should be willing to help you calculate your benefits.

WHAT $100 WORTH OF GOODS OR SERVICES WILL COST IN FUTURE YEARS

If you are saving or investing dollars today for some future purpose—retirement, college educations, a new home—the rate of inflation is a key to whether your accumulation fund will meet your goals. The following chart shows why.

Annual rate of inflation	10 Years	20 Years	30 Years
2%	$122	$149	$ 181
4	148	219	324
6	179	321	574
8	216	466	1,006

WILLS

You don't have to be rich to need a will. It's the only way to be certain your property goes to those you want to have it. And only in a will can you appoint a guardian for your children.

If you don't have a will or if yours was drawn up prior to 1981, you need the assistance of a lawyer as soon as possible. Don't rely on stationery-store forms—only a lawyer knows what constitutes a valid document in the state in which you live. For a relatively simple will, a legal clinic may be a good choice.

In case your fortunes change, it's sensible when making bequests of money in a will to use percentages rather than dollar amounts.

Review your will every now and then, and keep it up to date. It's an especially good idea to revise your will when you retire. Also, as the tax laws change, it may be advantageous to change some of your bequests.

If you have moved, be sure that your will conforms to the laws of the state in which you now live. Your will is administered according to the state of your legal residence at the time of your death.

WHAT YOU SHOULD HAVE BESIDES A WILL

In addition to your will, you should keep lists of close family members and associates and of important personal documents. This inventory should be updated at least once a year. Make enough copies so that it's readily available if an emergency occurs, and make sure that family members know where to locate a copy quickly. The inventory should include:

The names, addresses, and dates of birth of you and your immediate family.

The location of your birth certificate, citizenship papers, military-discharge papers, tax returns.

Your Social Security number and the location of your card.

The location of your marriage license and prenuptial agreement, if any. If you have been married previously, your deceased or former spouse's name. If divorced, the location of your divorce papers.

The location of the originals of any wills.

The names and addresses of those you intend as executors, trustees, beneficiaries of your will.

The names and addresses of your doctor, attorney, accountant, employer, banker, insurance agent, stockbroker, landlord.

The location of any insurance policies.

The location and enumeration of stocks, bonds, and other securities.

A complete rundown of other assets, including bank accounts, businesses, real estate, jewelry.

A complete outline of your debts and other obligations.

The location of your safe-deposit box and its key.

The funeral arrangements you prefer and any arrangements you have made.

It may also be desirable to have available a list of instructions on what is to be done immediately upon the event of your death or disability—anything from "Call my office" (give phone number) and "Stop the newspaper" (give phone number) to "Call the appraiser (give phone number) to appraise the worth of my business."

Storing It All Away

STORAGE GUIDELINES

Organize existing storage space before increasing it. New storage often creates more places for disorganized clutter and more surfaces to collect unneeded items.

To determine whether you really need more storage space, draw a floor plan and list what you want to have on hand in each room. See if something can be shifted to a room with more free space.

Strive to create "one-motion" storage. That means you can open a cabinet, closet, or drawer, reach in, and grab what you want in one motion without having to move anything out of the way.

You won't outgrow storage if it's flexible. Adjustable shelves easily adapt to changing book, music, or video collections and new electronic gear. Modular storage units can be regrouped, added to, or used separately.

FINDING NEW STORAGE SPACE

Most homes abound in overlooked storage spaces. This typical home shows just some of the possible locations you may have missed. In making your own search, look especially for places that you can use without losing too much floor space.

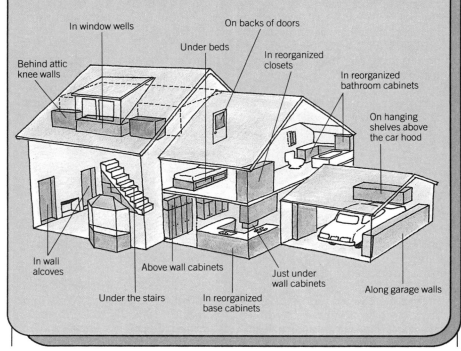

In window wells

On backs of doors

Under beds

In reorganized closets

Behind attic knee walls

In reorganized bathroom cabinets

On hanging shelves above the car hood

In wall alcoves

Above wall cabinets

Just under wall cabinets

Along garage walls

Under the stairs

In reorganized base cabinets

Keep a flexible attitude toward a storage piece's use. A chest can move from room to room, storing different materials as your needs change over time.

Having many small shelves or compartments results in neater, easier-to-use storage than having just a few large ones.

FROM THIS . . .   **TO THIS . . .**

Avoid piling. A good rule is never to stack more than three pieces that are not part of a set.

In small rooms, use open storage, such as shelves and racks. They won't take away from the room's apparent size.

If space is tight, make sure you really need a piece of furniture. You may not need a bureau, for example, if you substitute enough shelves, trays, and baskets.

WHERE TO STORE THINGS

Be honest with yourself about which items should go where. Just because you are fond of something, don't assume it deserves a prime location.

To find the best storage place for an item, take it to the spot where you use it most. Then determine a way to store it there or close by.

Keep frequently used items between knee level and no more than 10 inches above your head. Put items you use less regularly on higher and lower shelves.

Seldom needed lighter items

Frequently needed lighter items

Frequently needed heavier items

Seldom needed heavier items

10″

For both safety and convenience, store a heavy, regularly used article within a foot either way of waist level. Make sure that it has a sturdy support and can be removed and replaced without upsetting lighter things.

To gain more space for the things that you use every day, put rarely needed and out-of-season articles in clearly labeled boxes or bags and keep them in your home's less-accessible storage areas.

TO SPEED YOUR ENTRANCES AND EXITS

Store frequently needed gloves, scarves, and hats in a small chest of drawers by the door. Or hang small baskets for them on the back of the closet door.

Store extra outdoor accessories on an easily reached closet shelf in a box with labeled cubbyholes. A cardboard shoe-storage box from the five-and-ten is ideal.

String a clothesline with clothespins along the back of the coat-closet door for children's winter mittens. If you make the line low enough, the kids can learn to hang their own mittens.

Supplement your coat closet with a handsome wall rack or an old-fashioned freestanding coatrack. You'll find it's a lot more convenient for your guests' coats than squeezing them into the closet.

TO CONTROL WETNESS AND MUD AT YOUR ENTRYWAY

Keep boots and overshoes in a box or basket by the entrance. Line the bottom with a folded plastic trash bag.

Create storage for sports gear by the back door. Be sure the area includes a bench so that your family's athletes will be inspired to sit and remove their muddy shoes.

To keep water from collecting in an umbrella stand, cut a piece of sponge to fit inside the stand's bottom. Remove and squeeze the sponge dry when necessary.

IN YOUR SITTING AREA

Make your coffee table do double duty. Suspend a shelf 4 or 5 inches below the top. It's a handy place to store items ranging from magazines to games and puzzles.

For more storage space, consider using an attractive antique trunk as a coffee table or a wicker chest as an end table.

Next to your television-viewing chair, nail or hook a basket to the wall to hold mending supplies or small projects.

For the half-read newspaper or magazine, make a "pocket caddy" and attach it to your reading chair. Make a cloth envelope with a long tongue that you can secure under the seat cushion with Velcro strips. Use slipcover fabric or a compatible fabric.

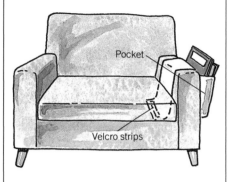

Pocket

Velcro strips

Almost any low storage unit can double as seating. A cushion can turn a storage cube into a seat. A cushion and pillows can turn a trunk into a cozy window seat.

Also consider turning a wall alcove or a window recess into a seating-storage area. Enclose the area with a plywood top and front attached to cleats on the wall. Attach the top with hinges.

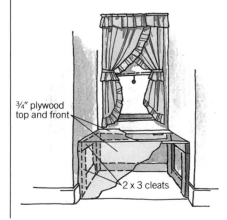

¾" plywood top and front

2 x 3 cleats

FOR YOUR AUDIOVISUAL GEAR

Don't stoop to find that album or movie. Store your records, tapes, and discs at eye level. Locate players just above waist level.

You can store audiocassettes, videotapes, and compact discs two deep on a conventional foot-deep shelf. Build a shelf insert to raise the back row up high enough to be reached easily.

1 x 6 shelf insert

Make sure that all your electronic equipment has adequate ventilation. Allow at least 2 inches of space on all sides.

Leave a 1-inch space for wires at the back of shelves that will carry electronic gear. And instead of running all the electric cords to a baseboard outlet, mount an extension strip outlet at shelf level.

KEEPING YOUR KITCHEN IN ORDER

Too much clutter? Go through each drawer and shelf, check for unnecessary duplications (do you really need three can openers?), and get rid of them.

Sort out useful, but rarely used, utensils—the egg slicer, lobster-claw crackers, Christmas-cookie cutters—and store them in an out-of-the-way drawer. Better yet, put them in a box on a top shelf.

Go to your local variety store and explore all the inexpensive storage items that might be useful in your kitchen. For example, get a wire rack for boxes of foil and plastic wrap or stacked plastic bins for potatoes and onions.

FOR KITCHEN EFFICIENCY

Whenever possible, keep toasters, mixers, and other small appliances within easy reach. If you store them away, it becomes a chore just to get them out.

To keep small appliances handy without extra clutter, put them behind small, hinged shutters or doors at the rear of the countertop.

Store cans, jars, and small boxes in single rows so that they're easy to find and reach. Consider installing narrow shelves for them along an inconspicuous wall or around a cabinet's interior.

ADDING A LAZY SUSAN TO A CUPBOARD

Revolving shelves under a counter put every item within easy reach. Making them is simpler than you might think. All you need is some ¾-inch plywood, a 4-inch lazy-susan bearing (stocked by many hardware stores), 6d finishing nails, white glue, and flexible metal countertop edging to put a lip on each shelf.

The trickiest part is cutting the plywood circles. Have your lumber dealer cut them for you unless you have a saber saw; in that case, try the technique on p.188. For a typical 24-inch-deep cupboard, you'll need circles 22 inches in diameter. But always measure your cupboard first and make sure the unit will clear all sides by at least ½ inch. One crosspiece should measure the same as the diameter of the circles. The other is actually two short pieces, each measuring half the diameter minus ⅜ inch.

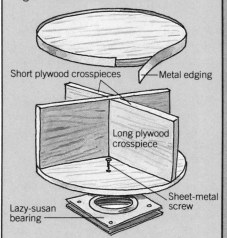

Short plywood crosspieces — Metal edging

Long plywood crosspiece

Lazy-susan bearing

Sheet-metal screw

To install the lazy susan, screw the bracket to the cupboard and then attach the unit to the bracket with sheet-metal screws. Before attaching the bracket to the cupboard, however, use the tiny holes in the bracket as guides for marking and drilling screw holes in the bottom circle. Then temporarily screw the unit to the bracket to check that the sheet-metal screws are the right length.

You can make a smaller lazy susan for a wall cupboard the same way. Just use ½-inch plywood and a 3-inch bracket.

No more misplaced rings, watches, or bracelets! Hang a cup hook near the sink to hold them while you're cooking or cleaning.

The place mats on top of the pile won't get messed up when you pull out the set below if you put sheets of cardboard between sets.

TO FREE COUNTER SPACE

Put away the clean dishes as soon as you walk into the kitchen. This will give you a larger, clearer work area and make room for the next batch of dishes.

Mount items under your cabinets. You can buy fold-down racks that will hold spices, knives, and cookbooks. You can also get drawers and appliances designed to be installed under cabinets.

Fold-down rack

Install tall or bulky appliances, such as blenders and food processors, on pop-up shelves near their point of use. Get a mechanism of the appropriate size and mount it according to directions.

Pop-up mechanism

A wire dish rack that mounts directly over the sink not only frees space but also reduces moisture problems by draining your dishes directly into the sink. They're carried by kitchen speciality shops.

STORING CHINA

All china of the same pattern need not be stored together. If you have a family of four and a service for 12, move some of the place settings to a higher shelf (or even to another room).

Add a new shelf for china between existing ones. Attach it to the cabinet sides with cleats (p.64) or make an insert with legs from boards or plywood.

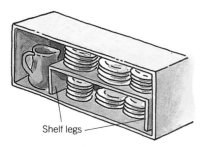

Shelf legs

Use wire racks that let you store plates, saucers, and bowls vertically. Hang cups from cup hooks or pullout cup racks.

KEEPING UTENSILS HANDY

For a simple but effective knife organizer, saw slots in a 2 x 3 about 1½ inches apart. Then glue it to the bottom of a drawer.

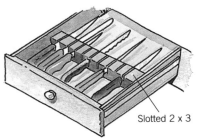

Slotted 2 x 3

Keep spatulas and other cooking utensils near your stove, and store whisks and other mixing utensils near your food-preparation area. Hang them on pegboard (p.55) or a rack with hooks.

Also consider keeping "bouquets" of small utensils in wide-mouthed jugs, or hanging steel utensils on a magnetic steel bar.

You can make almost any utensil hangable by drilling a hole in its handle. If it's too thick to fit over a hook, run a loop of cord (or a leather thong) through the hole.

To put pots and pans where you really need them, install pullout shelves or rollout bins (pp.68–69) in the cabinet next to your stove or under your built-in cooktop.

A vertical rollout with pegboard is a convenient way to store pots and pans and to take advantage of an otherwise wasted narrow space.

Run out of space in cabinets and on the wall? Hang attractive, frequently used cookware from a metal rack suspended from the ceiling. Such racks are available in most cookware departments.

Store baking pans, trays, and platters vertically in that hard-to-reach cabinet over the refrigerator. Make dividers from ¼-inch plywood; install them between spacers of the same material on the cabinet's top and bottom.

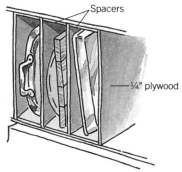

Spacers

¼" plywood

You can also create vertical dividers with wooden dowels (p.63). They're especially good for organizing pan lids.

CREATING NEW KITCHEN STORAGE

Put the inside of cabinet doors to work. Hang measuring cups and spoons and other utensils from hooks, and store spices and small packages in racks. But first make sure they won't interfere with the shelves when you close the door.

Make shallow open shelves for spices and storage jars at the rear of your countertop.

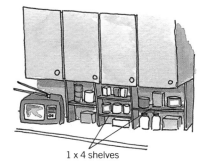

1 x 4 shelves

The space next to a refrigerator can house a rollout pantry if there is 4 inches of ventilation between the refrigerator and the pantry and 2 inches around the other two sides. Just mount a basic case (p.64) on two pairs of sturdy casters.

Lattice shelf lip

Make a hang-up spice rack easily with 1 x 4's and ¼-inch dowels. Clamp two 1 x 4's together and drill holes through both at once. Glue in the dowels.

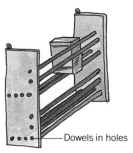

Dowels in holes

Add a bookcase to your kitchen. Use it to organize cookbooks and canisters. Convert the top into extra counter space by covering it with waterproof wallpaper.

Another helpful addition is a roll-around cart. It provides extra work and storage space that you can wheel from sink to stove to table.

To convert a cabinet into a wine cellar, replace the existing shelves with two large plywood pieces, each slotted halfway through and fitted together to form an X.

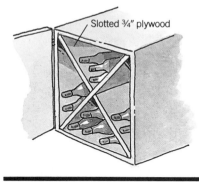

Slotted ¾" plywood

CLEANING SUPPLIES

Store your cleaning materials in a plastic carrying tray. They'll be much easier to take out and put away and to move about.

When arranging your cleaning supplies in a closet, give first consideration to making large and awkward items, such as vacuums and rolling buckets, easy to reach.

FOR THE LAUNDRY

Install a clothes rod below a high shelf in your laundry room and you'll have a handy place to hang drip-dry or freshly ironed clothes.

If space is tight, get a pop-up ironing board at a home center. Install it in place of a cabinet drawer.

Pop-up ironing board

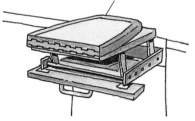

Construct a simple cabinet with shelves or cleats to hold plastic laundry baskets. Have each family member be responsible for bringing his or her own basket to the cabinet on laundry day, and for removing it—full of clean laundry—afterward.

GETTING THE MOST FROM YOUR BEDROOM CLOSET

Always hang coat hangers so that all the hooks point away from you. This makes it easy to remove several articles at once—or all of them in an emergency.

Hang all your short things at one side of the closet. Usually you'll create enough space underneath for a shoe rack, a small chest of drawers, or a second clothes rod.

Rub a bit of paste furniture wax on a wooden clothes rod. You'll find that hangers slide back and forth more easily.

Whenever you remove a garment from a hanger, put the hanger at the end of the rod. When you rehang the garment, you won't have to search for a hanger or create a tangle.

If you're annoyed by hangers getting tangled, remove the pole and saw shallow notches at ½-inch intervals along its top edge.

Consider storing folded clothes on shelves that pull out (pp.68–69). They are more flexible than dresser drawers, and they can be used at greater heights than drawers.

If you have a closet without a light fixture, you can get an inexpensive battery-operated light unit that mounts on the wall or ceiling.

REMODELING A CLOSET

You can store more in a bedroom closet by hanging clothes on bilevel rods. In a closet used only by a man—or a child— you can devote the entire hanging space to bilevel rods, assuming coats and bathrobes are kept elsewhere. But a woman will also need a single rod at the standard 6-foot height for dresses.

In revamping a closet, first take out all the existing rods and shelves. For folded items and accessories, build a narrow case of ¾-inch plywood from floor to ceiling. Outfit it with shelves and drawers (pp.64–67). Secure it to the floor and wall studs (p.49) with L-brackets.

For clothes rods, use 1-inch wood dowels. Mount each rod in metal clothes-rod sockets on 1 x 4 cleats. Mount each socket so that its center is 11 inches from the back wall. If a shelf will rest on the cleat, put the socket near the cleat's lower edge so that you'll have space above the rod for putting in and taking out hangers. To make sure a rod is straight, mount the socket for one end; then insert the rod and place a level on the rod to determine the exact position of the other socket.

The shelves in most closets can be up to 22 inches deep. But if your closet door doesn't extend to the ceiling, shelves at higher levels may have to be shallower for you to reach them. Use ¾-inch plywood for the shelves, and mount shelves other than those above rods with 1 x 2 cleats. Secure all wall cleats to the studs. Finish plywood edges with ¼-inch-thick molding, or if you plan to paint the closet, fill the edges with wood putty.

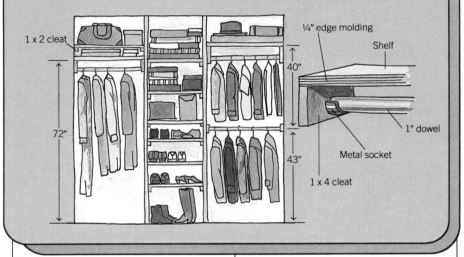

1 x 2 cleat · 72″ · ¼″ edge molding · Shelf · 40″ · 1″ dowel · Metal socket · 43″ · 1 x 4 cleat

PLANNING NEW CLOSET SPACE

A walk-in closet is luxurious but wasteful of space; a reach-in closet uses all of its space for storage.

Unlike sliding doors, folding and accordion doors allow easy access to the full front of a closet. They also require less free space in front of the closet than a regular side-hinged door that swings out.

You can create a new closet in a deep wall alcove or across the end of a small room by simply hanging full-length folding or accordion doors from the ceiling. Equip it with shelves and clothes rods as shown in the box above.

If mildew is a problem, make sure your closet has plenty of ventilation by using wire shelving (p.63) and louvered doors. In an extreme case, insulate the back wall.

KEEPING ACCESSORIES NEAT

Golf tees make fine pegs for a belt or tie rack. Just drill rows of holes in an attractive board and glue the pointed ends of the tees into them.

Golf tees

Shoes won't disappear into the back of the closet if you store them in wire racks or shoe bags. Or make your own simple stacking shelves for them.

Clear plastic drawers and boxes that stack on closet shelves create see-through storage that's perfect for shoes, hats, and sweaters.

If your closet lacks shelves, hang your accessories. Closet shops carry hanging cases with pockets for shoes and handbags as well as special hangers for ties and belts.

PLANNING A CHILD'S ROOM

Keep storage at your child's level. Install low horizontal shelves, cabinets, and other units instead of tall vertical ones.

If storage is flexible, it can change as your child grows. Use adjustable shelves, modular units, and easily moved chests of drawers. Avoid built-in storage units that you can't adjust.

STORING PLAYTHINGS

A very young child has trouble putting toys away precisely. Your toddler will clean up with less fuss if you provide roomy, catchall storage bins and baskets.

As your child gets older, keep playthings on shelves; they permit a toy to be found without rummaging. But use catchall units for storing quantities of related items, such as building sets.

Some playthings are unwieldy. Be sure your storage has deep shelves for storing large toys and hooks for hanging awkward ones.

For quick, inexpensive storage, cover cardboard boxes with stick-on paper. Use them as bins or stack them for shelves. Replace them when they become tattered.

Modular plastic storage cases—or wooden cubes—can also serve as either bins or shelves and when empty can even be flipped over to form a stool.

Plastic dishpans and vegetable bins make handy storage drawers for toys. Mount them on cleats (p.67) or suspend them beneath a shelf from simple runners.

Mount a racing-car set on a piece of ½-inch plywood with a simple 1 x 2 frame around the edges. Add casters so that it can be rolled under the bed when not in use.

If you have two heavy, solid storage units, you can install a play table between them on adjustable tracks (p.67). This allows the table to grow with your child.

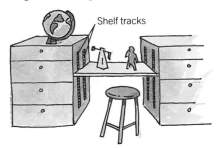
Shelf tracks

YOUR CHILD'S CLOTHING

To put your child's clothes within reach, add a second, lower rod in the closet. Install new clothes-rod sockets on a cleat (p.43). Or simply suspend the rod on chains from the higher rod. Use the upper rod for out-of-season wear.

S-hooks

AN UNDERBED CART

Just over 6 inches high, this low rollaway fits under most beds and is ideal for such items as shoes, blankets, and toys. Measure to determine the best front-to-back and side-to-side dimensions for your bed. Plan to recess the cart's front 4 to 6 inches to give you toe space under the bed. For a full-size or larger bed, make two carts, one for each side.

Cut the 1 x 6 front and back each 3 inches longer than the plywood bottom's side-to-side dimension. Cut the 1 x 4 sides and 2 x 2 cleats the same length as the bottom's front-to-back dimension.

Before assembling the unit, make sure that when the casters are screwed to the cleats, the bottom will be at least ½ inch above the floor. If not, or if your carpet has a deep pile, lower the cleats.

Assemble the unit with 2-inch No. 8 woods screws (p.66) and white glue in the sequence given below.

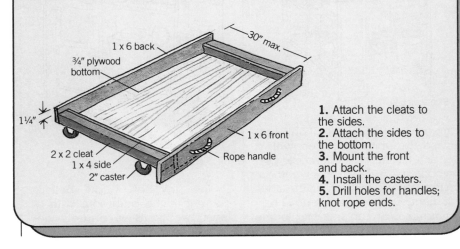

1 x 6 back
¾" plywood bottom
30" max.
1¼"
2 x 2 cleat
1 x 4 side
2" caster
1 x 6 front
Rope handle

1. Attach the cleats to the sides.
2. Attach the sides to the bottom.
3. Mount the front and back.
4. Install the casters.
5. Drill holes for handles; knot rope ends.

Shallow drawers enable a child to find socks, underwear, and shirts more easily. To prevent a deep drawer from becoming cluttered, add dividers (p.68).

Keep a clothes hamper in your child's room rather than the bathroom. It's complicated for a child to move clothes between rooms. Put it near the closet to collect dirty clothes as soon as they come off.

MAKING NEW BATHROOM STORAGE

Install a shelf just above the sink. It'll give you a handy, dry place for cosmetics, toiletries, and grooming aids. Place the shelf high enough so that it doesn't interfere with turning the water on and off.

Fill the area below an open sink with shelf units that fit around the plumbing and open onto all the reachable sides.

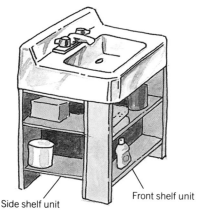

Side shelf unit

Front shelf unit

If you feel more ambitious, enclose the undersink area with a cabinet version of the basic plywood case (p.64). Make it without a top or back, and attach the sides to cleats on the wall. Remove any metal legs on the sink and let the cabinet support it.

For a bath fixture that will do double duty, make a shelf unit that incorporates a towel bar. Use 1 x 6's with a 1-inch-diameter dowel. Make the hole for the dowel with a hole-saw drill attachment (p.188).

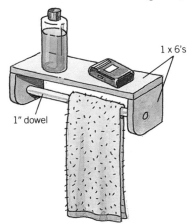

1 x 6's

1" dowel

Fill any unused space around a toilet with storage that combines shelves and towel bars in a space-saving ladder arrangement. Be sure to leave space above the tank so that you can take the top off.

Towel ladder

Protect any new wood shelf or cabinet in the bathroom with at least two coats of a urethane-based enamel or varnish.

AN UNDERSTAIRS ROLLOUT BIN

The best way to use that hard-to-reach space under the front edge of a stairway is with a rollout bin. You'll find it a perfect place to store awkward items ranging from cleaning supplies to boots and sports equipment. The bin is a simple box of ¾-inch plywood on casters. Assemble it with 2-inch and 1¼-inch No. 8 screws and white glue, reinforcing all of the corners with ¾-inch square molding (p.64).

To cut the front, back, and filler pieces at the correct angle, trace the slope of the stairs on a piece of cardboard. Then make it into a pattern for marking the plywood. The bin's front and back should clear the stairs by ¼ inch and the floor by ½ inch; the filler piece, which is nailed in place, fits flush.

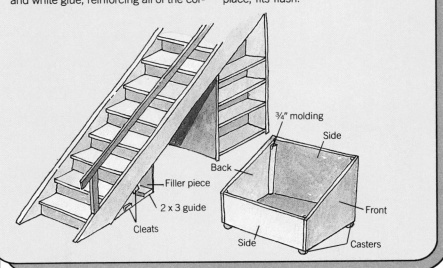

¾″ molding
Side
Back
Filler piece
2 x 3 guide
Front
Cleats
Side
Casters

Don't let hair dryers, curling irons, electric shavers, and other small appliances take up precious shelf space. Hang them from a pegboard or from hooks screwed into a shelf edge or bottom. Or put them in baskets on a wire grid.

Caution: Never use or store an electric appliance where it can be dropped or pulled into a sink or tub. Always unplug it after using.

DON'T FORGET HALLS

Even a narrow hall may have space for shelves. Consider lining a wall from floor to ceiling with shallow shelves for paperbacks or for your collection of figurines or other eye-catchers.

Construct a storage loft across the end of a hall or above a stairway. Use it for luggage and other lightweight, occasionally used items.

SUMMER CLOTHES

¾″ plywood

1 x 3 cleats

UNDER THE STAIRS

You'll have a much easier time dividing up the open space under stairs if you keep in mind that it's nothing more than a large triangle with a hard-to-use corner. One way to use that space is with a rollout bin (see box, p.47).

You can fill the space under stairs with shelves. Support the shelves at their stair ends with stepped vertical pieces. Use the space behind the shelves as a closet.

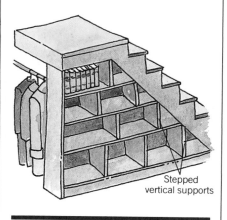

Stepped
vertical supports

IN THE ATTIC

Even if your attic is cramped and filled with cross members, you can probably find room for storage. Just cover accessible areas around the hatch with a floor of ¾-inch plywood. Don't store heavy items there if your joists are more than 16 inches apart.

If you have trouble getting plywood through the hatch to floor your attic, saw the sheets into widths that will go through. Then fit them back together in the attic.

Attic searches will be easier if you arrange items so that you can quickly survey everything from the attic hatch or doorway. Keep related articles near one another, and label cartons in large letters.

To protect attic-stored items from dust, put smaller articles in tightly closed or sealed boxes. Cover furniture and other large items with plastic drop cloths.

For storage along a gable wall, simply install shelves with brackets or with standards and brackets (p.60). Make each shelf progressively shorter to fit between the sloping sides at each end.

To make shelves under eaves, run uprights between the rafters and the joists (or floor). Then run shelf supports from the upright to the rafters. You can make shelves the same way under stairs with exposed stringers.

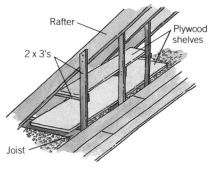

Rafter
Plywood shelves
2 x 3's
Joist

FASTENING TO STUDS

In most homes the safest way to mount any wall storage is to attach it with screws or nails that go at least 1 inch into the studs—the wooden uprights that support the wall. The box on the facing page gives clues to help locate studs.

Another way of finding studs in plasterboard walls is to move a magnetic compass or a magnet on string back and forth and up

LOCATING WALL STUDS

In most homes the distance from the center of one wall stud to the center of the next is 16 inches. But sometimes it's 24 inches—or some other interval. In an older building the spacing may be irregular. Here are some clues for finding studs.

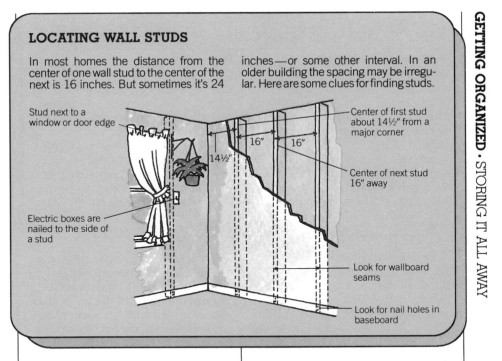

Stud next to a window or door edge

14½"

16"   16"

Center of first stud about 14½" from a major corner

Center of next stud 16" away

Electric boxes are nailed to the side of a stud

Look for wallboard seams

Look for nail holes in baseboard

and down over a wall until the compass needle or the magnet is attracted by the metal of the nails in the stud. Magnetic stud finders use the same principle.

If all else fails, you can find a stud by drilling a tiny hole angled sharply to one side. Feed a piece of coat-hanger wire into the hole until it hits a stud. Pinch the wire between your fingers; then pull the wire out and transfer the measurement to the wall. The stud's center should be only ¾ inch farther away, but drill a tiny test hole.

Whenever possible, make a stud-locating hole where the storage unit will hide it. Otherwise, drill the hole low on the wall so that it will not be very noticeable when you patch and paint it. Use a weighted plumb line to transfer the exact location of the stud to a higher position.

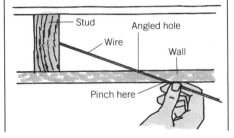

Stud

Angled hole

Wire

Wall

Pinch here

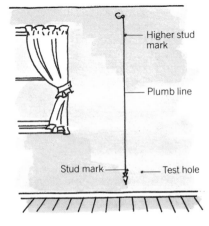

Higher stud mark

Plumb line

Stud mark

Test hole

WHAT IS YOUR WALL MADE OF?

When you drill a test hole into . . .	You will find . . .
Wall coverings:	
Wallboard or plaster only	White dust, quick breakthrough
Thick plaster	White dust, delayed or no breakthrough
Thin plaster over wood lath	White dust, then gray, then breakthrough
Behind-wall materials:	
Wood stud	Moderate resistance, light wood shavings
Metal stud	Heavy resistance, silver shavings
Cinder block or concrete	Very heavy resistance, gray-brown dust
Brick or hollow tiles	Heavy resistance, red dust
Mortar between bricks or blocks	Moderate resistance, gray dust

Attach a heavy item, such as a cabinet, to a board screwed into the studs with lag bolts (see chart, facing page). For each lag bolt, drill a hole in the board slightly larger than the bolt's diameter; then use the hole as a guide to drill a hole into the stud that's slightly smaller than the bolt's diameter.

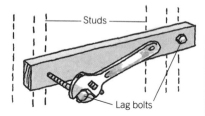

Studs — Lag bolts

You can also attach a heavy load with hanger bolts. You screw a hanger bolt into a stud and then attach an object to it with a nut. To install a bolt, drill a pilot hole and screw it in with locking-grip pliers on its unthreaded midsection.

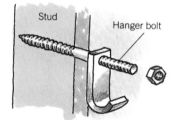

Stud — Hanger bolt

Modern buildings often have metal studs. To fasten an object to one, use a sheet-metal screw. Drill a hole until you hit the stud. Then dent the stud with a large nail and drill a hole half your screw's diameter. Use a No. 4 screw for light loads and up to a No. 8 for heavier ones. Screw sizes are the same as for wood screws (p.66).

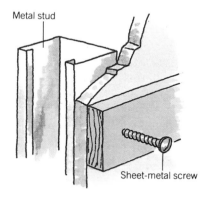

Metal stud — Sheet-metal screw

HOLLOW-WALL FASTENERS

To mount light loads between studs on a plaster or plasterboard wall, use hollow-wall anchors or toggle bolts. Reserve plastic anchors for very light loads. Putting heavy loads on these fasteners could cause the wall to give way.

WALL FASTENERS

Fastener	Use
Plastic anchor	Very light loads on hollow and masonry walls; use with a sheet-metal or round-head screw
Sheet-metal screw	Light to heavy loads on walls with metal studs; screws directly into stud
Hollow-wall anchor	Light loads on hollow walls; comes with its own bolt
Toggle bolt	Light loads on hollow walls; heavy loads on cinder-block walls; comes with its own bolt
Lag bolt	Heavy loads on walls with wood studs; screws directly into stud
Cut nail	Light loads on masonry walls; goes through a board into wall
Masonry nail	Light loads on masonry walls; goes through a board into wall
Fiber plug	Light loads on masonry walls; use with wood or sheet-metal screw; also comes in plastic
Lead anchor	Medium loads on masonry walls; use with wood screws (see chart p.66)
Expansion shield	Heavy loads on masonry walls; comes with its own bolt

The more hollow-wall fasteners you use to hold an object, the lighter the load on each fastener. For all but the lightest loads, try to use at least two fasteners for each item that you put up.

The length of the hollow-wall anchors or toggle bolts you need depends on how thick the plaster or plasterboard on your wall is. To determine a wall's thickness, drill a small hole in it, then bend thin, stiff wire into a hook and curve the hook through the hole. Pull the hook against the inside of the wall and mark the wire at the point it comes out of the wall. Remove the hook and measure between the end of the hook and your mark.

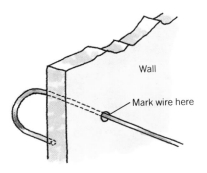

Wall

Mark wire here

To install a hollow-wall anchor, drill a hole the same size as the anchor; then insert the anchor and tighten the screw to flatten the end of the anchor against the inside of the wall. After that, you can take out and put in the screw as often as you like.

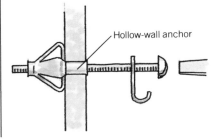

Hollow-wall anchor

A toggle bolt holds an object more securely than a hollow-wall anchor. But a toggle bolt is trickier to install. You must drill a hole large enough for its folded wings to pass through, and you must attach the object to the toggle bolt before you put the bolt into the wall. Once the bolt is installed, you can't remove it without losing the winged toggle inside the wall.

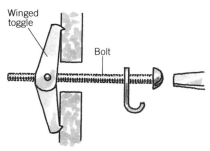

Winged toggle

Bolt

You can make a hole for a small plastic anchor in many walls by simply driving in a large common nail. Experiment to see which nail size is best for your combination of anchor and wall.

Interior doors are often hollow. To attach an object to one, get a small version of the hollow-wall anchor, known as a hollow-door anchor.

If you have trouble attaching an object to a wall because the item itself is unusual or because the wall is made of an unusual material, chances are good that specialized fasteners are available. Ask for help at a building-supply or hardware store or home center.

FASTENING TO MASONRY

To secure most items to a concrete, brick, or cinder-block wall, you'll need to drill a hole and insert a wall fastener. Use lead anchors for most loads and expansion shields for exceptionally heavy

ones. Use plastic anchors and fiber plugs for very light items (see chart, p.51).

To drill a hole in masonry, use a carbide-tipped bit on an electric drill, preferably a variable-speed model that will let you drill at a low speed. As you drill, move the bit in and out rather than pushing hard and continuously on it. If the drill begins to stall, release the trigger, or you'll burn out the motor.
Caution: When drilling into masonry, always wear safety goggles and work gloves.

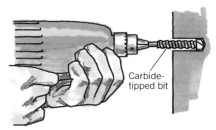

Carbide-tipped bit

If your drill lacks the power to drive a big bit into solid concrete or brick, try drilling a small hole first, then a larger one. Or rent a ½-inch variable-speed drill.

On a cinder-block or a hollow-tile wall, another good fastener is a toggle bolt. Drill a hole for it with a carbide-tipped bit. Then install the fastener as you would on a hollow wall. Drill a test hole first to make sure the block's hollow interior has enough space to accommodate the bolt's wings.

You can attach boards that will carry light loads with either cut nails or masonry nails (p.51). Because these nails tend to split wood, first drill a hole in the board for each nail. Make it slightly smaller than the widest part of the nail. If a wall is very hard, drill holes for the nails in the wall too.

Cut nails and masonry nails can chip a claw hammer, causing flying metal particles. Always drive them in with a ball peen hammer or light sledgehammer. And wear safety goggles and work gloves.

If a fastener will carry a heavy load, don't install it in the mortar between masonry blocks. Under stress, the mortar is likely to crumble, and the fastener will pull out.

FAST FASTENERS

You can drive a special sharp-tipped hollow-wall anchor into plasterboard with a hammer. After that, you flatten the anchor inside the wall as you do with a regular hollow-wall anchor (p. 51).

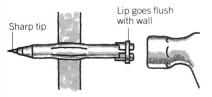

Sharp tip

Lip goes flush with wall

To put up hardware quickly, use rivetlike expanding fasteners that shoot directly into plasterboard from an inexpensive tool that you squeeze or from an attachment on a stapler. On plaster or masonry, drill a small pilot hole first.

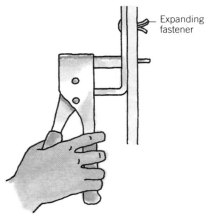

Expanding fastener

HOOKS AND HANGERS

In an open storage area, well-designed hangers can contribute nicely to the decorative scheme, especially if you coordinate their style and color. Designer hangers come in a wide variety of styles and materials.

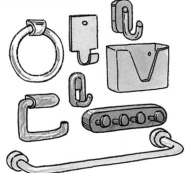

In utilitarian storage areas, it's more economical and efficient to use screw hooks, wire coat hooks, and other traditional hardware. Most have screw-in tips that are simple to install.

One especially good longtime favorite is the spring clip. A typical clip holds handles ranging from ¾ to 1¼ inches in diameter, and you put it up with a single screw. You can also get spring clips mounted on a sliding track. There are even ones that hook onto pegboard.

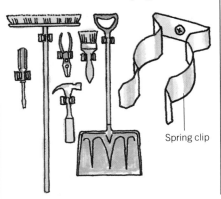

Spring clip

53

The best solution for many items that won't fit easily in regular storage areas is to hang them. An eggbeater won't take up drawer space if you hook it on a pegboard. Even a large item that's not too heavy to lift, such as a bike, can be hung from large vinyl-coated wall or ceiling hooks.

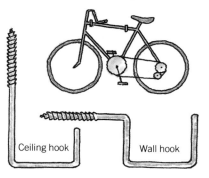

Ceiling hook   Wall hook

An easy way to make a pegboard is with Shaker pegs, which you can get from woodworking supply stores. Just drill a hole in a board for the tenon and put the peg in with white glue. Mount the board with wall fasteners or with screws extending into the studs.

Mounting screws
1 x 4
Hole
Pegs
Tenon

The back of any door is a natural spot for hooks and pegs. Another storage device that works well there is a shoe bag. You can use its pockets for objects ranging from gloves to toiletries.

Sometimes you can also put the front of a door to work. Consider putting attractive hooks or racks there. Or cover it with pegboard.

INSTALLING HOOKS AND HANGERS

To put a hook into solid wood, first make a pilot hole. For all but the largest hooks, the quickest way to do this is with a push drill (p.184). You can make a small hole with a nail or an ice pick.

If a hook is hard to screw in, angle the end of a screwdriver through it and use the screwdriver as a lever to finish screwing it in. If the hook is too open for this to work, clamp locking-grip pliers on the hook and use them to turn it.

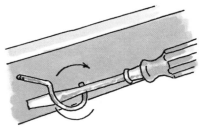

A screwdriver or locking-grip pliers can be used in the same manner to take out hooks that are locked in place by rust or paint.

If you're hanging a heavy object, make sure that your hook is long enough to screw into a wall stud (p.49). And if you want to hang anything—heavy or light—from the ceiling, use a hook that goes into a joist.

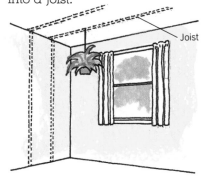

Joist

If you want to put up a hook for a light object on a plaster or plasterboard wall, get one that has a screw hole so that you can put it up with a wall fastener (p.51). Or mount hooks with screw-in tips on a board; then attach the board with screws going into the studs.

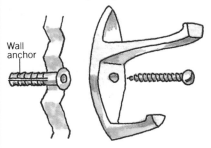

Wall anchor

PEGBOARD: A RELIABLE STANDBY

Putting up perforated hardboard, commonly known as pegboard, is still one of the easiest, fastest, and cheapest ways to create storage for flat, hangable items that you need within reach.

For hanging hand tools, kitchen utensils, and other lightweight objects, ordinary ⅛-inch-thick pegboard is fine. For heavy loads, get sturdier ¼-inch-thick pegboard. Tempered pegboard is stronger than untempered.

When selecting pegboard attachments, make sure they'll fit on your pegboard. Some can be used only on ⅛-inch pegboard and others only on ¼-inch panels. Some will fit both types.

Brownish, unpainted pegboard is a good buy for workshops and garage walls. Elsewhere you'll be better off using prepainted pegboard, available in white and many colors. Its wipe-clean factory finish is more durable than any paint you could apply.

If your decorating scheme dictates a color not available on prefinished pegboard, paint smooth, unfinished pegboard, using a urethane enamel for a hard finish. Apply it with a roller and take care not to clog the holes.

Pegboard panels come in various dimensions, up to sheets 4 feet by 8 feet for covering large wall areas. If you need a special size, look for a building-supply dealer who will cut a panel to the measurements you want.

If you cut pegboard yourself, you can prevent fraying and damage to the finish by clamping the panel between boards along the cut line and using a fine-tooth 12- or 15-point crosscut saw. Make sure the springy panel is supported evenly from below.

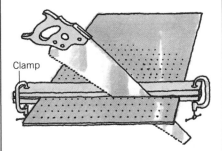

Clamp

PUTTING UP PEGBOARD

It's easy to install pegboard with plastic anchors, long screws, and ⅜-inch spacers. First mark the wall through the panel's holes. Mark at the corners and every 16 inches along the edges and at points in between. Put plastic anchors in the wall (p.51) at these points. When mounting the panel, put a screw through the pegboard hole, then through the spacer.

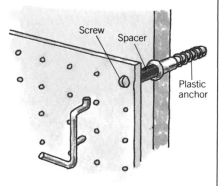

Screw Spacer Plastic anchor

If you have trouble fitting a spacer under a panel, glue it to the anchor in the wall. Use masking tape to hold it while the glue sets. Even better, look for a hardware dealer who carries a special pegboard anchor with a built-in spacer.

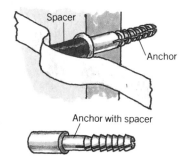

Spacer Anchor

Anchor with spacer

Heavy-duty ¼-inch pegboard and large sheets of regular ⅛-inch pegboard require extra support. Mount them with ¾-inch furring strips instead of spacers. Nail the strips to the studs. Then screw the pegboard to them. Put strips along all the panel's edges and along every stud in the middle. Plan them so that they'll fall between rows of holes.

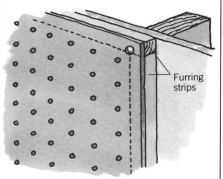

Furring strips

Furring strips are also best for mounting pegboard on rough and uneven masonry walls. Attach them with cut nails or masonry nails (p.51), using scraps of wood as shims to level them.

Shim

In garages and other areas with unfinished walls, screw pegboard directly to the exposed studs.

If either studs or furring strips will be visible through a panel's holes, paint them black; they won't be noticeable that way.

Put pegboard on the back of an open bookcase, and you'll have a dual-purpose room divider with shelves on one side and hooks on the other.

SHELF MATERIALS

For shelves less than a foot deep, the strongest and most rigid commonly available material is nominal 1-inch softwood lumber (see box at right). It's also easy to cut, nail, and finish.

To reduce the tendency of a wide board to curve along its length, check its growth rings and install it so that its heart side—the side that was closest to the center of the tree—faces upward. The weight of materials on the shelf will then work against the warping.

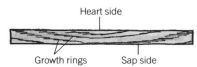

Heart side

Growth rings   Sap side

Another good shelving material is ¾-inch plywood (see box, p.58). It's ideal when you want deep shelves or shelves of a depth other than standard wood widths. It's also generally more economical for a large number of shelves.

To cut plywood most efficiently, use shelf widths that divide easily into a sheet's 48- x 96-inch dimensions, notably 8, 12, 16, 24, 32.

Plan to cut each plywood shelf ⅛ inch shorter than its potential maximum size to provide leeway for sawing. This typical plywood cutting diagram shows one way a sheet can yield 12 shelves.

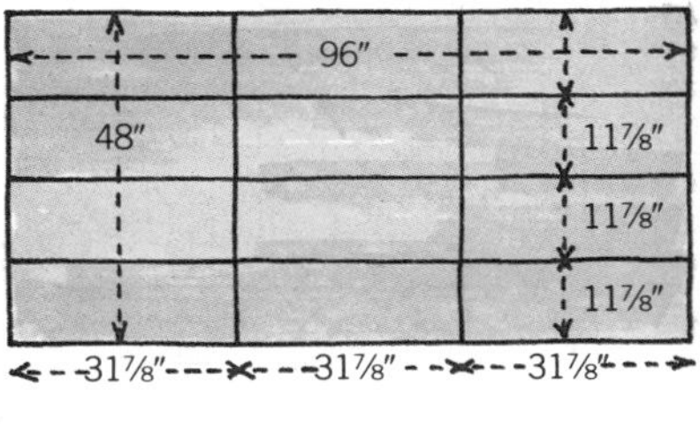

←——— Surface grain ———→

	96"	
48"		11⅞"
		11⅞"
		11⅞"

←– -31⅞"- --×- - -31⅞" - -→×- - -31⅞"- - -→

BUYING LUMBER

When buying board lumber, remember that the size you ask for isn't the size you'll get. For example, a 1 x 8 really measures ¾ inch thick by 7¼ inches wide—as the chart below shows. A board's length, however, is always exact. Most boards come in 8-foot lengths; you can get longer pieces in even-numbered feet. For an additional charge, dealers will usually cut boards to any length and width you order.

Most dealers carry one or two grades of "select" or "clear" lumber—boards with few or no knots or other defects. They are ideal for highly visible shelves that will receive a natural finish. But consider a less expensive and knottier "common" grade when you're planning to paint or to put the boards in the back of a closet. Buy from a dealer who'll let you inspect the lumber. And always sight along a board's edges to make sure it's straight.

STANDARD LUMBER SIZES

Size to order	Actual size in inches
1 x 2	¾ x 1½
1 x 3	¾ x 2½
1 x 4	¾ x 3½
1 x 6	¾ x 5½
1 x 8	¾ x 7¼
1 x 10	¾ x 9¼
1 x 12	¾ x 11¼
2 x 2	1½ x 1½
2 x 3	1½ x 2½
2 x 4	1½ x 3½
2 x 6	1½ x 5½
2 x 8	1½ x 7¼
2 x 10	1½ x 9¼
2 x 12	1½ x 11¼

BUYING PLYWOOD

Plywood usually comes in sheets measuring 4 feet by 8 feet, in thicknesses of ¼, ½, or ¾ inch. Some dealers sell half and quarter sheets. Most sheets consist of layers of softwood, usually Douglas fir. They are graded from A to D, depending mainly on how well patches (used to fix knots and other blemishes on front and back surfaces) match the original grain.

For most storage projects, a good choice is a lumberyard standby graded A–B (good front, fairly good back). On rough storage, you'll save by using a sheet with a face known as C-plugged (only moderate quality but knotholes are filled, or plugged). At the other extreme, a top-quality project may deserve plywood

faced with a special flawless N grade (no knots) softwood surface—or with a hardwood veneer, such as birch. If your project will be exposed to water—in a kitchen, for example—buy exterior plywood; it's made with waterproof glues.

Cutting plywood is tricky. If you don't have a circular saw with a carbide-tipped plywood blade, find a lumber dealer who will cut pieces to size for you. Supply exact measurements and indicate the direction of each piece's surface grain. For strength and looks, you'll usually want this grain to run in the longer direction—along a shelf's length, for example. When you pick up your order, check each piece's dimensions.

Cover any visible plywood shelf edge with veneer tape (step 6, p.64)—or with strips of ¼-inch lumber if it will be used heavily.

For utility shelving, an inexpensive substitute is ¾-inch particleboard, which comes in sheets like plywood. But reserve this less rigid material for light loads or else support it at close intervals.

For quick shelving, prefinished shelves are a great convenience. But most have cores of particleboard and should carry only light loads or be well supported.

STRENGTHENING SHELVES

To strengthen a shelf, attach a 1 x 2 or a larger wood strip along its front edge. If the shelf's supports permit, consider putting a strip under its rear edge or providing support from below at midspan.

Rear cleat

1 x 2

Vertical divider

If you want a shelf to span a distance greater than recommended (p.60), use nominal 2-inch board lumber. Or glue two pieces of ¾-inch plywood surface to surface and glue and nail 1 x 2's on the exposed edges.

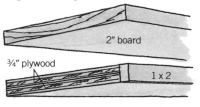

2" board

¾" plywood

1 x 2

SHELVES ON INDIVIDUAL BRACKETS

On shelves that will carry light loads, the brackets will be almost unnoticeable if you use large L-brackets and install them upside down so that the items you put on the shelf will hide them.

L-bracket

When putting up shelf brackets, always attach the longer leg to the wall. And for heavy loads use brackets with angled gussets between the legs.

SHELVES ON STANDARDS

One of the fastest, least costly ways to cover a wall with shelves is to use standards and brackets. Many versions are available, including heavy-duty metal ones and decorative wood ones. Most are installed like regular standards and brackets (p.60).

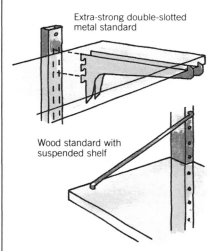

Extra-strong double-slotted metal standard

Wood standard with suspended shelf

When planning to install shelves on standards, be sure to investigate adjustable angle brackets for a magazine or book rack and long brackets for a desk or cabinet.

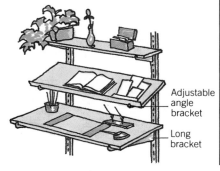

Adjustable angle bracket

Long bracket

PUTTING UP SHELF STANDARDS

If you don't have a level, you can still install a shelf standard that's perfectly vertical. Just mount it loosely from its top screw and let it swing back and forth. When it stops moving, install the bottom screw and tighten both screws.

Which end is up? If your shelf standards have no slots at one end, that end is the top. That way, the lowest shelf can be mounted at the very bottom of the standards.

On a masonry wall, it's difficult to install lead anchors that precisely match the holes on a shelf standard. It's easier to secure a 1 x 3 to the wall with cut or masonry nails and then screw the standards to it.

TYPICAL SHELF REQUIREMENTS

Kinds of objects	Depth in inches	Height in inches
Audiovisual materials		
Audiocassettes	3¼	5
Compact discs	6¼	5½
LP records	13½	13½
Videocassettes	5¾	9
Books and magazines		
Art and picture books	12	13
Novels, general books	8–12	10
Magazines	9½	12
Paperbacks	6	8
Clothing		
Men's shirts	15	10
Men's shoes	13	6
Men's sweaters	15	12
Women's blouses	14	10
Women's shoes	10½	8
Kitchen items		
Beverages	6	13
Bowls	8–12	5
Boxed foods	6–8	8–12
Canned goods	4½	5½
Cups and glasses	10	6–10
Plates (stacked)	12	5–7
Pots and pans	9–12	5–9
Trays (on edge)	11	16
Linens and bath items		
Bath towels	16–24	14
Sheets	16–24	12
Toiletries	4–8	4–10

SPACING SHELF SUPPORTS

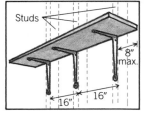

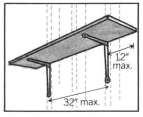

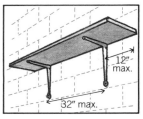

Heavy loads should have their supports held by long screws going well into the wall studs. Supports should be screwed to every stud. In most homes, the studs are spaced at 16-inch intervals (see box, p.49). Keep the overhang at each end of a shelf to 8 inches or less.

Lighter loads can be held by supports screwed into every other stud, and the overhang can extend 12 inches. But if your home has studs 24 inches apart, attach a support to each stud, whatever the load. You can attach a shelf carrying a very light load with wall fasteners (p.51).

Masonry walls call for inserting either expansion shields or lead anchors to hold the supports (p.52). For heavy loads, put supports at least every 16 inches, and keep the overhang less than 8 inches. Lighter loads need support at 32-inch intervals and an overhang of 1 foot or less.

SINGLE SHELF ON BRACKETS

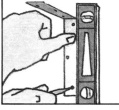

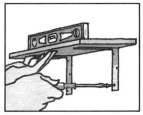

1. Position a shelf bracket on the wall. Use a level or a combination square to check that it's vertical. Mark the position of the screw holes. With a bit that's slightly smaller in diameter than the screw, drill screw holes. Screw the bracket to the wall.

2. Measure and mark the positions of both brackets on the shelf. Then drill holes and screw the other bracket to the shelf. Make sure that the bracket is square and even with the shelf's back edge. Be careful not to drill all the way through the shelf.

3. Position the shelf on the wall and check that it's level. Then attach the bracket that's on the shelf to the wall. Finally, attach the first bracket to the shelf. Each time, mark and drill holes for the screws as you did in the first two steps.

SHELVES ON STANDARDS

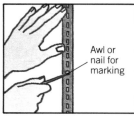

Awl or nail for marking

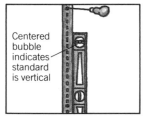

Centered bubble indicates standard is vertical

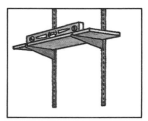

1. Position a slotted standard on the wall. Find a screw hole in the middle of the standard and mark its position. Using a bit that's slightly smaller than the screw, drill a hole at that point. Attach the standard but don't tighten the screw all the way.

2. Adjust the standard's position until the bubble in a level shows that it's perfectly vertical. Then mark and drill holes for the other screws and finish attaching the standard. If necessary, you can swing the standard out of the way while you're drilling.

3. Put a bracket on the standard and in the matching slot holes of another standard. Hold the second standard against the wall and put a shelf on the brackets. Level the shelf, then put up the standard the same way you did the first.

DISGUISING SHELF HARDWARE

Camouflage brackets for a single shelf or standards by painting them the same color as the wall.

To conceal brackets on standards, use brackets an inch or so shorter than the shelf width. Drill a hole partway into the shelf's underside for each bracket's front tip. A 1 x 2 nailed to the shelf's front edge hides the brackets even more.

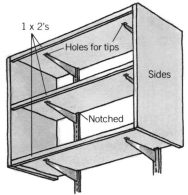

To make shelves on standards and brackets look built-in, install sides at each end. Attach them to just the top and bottom shelves so that you can still adjust the others. Notching the shelves to fit around the standards also helps.

SHELVES ON UPRIGHTS

Uprights that fit by screw or spring pressure between the ceiling and the floor provide another quick way to cover a wall—or divide a room—with shelves. Poles slotted to accept brackets are available for standard 8-foot ceilings. Higher ceilings need extensions.

Install tension poles with their brackets toward the wall. This helps conceal the slots and brackets, creating a more finished look.

Whenever possible install a tension pole directly beneath a joist in the ceiling. You can usually locate joists as you do studs (p.49).

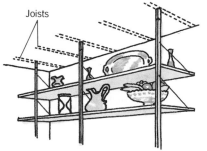

You can make your own tension poles from 2 x 4's. Cut each an inch shorter than ceiling height and screw a shelf standard to it. Then drill a hole in the top and install a screw-out furniture leveler. Put an extra nut on the leveler to lock it in place. Secure the 2 x 4 to the floor with an L-bracket.

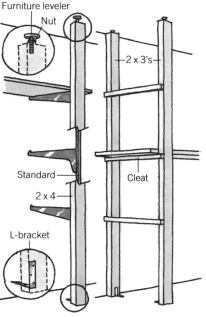

For deeper shelves, use pairs of tension poles made from 2 x 3's. Support the shelves with cleats or with clips on tracks (p.67).

If appearance doesn't matter, you can install uprights quickly with spring-loaded metal caps that top 2 x 3's. But make sure the fit between floor and ceiling is tight and that each upright is under a joist.

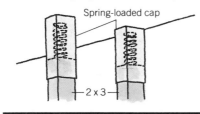

Spring-loaded cap

2 x 3

INDUSTRIAL SHELVING

Don't limit steel utility shelves to rough storage. Spray-paint a unit in a bright color and outfit it with plastic or wire bins for a bathroom. Or finish it in a subdued color and use it for large books and vases in the living room.

Industrial wire shelving may also be the answer to storage in any room—and a unit can carry a lot of weight. Many home centers carry chrome-plated units, and you can get plainer versions from commerical shelving stores.

IMPROVISED SHELVES

Create an entire storage wall by grouping together sturdy wood and plastic cartons or by combining them with boards. Keep larger and stronger cartons near the bottom, and secure higher ones to the wall and to one another. For a unified effect, paint all the containers the same color.

Bricks, cinder blocks, tile flues, wood blocks, and decorative cement blocks are all time-honored shelf spacers. Be sure to stack them straight. Locate a tall unit along a wall and secure the higher shelves to the wall.

You can make hanging shelves for light loads with rope, chain, threaded metal rods, and either woven nylon lawn-chair webbing or jute upholstery webbing. Be sure to secure the supports to ceiling joists or wall studs.

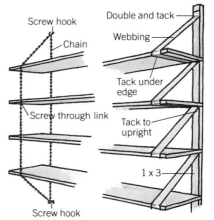

Screw hook

Chain

Double and tack

Webbing

Tack under edge

Screw through link

Tack to upright

1 x 3

Screw hook

Create a wall unit with a pair of straight ladders. Secure one side of each ladder to a stud in the wall and rest shelves on the rungs.

SHELF TIDIERS

To keep items from falling off a shelf, make shelf ends by attaching a short length of board or plywood to each end.

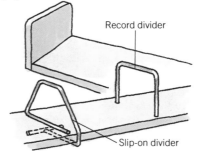

Record divider

Slip-on divider

Wire dividers that slip on and grip the shelf are a nice alternative to regular bookends. And wire LP-record dividers that fit into holes drilled in a shelf make good dividers and ends on any shelf.

Dowels make good vertical shelf dividers. To fit a dowel between two shelves, cut it ½ inch longer than the distance between the shelves. Then drill a hole ½ inch deep in the upper shelf and another hole ¼ inch deep in the lower shelf. Shove the dowel all the way into the upper hole; then drop it into the lower one.

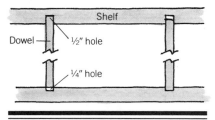

WIRE WALL SYSTEMS

Consider using a wire grid instead of pegboard. Its waterproof vinyl finish makes it especially useful in a kitchen or bath. An assortment of hooks, baskets, and other clip-ons are available.

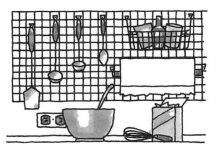

Vinyl-coated wire shelving provides a fast way to create shelves in a kitchen, bathroom, pantry, child's room, laundry room, or garage. It comes in various lengths, and you can quickly cut it to any length with a hacksaw. Mount it with the lip upward to keep items such as bottles from falling off.

You can also quickly remodel a closet with wire shelving. Get shelves with a bare front rod for hanging clothing.

Install a wire system with closely spaced plastic anchors or other hollow-wall fasteners. The design of most systems requires fasteners at set intervals, usually making it impossible to fasten to studs.

CABINETS AND CASES

Before building a cabinet or case, check stores that carry unfinished furniture or prefabricated kits. A standard unit, such as a bookcase, can cost little more than the building materials.

To avoid an unpleasant surprise, plan your cabinet or bookcase on paper before sawing the pieces. Measure the space where the unit will go and make sketches with dimensions, showing front, side, and top views.

If you're fitting a cabinet in a tight space, be sure to allow enough room to get it into position. Usually a ⅛-inch clearance on each side is all you need.

If a space requires a storage unit wider than 32 inches, put in a vertical partition, or consider having two units side by side.

A BASIC PLYWOOD STORAGE UNIT

Here's an easily adaptable storage unit with a frame and shelves made of ¾-inch plywood. For the back, order a piece of ¼-inch plywood that's ¼ inch less than the unit's overall measurements from side to side and from top to bottom shelf. Get a 1 x 3 (see box, p.57) for the toeboard and ¾-inch-square molding for the cleats. Also buy white glue, 3d and 6d finishing nails, and veneer tape to cover the plywood edges.

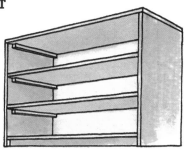

Tips on tools and wood joining are on pp.183–192; on buying and cutting plywood, p.58.

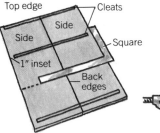

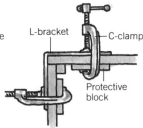

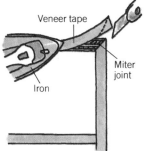

1. Align top and bottom edges of the side pieces. Mark each cleat position, making a line across both pieces at once. Make sure lowest cleat will be even with toeboard top. Cut cleats 1 inch shorter than shelf depth. Nail and glue a cleat along each line and at each side's top edge. Use 3d nails 2 inches apart.

2. Join the top and sides. At each corner apply glue and clamp the pieces together at a right angle. Use an oversize L-bracket with C-clamps to get a right angle. (For more on gluing and clamping techniques, see pp.191–192.) Secure the top to the sides with 6d nails and to the cleats with 3d nails.

3. Set the bottom shelf in place. Glue and clamp each bottom corner. Use 3d nails to secure the bottom shelf to the cleats and 6d nails to secure the sides to the shelf. Then install the toe-board, using glue and 6d nails.

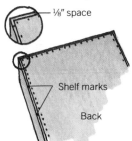

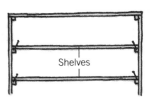

4. Turn the unit over. Measure up ⅜ inch from the top of each cleat, and make a mark across the frame's back edges to indicate where each shelf's center-line will be. Apply glue along the frame's edges. Then position the back so that it is set in ⅛ inch along all edges. Attach the back with 3d nails at 4-inch intervals.

5. Install the shelves. Put glue along each shelf's back edge and along each cleat top. Then secure the shelves to the cleats with 3d nails. Then turn the unit over. Using the marks you made earlier, draw a line across the back along each shelf's center-line. Nail the back to the shelves along the line.

6. Cover the raw plywood edges on the front of the unit with veneer tape. Use a clothing iron on a warm, nonsteam setting to smooth the tape along the entire length of an edge. Do the shelf edges first and trim the tape ends with a utility knife. Then do the sides and the top. Miter the tape at the top corners.

MAKING A CABINET

After assembling a cabinet's basic frame, measure diagonally between corners. If both measurements are exactly the same, the frame is square. If not, shift the sides until the corners are square.

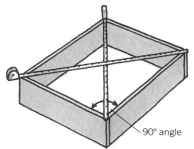

90° angle

For a case that you can dismantle and move easily, connect the four major joints with bolts and nuts. Attach the back with screws and have shelves that just lift out.

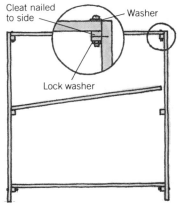

Cleat nailed to side
Washer
Lock washer

When nailing cleats to a unit's side, angle the nails downward for greater holding power.

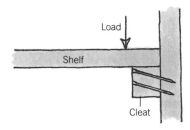

Load
Shelf
Cleat

BUYING NAILS

You can do most projects with either common nails or finishing nails. Common nails have large, flat heads and are fine for rough work. But when appearance counts, select the thinner finishing nails. You can drive a finishing nail's head below the wood's surface with a nail set and fill the hole with wood putty.

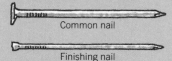

Common nail

Finishing nail

Nails are sized according to the penny system, designated by a number and a *d*. For sizes up to 10d (10 penny), you can calculate a nail's length by dividing the penny size by four, then adding ½ inch. An 8d nail, for example, is 2½ inches long. If you can, buy nails in 1-pound quantities—the cost per nail is much less than when you buy small packets.

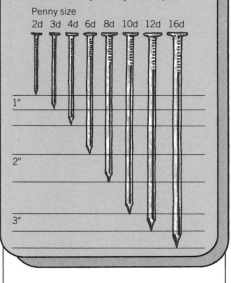

Penny size
2d 3d 4d 6d 8d 10d 12d 16d
1"
2"
3"

For stacking modular units, make the basic case (facing page) without a toeboard. Attach the bottom with corner cleats like the top.

For added strength, use 1 x 2 (or larger) cleats and attach them with glue and screws (p.66). Reinforce each shelf's edges (p.58).

To create an open bookcase, simply nail shelves between four L-shaped corners, each made by gluing and nailing a 1 x 4 to a 1 x 3.

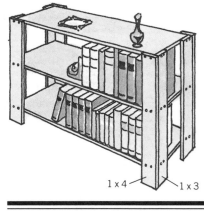

1 x 4   1 x 3

VARYING THE BASIC CABINET

Since a bookcase is narrow, you can make it from board lumber, following the steps for making a plywood case (p.64). Either 1 x 10's or 1 x 12's are good choices.

If you're building a tall bookcase, make the sides overlap the top so that the top's edge can't be seen. For added strength, nail through the sides into a middle shelf.

For a kitchen or bathroom cabinet, just make a basic case with a kick space. Notch the corners of the sides and nail a 1 x 4 toeboard over the sides.

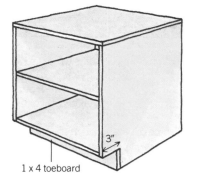

3″

1 x 4 toeboard

BUYING WOOD SCREWS

Match a screw to the type of job it will do. A flathead screw is fine for most joints. You can drive its head flush with the surface or sink it below and hide it with wood putty or a wood plug (p.190). When a screw must be exposed, an ovalhead screw is attractive and can be easily removed without marring a surface. A roundhead screw is most useful for attaching thin material, such as a metal bracket or pegboard, to wood.

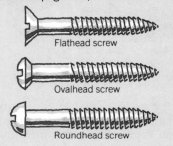

Flathead screw

Ovalhead screw

Roundhead screw

Screws usually come in lengths ranging from ¼ inch to 3 inches. Diameters are indicated by a gauge number. Many length and gauge combinations are available. When buying screws, state the length and gauge number you want—for example, a 1¼-inch, No. 7 screw. Get stainless steel or aluminum screws for a project that will be exposed to moisture and brass or bronze ones to match hardware. Otherwise, you'll save using plain, plated, or galvanized screws. Like nails, screws are most economical when you buy them in pound quantities.

Gauge number

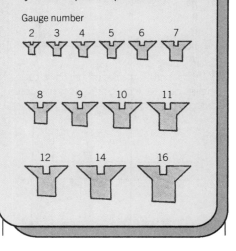

For a wall-hung case, replace the basic case's back with mounting boards—a 1 x 4 nailed and glued under the top and a 1 x 2 under the bottom shelf. Mount a 1 x 2 under the front of the bottom shelf too.

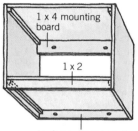

1 x 4 mounting board

1 x 2

1 x 2 mounting board

Use screw eyes to support a shelf that you may later want to move. Screw eyes are also great for adding a shelf to a finished cabinet.

For movable shelves, use metal spade pins or bracket pins that fit in rows of holes in the sides.

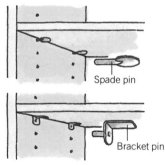

Spade pin

Bracket pin

Drill holes for pins before assembling a unit. For perfectly aligned holes, use pegboard as a guide.

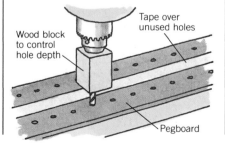

Wood block to control hole depth

Tape over unused holes

Pegboard

You can also create adjustable shelves with metal tracks and clips. Attach two tracks to each side before assembly. Notch the shelves to fit around the tracks.

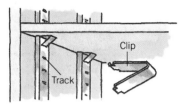

Clip

Track

Use pliers to squeeze troublesome clips into tracks.

Putting doors on a cabinet is tricky. It's easier to build the case to fit precut doors. A good choice for doors is ¾-inch-thick unfinished slat shutters. Put them between 1 x 2's nailed to the unit's front edges. Use attractive hinges.

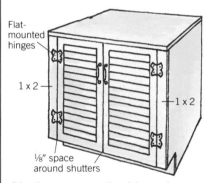

Flat-mounted hinges

1 x 2

1 x 2

⅛" space around shutters

It's also easier to build a cabinet to fit ready-made drawers. Use plastic bins and fit their rims between pairs of cleats on each side. Or use wire baskets on their own metal runners or frame.

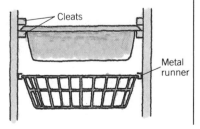

Cleats

Metal runner

To make cabinets look built in, install molding that covers the cracks along walls, ceiling, and floor and between units. Span wide gaps between units with shelves or false panels. These are great ways to adapt old or purchased units to a new space.

ORGANIZING DRAWERS

You can increase a deep drawer's usable space with a sliding tray. A simple box of ½-inch plywood on hardwood runners will do.

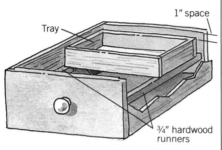

Tray · 1" space · ¾" hardwood runners

Make a tray half of the drawer's width or depth so that you can slide it and gain full access to the bottom. Or make it with handles so that you can easily lift it out.

Here is a versatile divider arrangement that can benefit both wide and deep drawers. Nail and glue the rear divider to the front-to-back dividers first. Then nail and glue the spacers on the drawer's front, and glue the dividers' front ends between them. Nail the rear piece through the sides.

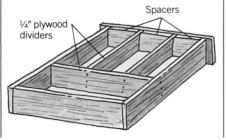

Spacers · ¼" plywood dividers

To find the best arrangement for dividers, try temporary ones for a few weeks. Just use doubled-over cardboard with flaps at the bottom and ends. Use the flaps to attach the pieces to the drawer and to each other with duct tape.

Plastic trays with compartments needn't be limited to desk and kitchen drawers. Use them in any shallow drawer to organize jewelry, cosmetics, sewing supplies, tools, keys, and pocket change.

Another way to create small compartments in a shallow drawer is to notch and join strips of lattice, which you can buy at a lumberyard. Clamp the crosspieces together and cut the notches all at once so that they'll align exactly.

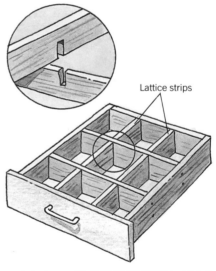

Lattice strips

ROLLOUTS AND PULLOUTS

Rollouts and pullouts are great space savers. Because you don't have to reach in, you don't have to leave room above items, and you can take out bulky items in the rear without disturbing small ones in the front.

An easy way to make a pullout shelf is to mount plywood between hardwood cleats with other pieces of cleat material on the shelf as guides. To clear your cabinet's front frame, you may have to put a spacer behind the cleats.

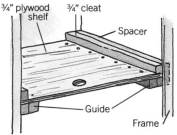

¾" plywood shelf ¾" cleat Spacer Guide Frame

For a simple rollout tray, nail and glue 1 x 4's around the edges of a piece of ¾-inch plywood. Then mount the tray to the bottom of a cabinet, using a pair of base-mounted drawer slides.

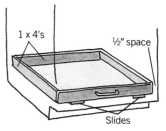

1 x 4's ½" space Slides

A rollout with shelves is just a simple case on drawer slides. You can build one to fit any cabinet, using ¾-inch plywood, 1 x 4's, and trim for the plywood's edges.

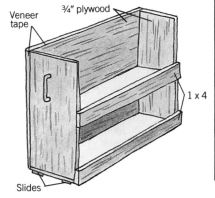

Veneer tape ¾" plywood 1 x 4 Slides

Custom design other rollouts to fit your needs. Make a rollout with a center partition and shelves on two sides. Or, instead of shelves, install dowels like towel bars for hanging clothing or linens.

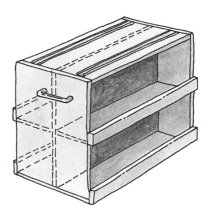

Also consider supporting a rollout from slides attached to a cabinet's top or side. If a cabinet wall is thin, mount a slide on a sturdy cleat.

SELECTING DRAWER SLIDES

After planning a rollout, show your design to a hardware dealer to find out exactly what type of drawer slides you need. If your local dealer doesn't have the kind you need, try a store specializing in cabinet hardware.

Drawer slides vary in the amount of clearance they need. Buy them *before* you cut the pieces for a rollout. They should be slightly shorter than your cabinet's depth.

Drawer slides that pull out most, but not all, of the way are less expensive and generally easier to install. But consider full-extension slides if you'll need to take heavy items out of the rear of a rollout.

69

CHAPTER TWO

INDOORS

Discover how to keep your entire home—from floors to ceilings and from basement to attic—sparkling clean and running smoothly. Then learn all about selecting and maintaining appliances and what to do before calling for service when a problem arises.

All Around the House

Page 71

Planning your cleaning and making it easier; how to clean in layers; choosing and using cleaning products and equipment; safety measures; washing walls and ceilings; cleaning wall coverings; treating tiles; caring for paneling; washing, waxing, and protecting floors; how to replace vinyl floor tiles; cleaning curtains; caring for window shades and venetian blinds; cleaning windows; replacing a windowpane; fixing a broken sash cord; caring for window screens; making windows energy-efficient; how to deal with a sticking door; sliding doors; fixing a door that binds; how to choose a vacuum cleaner and its attachments; vacuum maintenance, problems, and repair; cleaning and preserving carpets; patching a carpet; repairing a carpet burn; Oriental rugs; caring for your furniture and light fixtures; cleaning special objects; cleaning the fireplace; home entertainment systems; what to do before calling for a tele-

phone repairman; keeping the dining room clean; cut flowers and houseplants; bedroom upkeep; kitchen cleaning basics; kitchen safety; range and microwave maintenance; cleaning an exhaust fan; caring for refrigerators and small appliances; clean kitchen counters; sink care; handling the garbage; unclogging drains; washing the dishes; vacuum bottles, pots, and pans; sharpening knives; safety in the bathroom; keeping a bathroom spotless; repairing a leaking spout; toilet problems; attic hints; controlling dampness in basements and flooding; patching an inactive crack in a basement wall; leaks and seepage; fixing leaky pipes; frozen pipes; conserving energy; heating system problems; oil burner maintenance; attic and room fans; air conditioning hints; noise-busting a room air conditioner; pest control; do's and dont's of using pesticides; sorting out security systems and alarms.

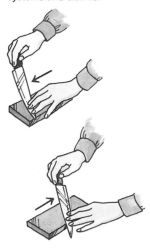

Those Wonderful Appliances

Page 131

How long you will have an appliance; what to check before calling for service on an appliance; getting the most from a refrigerator and freezer; how to replace a refrigerator door gasket; selecting a range; adjusting your oven's temperature control; what to do if you smell gas; adjusting the flame on a gas range; selecting a dishwasher and loading it properly; getting the most from dishwasher detergent; buying and connecting your new clothes washer; saving on water-heating bills; water-heater upkeep; setting up and maintaining a new dryer; toasters and toaster ovens; cooking with a microwave; mixers, blenders, and food processors; coffee makers, percolators, and urns; caring for steam irons; humidifiers and dehumidifiers; trash compactors and garbage disposers; electric lights, plugs, and cords; testing and replacing an appliance power cord; replacing a plug; light switches; fuses and circuit breakers; shutting off electric power.

All Around the House

PLANNING YOUR CLEANING

Decide what "clean" means to you and then keep house accordingly. Clean things because they're dirty, not because it's time. If you don't notice a difference when you're cleaning something, *stop!*

It may be more practical for you to do your spring cleaning in the fall—the temperature's right for hard work, and it's more efficient to remove summer dirt that's come in through open windows before closing up the house for winter.

On the other hand, you may wish to clean and air out the house in the spring after it has been closed all winter.

Few cleaning jobs need to be done at a set time of year. Aside from cleaning screens and storm windows, and laundering summer or winter blankets, how you set up a seasonal cleaning schedule is strictly up to you. (To find out the best times for tackling exterior chores, turn to p. 166.)

CLEANING IN LAYERS

When you clean according to a schedule, you build up a momentum that you don't have to break while deciding what to do next. One way to organize your cleaning schedule is to think of cleaning in layers. Adjust the following schedule to suit your specific needs, taking into account the size of your family and your home.

Layer 1 covers everyday jobs: washing the dishes, sweeping the floor, emptying the garbage, making the beds, picking up. These tasks should add up to no more than half an hour for a one-bedroom, single-level home. Add 10 minutes for each additional bedroom and level.

Layer 2 tasks are done once or twice a week: vacuuming, watering the plants, cleaning the garbage pail, wiping down the bathroom, cleaning the toilet, dusting the furniture.

Layer 3 is once-a-week deep cleaning: scrubbing the floors, polishing the furniture, cleaning the refrigerator, changing the linens. Set aside several hours to do all these jobs at once. Or add one deep-cleaning job to your list of Layer-1 tasks each day.

Layer 4 involves special projects: washing the windows and the woodwork, cleaning the oven, polishing the silver, cleaning the silver, washing summer and winter blankets, cleaning the screens and storm windows. Either choose a fixed 2 hours a week for these or add them to your Layer-3 list of things to do each week as they come up.

MAKING CLEANING EASIER

Where to begin? To see real progress fast, start with the areas that tend to go the fastest—the living and dining rooms and the halls—they're usually less cluttered and less dirty.

71

To make sure that you don't miss anything when dusting a room, start at the door and work around the room in one direction.

Eliminating clutter cuts down on the need to clean because an uncluttered home, even though not spotless, looks better than one that is dust-free but strewn with odds and ends.

Clean faster by clustering your activities; do as many tasks as you can in one place before you move on to the next area.

CHOOSING AND USING EQUIPMENT

No need to return to the cleaning closet every time you need something. Carry all your supplies from one room to the next in a "maid's basket"—a plastic bin with a handle—or a cleaning cart.

For spills and daily cleanup, install paper-towel racks in key places—the garage, workbench, baby's room, and bathroom, as well as the kitchen where they're usually kept.

Be choosy about your cleaning rags. Use cotton fabrics, such as old towels, diapers, or undershirts, and avoid cloths that contain less absorbent synthetic fibers, such as old slips.

Use clean cloths for damp or dry dusting; dirty ones will scratch surfaces.

To prevent dust from rolling out of your dustpan, dampen the pan before you start dusting.

If the edge of your dustpan becomes bent, take time to straighten it out, or you'll end up chasing dirt across the floor every time you use it.

Once you've collected the dirt and dust, you'll have to get rid of it. If you can't shake the dust mop outdoors, try shaking it into a paper or plastic bag—or try vacuuming instead of dusting.

CHOOSING CLEANING PRODUCTS

Resist the temptation to buy more types of cleaning products than you need. The more products you accumulate in your home, the greater the chance they'll be misused by children and adults.

Read all product labels before using the product. As a general rule, do not mix cleaning substances unless the directions instruct you to do so.

THE USE AND CARE OF BASIC CLEANING TOOLS

Tool	Use	Care
Dustcloths	For dry dusting of lightly soiled surfaces, use lintless cloths. Dampen absorbent terry or other cotton cloths with water or a little furniture polish to clean dust, smears, fingerprints, or soot. Follow the grain of wood surfaces	Wash in hot sudsy water after each use. Hang to dry. Cloths used for waxing and polishing should not be machine-dried because flammable fluids or fumes may remain in them
Broom	For quick, routine cleanup of hard floors. Keep broom firmly on surface and sweep slowly in one direction, collecting dirt in dustpan	Always hang to store. When soiled, dip it in hot sudsy water, rinse, and dry with rubber band around bristles to straighten them
Dust mop	For dusting bare floors between vacuum cleanings. Push across floor without raising mop, following grain of wood	Always hang to store. Shake into a large moistened bag after each use or vacuum clean. Wash in hot sudsy water, rinse, and dry in breezy, shady place. Or run through the washer and dryer in a net bag
Wet mop	For cleaning dirt and grime from washable resilient floors. Use with all-purpose cleaner or detergent and wring with wringer attached to bucket. Mop should be wet, but not sopping	Wash in hot sudsy water after each use, rinse thoroughly, shake to separate strings, and hang or turn upside down to dry (in sun if possible). Store in a cool, dry place. Never keep a damp mop on floor or in bucket
Sponge mop	For cleaning moderate-size, hard-surface floors. Soak in sudsy cleaning solution, then squeeze until just damp. Clean with firm strokes, covering no more than a 3-square-foot area at a time. Rinse, then repeat	Wash and rinse after each use, then stand upside down to dry. Moisten occasionally to keep from "drying hard." If detachable, follow care instructions for sponges
Scrub brushes	For cleaning rough surfaces, heavily soiled hard floors, and outdoor porches. Scrub with long strokes, using hot water and all-purpose cleaner	Wash in hot sudsy water after each use. Rinse in clear water; shake and let dry, bristles down. Store only when completely dry
Sponge	For all washable surfaces. Dip into hot or warm sudsy water, squeeze thoroughly, and rub with firm strokes	Clean in hot sudsy water, rinsing completely and squeezing dry. Throw in the washing machine with a general load (zip into a net bag to keep sponges from falling apart) or with a bleach load if sponges are smelly
Dry sponge	For flat-painted walls and ceilings, wallpaper, lampshades, and other areas where liquid cleaners are unsuitable. Use dry, turning and folding so that a clean part of the sponge is always in contact with the surface	Dry sponges are not reusable. Discard when saturated with dirt
Bucket	For all wet cleaning. Use two buckets—one for cleaner and one for rinse solution. Choose one with a wringer attached for wet-mopping	Rinse thoroughly after each use. Let rubber buckets air-dry; to avoid rust, dry metal buckets with paper towels after rinsing

Many people recommend making your own cleaning products. This is worthwhile only if the homemade products are much less costly and work just as safely and effectively as the commercial versions. They seldom do.

SAFETY MEASURES

Find a safe storage area for cleaning products out of the reach of children and pets—not a cabinet where food supplies are kept. Return products to this area immediately after use. Never put a cleaning product down within a small child's reach and walk away, not even for a minute.

Always keep household cleaning products in the containers they came in. Never transfer them to containers that you normally use for food. Throw out empty cleaning-product containers immediately; they're not suitable for storing anything else.

Before throwing away a cleaning product, check the label on the container; if it has "Caution," "Warning," or "Poison" on it, follow carefully the directions for the proper disposal of the empty container.

CLEANING METHODS

Avoid extra work; follow the manufacturers' directions on cleaning supplies. If the label says use only one capful, more won't be better—it will be harder to rinse off and more expensive to use.

Cover half the holes in the top of a can of scouring powder with masking tape and the can will probably last twice as long.

To avoid redepositing dirt on the surface, always use a clean solution. Mix up a new bucket of cleaner and water as soon as the first bucket becomes moderately dirty.

SUBSTITUTES FOR CLEANING PRODUCTS

Ammonia, diluted with 3 parts water in an empty pump-spray bottle, can be used instead of a commercial spray to clean windows, appliances, and countertops. Use full-strength ammonia to remove wax from floors or to clean the oven (not really dirty ones, however).
Caution: Always wear rubber gloves whenever cleaning with an ammonia solution. Also, when using it full strength, make sure that the work area is well ventilated.

An excellent substitute for metal cleaner to scour copper and brass is ½ cup vinegar mixed with 1 tablespoon salt.

Full-strength pine oil makes quick work of cleaning and deodorizing garbage pails and bathroom and kitchen floors. If you dilute the pine oil, you won't have to rinse.

Baking soda is milder than harsh scouring powders for cleaning kitchen and bath fixtures. It also removes odors and washes stains from refrigerators and freezers, coffeepots and teapots, and thermos bottles. Try it to deodorize diaper pails and kitty litter.

A sprinkling of dry baking soda before vacuuming will freshen carpeting as well as any commercial carpet deodorizer.

WALLS AND CEILINGS

Before washing a painted surface, dust it with a broom covered with a flannel cloth. Change the cloth when it gets dirty.

To dust hard-to-reach corners, slip an old sock over a yardstick and secure it with a rubber band.

Cobwebs can be sticky and stain surfaces. Lift them away from the wall rather than push them onto the surface, using a vacuum cleaner tool or a cloth-covered broom.

When vacuuming trim, plaster-work, or woodwork, protect the surface from scratches by attaching a "bumper," a strip of foam rubber secured with a rubber band, to the head of your vacuum's crevice attachment.

WASHING WALLS

Washing painted walls is faster and cheaper than painting them. If you have your walls professionally washed, you'll probably spend a third of what you would for a professional paint job.

Tie a washcloth around your wrist to catch wall-washing drips. An athlete's terry cloth wristband will work well too.

Practice the two-bucket technique to make your cleaning solution last longer. Rinse and squeeze the dirt from your wall-washing sponge into a bucket of water before dipping it into the clean solution. (The two-bucket technique works well for washing floors too.)

If you start at the bottom when washing walls, the cleaning solution will drip onto the part of the wall you've just cleaned. But if you start at the top, the cleaning solution may cause permanent stains as it drips down. The best way is to work rapidly in small areas with a well-wrung-out cloth or sponge, beginning at the bottom.

Use only white, off-white, or color-fast cloths or sponges to wash walls and ceilings; some dye in colored cloths or sponges may stain the surface.

Very dirty walls may need rinsing as well. Kids over 5 can help with this task, bringing clean water when you need it. (Make a mark on the rinse bucket and ask the child to fill it up to the mark.)

Wiping walls dry will prevent streaking. Use terry cloth towels with a high cotton content, tumble-dried for more absorbency.

As a resting place for lint, pet hair, and other residue, baseboards are usually the dirtiest part of the room. Wash them last after you've finished washing the walls and have damp cloths from wiping them. Clean the baseboards with the damp cloths; then follow with your sponge and a fresh towel.

WALL COVERINGS

Clean fabric wall coverings, including grass cloth, with a hand-held vacuum. Very delicate fabrics such as silk, however, may need a specialist's attention.

Transform regular wallpaper into washable wallpaper by giving it a coat of wallpaper sizing, then one of clear shellac.

Is your nonwashable wallpaper soiled? Rub it gently with an art-gum eraser, dough-type wallpaper cleaner (found in paint and hardware stores), or crustless slices of fresh, "doughy" bread.

Here's a novel way to clean washable wallpaper with dry detergent suds. Mix ¼ cup liquid dishwashing detergent with 1 cup warm water and beat with a rotary beater into a stiff foam. Scoop up only the dry suds and apply with a cloth or sponge.

SPOTS ON WALLPAPER

Clean fresh spots on wallpaper as soon as possible. Blot a new grease spot with a clean paper towel. Then, holding a fresh piece of absorbent paper on the spot, press with a warm (not hot) iron. Change the paper when it becomes greasy.

To remove old grease spots, buy a commercial stain remover (available at wallpaper stores).

Remove crayon marks on wallpaper by sponging them with dry-cleaning solvent. If the dye remains on the wall, mix 1 teaspoon liquid bleach in 1 cup water and apply to the colored stain. (Be sure to test this bleach solution on an inconspicuous spot to determine whether it will damage the pattern or the paper.)

Silver polish, applied with a clean cloth, will remove crayon marks on vinyl wall covering. Concentrated dishwashing detergent also works well.

Use chlorine bleach to remove ink spots on washable wallpaper. Pat the spots with a cloth or a cotton swab dampened with bleach, then rinse with a cloth or sponge dipped in clear water. Test this method in an inconspicuous spot first, since the bleach may remove wall covering color.

TILE TREATMENTS

Get rid of that soapy film on ceramic tile walls or floors—wipe household cleaner (either diluted or full strength) or a solution of 1 part vinegar and 4 parts water over them. Rinse thoroughly with clean water and buff tiles to prevent streaking.

For stained or mildewed grouting, apply a bleach solution (¾ cup liquid chlorine bleach to 1 gallon water) with a cloth, sponge, or toothbrush (wear rubber gloves and old clothes in case of spattering); rinse thoroughly.

Or run a typewriter eraser over grouting to make it come clean.

WOOD PANELING

To clean and polish unwaxed varnished or shellacked wood paneling, apply a mixture of ½ cup turpentine, ¾ cup boiled linseed oil, and 1 tablespoon vinegar; let stand for 15 minutes, then rub until all of the cleaner is removed. To test, rub with a clean, dry finger; it should leave no smudges behind.

For surface scratches on wood paneling, apply clear wax on a damp cloth and rub the scratched area with the grain. If the paneling is dark, you may have to re-stain the scratch mark, and for a uniform appearance, you may have to wax the entire area.

To prevent paneling from developing dark spots behind a picture, place corks at the bottom corners of the frame to allow air to circulate back of it. Cut the corks so that they hold the picture parallel to the wall.

GENERAL FLOOR CARE

Before buying cleaning and waxing products, know what type of floor you're maintaining. If you can't determine it at a glance, ask your home's previous owner or a flooring expert.

After purchasing a new floor covering, keep the maintenance literature in a special file, or write instructions on an index card and tape it to the inside of your cleaning-supplies cabinet door.

Dust-mopping or vacuuming floors daily gets rid of the fine grit that grinds the shine off both waxed and no-wax floor coverings. In the long run, you're putting off the day of a major cleaning.

Dust mops pick up more dirt than brooms and are especially suited to the smooth, glassy finishes used on wood and no-wax floors. To make the work go faster, buy a commercial 18-inch dust mop at a janitorial supply store.

An oiled dust mop ruins a waxed surface. Use a dry dust mop or, if the room itself is very dry, one slightly dampened with water (just a few sprays will do the trick).

When dust-mopping, sweeping, or vacuuming won't do the job, damp-mopping with clear, luke-warm water is safe for all protected surfaces. (Be sure that wood floors are well sealed, however, before damp-mopping them.)

WASHING FLOORS

More floors are washed away than worn away; so wring out your mop until it's almost dry. Excess water will penetrate the seams of sheet flooring or tiles, dissolve protective coatings, and raise the grain and make wood rough.

Use your kitchen trash container as your mop bucket; this way you can clean it at the same time you wash your floors.

Keep one mop just for rinsing; it's almost impossible to get all the cleaning solution out of a mop.

WAXING FLOORS

All floors need the protection of wax or special dressing. A waxed floor is easier to clean with fre-quent damp-mopping and occa-sional washing than one that's unwaxed.

Use water-base waxes and finishes on any surface not damaged by water (just about anything except wood and cork). Solvent-base wax-es can be used on most surfaces except asphalt and rubber.

Dampen the application pad or cloth with plain water before be-ginning to spread wax. This pre-vents excessive absorption of wax into the applicator, aids in spread-ing wax evenly, and makes appli-cation easier.

When a floor starts looking shab-by—usually after six to eight coats of wax (or about once a year)—it's time to remove the old wax.

A squeegee (not the one you use for windows) comes in handy when removing wax. After soaking and scrubbing the floor with detergent or wax remover, squeegee the resi-due into an uncleaned area. Scoop it into an empty bucket with a dust-pan; then damp-mop the squee-geed area with clear water.

If you're in doubt when applying fresh wax to your floors, remember that it's better to use too little than to use too much.

Avoid wax buildup on floor edges, under-furniture areas, and other light-traffic areas by only applying wax every other waxing session.

Keep track of where you do—and don't—want to wax. After you've moved the furniture and cleaned the floor, put a piece of newspaper the size of each piece of furniture on the floor where the furniture usually stands. Then wax around the newspaper.

Self-polishing floor wax hardens very quickly; wash the applicator immediately after each use.

For a quick shine between waxings, place a piece of wax paper under your mop and work around the room. (Be sure that you've dust-mopped thoroughly beforehand, since grit under the paper will scratch the waxed surface of the floor.)

To prevent worn spots on the polished floors in doorways or at the bottom of stairs, give them the following treatment once or twice a month: apply a thin coat of paste

wax with a cheesecloth, allow it to dry for 15 minutes, and then polish; repeat the procedure an hour or two later.

PROTECTING FLOORS

Keep dirt from being tracked into the house by stopping it at the door. A pair of rough-textured mats—one on the outside, the other inside the entryway—will catch a lot of it.

Use area rugs to protect carpets and waxed floors where traffic is heavy—the dining area, family room, and hallways, for example.

Glue bunion pads on the feet of tables and chairs so that they can be moved without scratching the finish of the floor.

If you fear that moving heavy furniture will damage your floors, slip a piece of plush carpet, pile side down, under the furniture legs. You'll protect the floor, *and* the furniture will slide easier.

Before moving furniture, slip heavy socks onto the legs, or place each leg into a "shoe" made from the bottom half of a clean milk carton.

RESILIENT-FLOOR CARE

When choosing a new resilient floor, remember that solid colors are harder to maintain and to keep looking good and that patterns with grooves and indentations collect dirt.

79

There's no need to fill the mop bucket just to clean the bathroom floor. Simply wipe the floor with a spray disinfectant and a clean cloth or paper towels.

The natural wax color of solvent-base products may mask the true color of light-colored resilient floors. Before using a product, test it in an inconspicuous place to be sure that the resulting color is acceptable and the flooring is solvent resistant.

If your floor is in bad condition, apply two or more thin coats of a self-polishing water-base product, allowing each application to dry at least 8 hours before recoating.

To restore pitted, rough asphalt tile, first smooth out the surface with very fine steel wool. Then wash with a mild detergent solution, and wax with a self-polishing water-base product (use several coats if the pitting is severe).

Even though it's called a no-wax floor, it will look better if you apply a vinyl dressing made especially for no-wax finishes. To keep the product from collecting in any depressed areas of the floor, don't pour it onto the floor directly; mop it on from a shallow pan.

Disguise bad scratches in vinyl flooring by rubbing them with a worn screwdriver blade and then waxing the area.

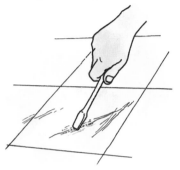

Do your vinyl tiles curl up at the edges? A simple way to cure this is to warm each problem tile with an electric iron just long enough to soften the adhesive underneath. Apply fresh adhesive to the curled area, then weight down the tile until the adhesive dries.

REPLACING VINYL FLOOR TILES

1. Warm the old floor tile with an iron to soften the adhesive beneath, then pry out the adhesive with a putty knife, working from the crack toward the edges of the tile.

2. Scrape away the old adhesive from the floor. Check the fit of the replacement tile; if it needs trimming, cut it with a utility knife or sand it lightly. Spread fresh adhesive on the floor.

3. Warm the replacement tile with an iron to make it more flexible before setting it in the fresh adhesive, then weight it down until the adhesive sets.

REMOVING STAINS

Remove black heel marks from a resilient floor by rubbing them with a typewriter eraser.

If a throw rug leaves stains on resilient flooring, a strong solution of chlorine bleach may remove it. (Test in an inconspicuous area first.) If this doesn't work, then rub with very fine steel wool; restore the dulled area with wax.

WOOD-FLOOR CARE

To keep a rocking chair from wearing the finish off a wood floor, place a strip of adhesive tape along the bottom of each rocker.

Remove mold from wood floors with dry-cleaning fluid; if the mold is deeply embedded in the wood, use bleach or disinfectant. Rewax to restore the shine. Since mold needs a damp environment, keep it from coming back by making sure that the area is well ventilated.

Severe yellowing and darkening of older wood floors is most likely caused by the buildup of many years of varnish applications. The only way to remedy this problem is to refinish the floor.

Self-cleaning, solvent-base polishes work by removing old wax and dirt. It's important to change the applicator pad or cloth often to prevent reapplying any of the old dirt.

CLEANING WOOD FLOORS

For a quick cleanup of a wood floor, go over a small area at a time with a well-wrung-out mop, wiping dry before moving on. Instead of plain water on natural or stained dark wood, try cleaning with cold tea.

For a more thorough cleaning of wood floors, use a liquid cleaning wax containing a solvent such as turpentine or nontoxic dry-cleaning fluid. Be sure that the room is well ventilated when you do this.

ELIMINATING STAINS

Rub alcohol stains on a wood floor with silver polish or an ammonia-dampened cloth, then rewax floor.

Need to get rid of those white spots that can show up on wood floors after waxing? Pour liquid wax over them, rub gently with fine steel wool, following the grain, then polish the area with a clean cloth.

MASONRY-FLOOR CARE

To make cleaning easier, seal stone, brick, and concrete floors with a penetrating masonry sealer, available at hardware stores and home centers. Left unsealed, a masonry floor absorbs cleaning materials beneath its surface.

Once you've sealed a masonry floor, apply several coats of a protective floor finish (a liquid acrylic finish or a paste wax) to give the floor smoothness and gloss.

Do not use harsh or abrasive cleaners on a masonry floor; it's not as durable as it seems and can be easily scratched. Clean it with water and washing soda or a mild detergent solution.

Sweep your concrete floor with industrial floor-cleaning compound (available in hardware or professional cleaning supply stores).

Wax your garage's concrete floor? Sounds crazy, but it makes sweeping easier and reduces the dust that gets tracked into the house. Be sure to seal the concrete first.

Remove grease stains on a concrete patio by wetting the stains and generously sprinkling them with dishwasher detergent. Let stand a few minutes before rinsing with boiling water.

Wet a stone floor with water before washing it with a cleaning product, then rinse well. Dried-on cleaner can cause stone surfaces to chip.

Clean brick or concrete floors with a rag mop—a sponge mop will break apart.

For stained grout between floor tiles, try rubbing the area lightly with folded sandpaper.

CLEANING CURTAINS

Wash fiberglass curtains in the bathtub. This way you don't have the unpleasant task of removing the tiny glass fibers from the washing machine, since you simply rinse them from the tub.

If just-washed curtains don't hang well, slip a curtain rod through the bottom hem of each panel and leave it there for a few days.

When you wash curtains, wash the rods as well. Then apply wax to the rods and the curtains will slip on and move more easily.

Before sending curtains to the dry cleaner, mark the places where the hooks should be reinserted. A dab of colored nail polish on the wrong side does the job neatly.

If curtains must be rehung on specific windows, mark them with colored thread on the wrong side of the bottom hem: one stitch for the first panel; two for the second panel; and so on.

WINDOW SHADES

Clean washable window shades by spreading them unrolled on a clean flat surface and scrubbing them with detergent and hot water and a brush or cloth. Rinse with a clean damp cloth and dry them thoroughly before rerolling.

When your nonwashable shades are dirty, try rubbing them gently with a dough-type wallpaper cleaner or with an art-gum eraser.

If a shade winds up with a bang, take it down and partially unroll it, then put it back. If tension is still too great, repeat.

If a shade doesn't roll up tightly enough, remove it from its brackets and increase the spring tension by rolling up the shade by hand. Replace the shade in the brackets; if the tension is still too slack, repeat the process.

Worn or stained shades can be turned: tack the worn bottom to the top and turn a hem on the old top to make a new bottom.

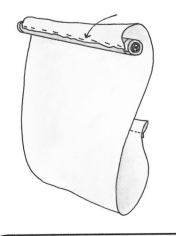

CLEANING VENETIAN BLINDS

There's no magic way to wash venetian blinds; to get them really clean, you must take them down and wash them in water and detergent in the bathtub. Scrub if necessary. When the blinds are clean, rinse them thoroughly with clear water and hang them over the shower-curtain rod to dry. (Protect the floor with old towels.) Shake the excess water from the blinds and let them dry thoroughly before rehanging them.

An alternative method is to lay the blinds flat on a large piece of canvas (preferably outdoors) and scrub one side at a time with a mild detergent solution. Hang the blinds on a clothesline and rinse them with the hose. Shake off the excess water and let them dry before rehanging them.

BLINDS

If you don't have a special venetian blind duster, wear thick absorbent cloth gloves and wipe the slats by hand.

Touch up soiled areas on white venetian blind tapes with liquid white shoe polish.

REPLACING VENETIAN BLIND CORDS AND TAPES

1. With the blinds drawn and the slats horizontal, remove the end caps and the metal cover from the bottom bar.
2. Unknot the cord ends and pull them out of the slats, but leave them on the pulleys. Reknot the cord ends.
3. Slide the slats out one by one.
4. Detach the tapes from their clamps on the top and bottom bars and attach new tapes of the same length.
5. Cut new cord the same length as the old. Thread it on the pulleys, following and then unthreading the old cord.
6. Put back the slats and run the new cord through the slat holes on alternate sides of the tape rungs.

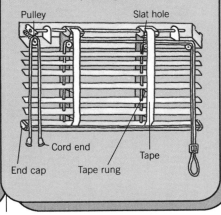

BEFORE CLEANING WINDOWS

Wash windows on a day that's cloudy, but not rainy. Working in direct sunlight causes streaks because the cleaning solution dries before you can wipe it off.

The best time to vacuum window frames and sills is before you wash windows. Use the brush attachment of your vacuum cleaner to remove dust, soot, cobwebs, and dead insects.

If you live in an upper-story apartment or a multilevel house, consider hiring a professional window washer. Doing the job yourself may not be worth the risk.

When cleaning the outsides of double-hung windows, don't take chances sitting on windowsills. Instead, raise and lower both sashes so that you can clean each outside surface from the inside.

Cool, clear water is the choice of most professional window washers. If windows are very dirty, add 2 to 3 tablespoons of ammonia or vinegar per gallon of wash water. Choose only one; if combined, they'll neutralize each other.

Sudsy ammonia leaves streaks on windows and mirrors. Use clear ammonia instead.

One of the best window-cleaning solutions can be found right in your medicine cabinet. Pure rubbing alcohol removes dirt easily and leaves windows crystal clear.

If you do a lot of window washing, invest in a professional-quality squeegee with a brass or stainless-steel holder. When the rubber blade wears out, turn it over and use the opposite edge.

Washing small windows will be much easier if you use a squeegee that's custom-fit to the windowpane. To make one, remove the rubber blade from its holder and trim it to a length that's slightly wider than the width of the windowpane. Then use a hacksaw to cut the holder to the exact width of the windowpane.

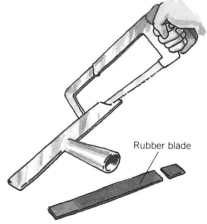

Rubber blade

WASHING AND DRYING WINDOWS

Here's an easy way to tell whether the spots you've missed are on the inside of the window or the outside. Use horizontal strokes to clean one side of the window and vertical strokes for the other.

To clean the corners of small window frames, use a cotton swab dipped in cleaning solution.

For drying windows, a wad of crumpled newspaper works just as well as expensive paper towels. Wear rubber gloves to keep your hands free of ink.

Want to prevent frost from forming on windows? Add ½ cup of rubbing alcohol or antifreeze to each quart of wash water. Or moisten a cloth with glycerin and rub it across the insides of the windows.

SPECIAL WINDOW PROBLEMS

Having a hard time removing dried paint from window glass? Soften the paint with soapy water or warm vinegar. Then scrape the paint off gently, using a sharp single-edge razor blade in a holder.

WASHING A WINDOW WITH A SQUEEGEE

Using a spray container, a clean sponge, or a brush with soft bristles, wet the window lightly with cleaning solution. Wipe the rubber blade of the squeegee with a damp cloth or chamois to make the blade glide smoothly across the glass.

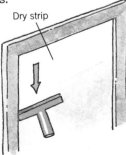

Dry strip

1. Tilting the squeegee at a 45-degree angle, press one end against a corner of the window and pull it across horizontally.

2. After wiping the blade, place the squeegee at the bottom end of the dry strip and pull it down to the bottom edge of the window.

3. Repeat across the window, slightly overlapping the adjacent dry area with each pass. Dab water drops with a dry cloth.

To remove oxidation deposits from the frames of aluminum windows, use a light household abrasive cleaner, a mild detergent, or fine steel wool. After cleaning, apply automobile paste wax. Reapply wax annually.

To remove hard-water spots from windows, use vinegar or a mild organic acid cleaner (available at janitorial supply houses). Scrub the spots gently, using a non-abrasive nylon pad. Then clean the window with a squeegee.

REPLACING A WINDOWPANE

Wearing heavy gloves, remove broken glass from the frame. Then scrape away old putty (soften it with a hair dryer if necessary) and remove the glazier's points with pliers. Sand all surfaces smooth. Have the new pane cut ⅛ inch smaller than the groove's length and width. Coat the groove with linseed oil or thinned alkyd (oil-base) paint to prevent absorption of oil from the glazing compound.

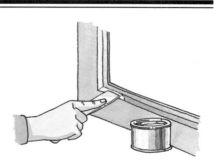

1. Apply a thin bed of glazing compound along all four sides to cushion the glass against stress and leakage.

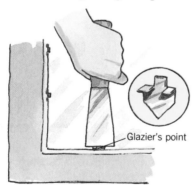

Glazier's point

2. Gently press the glass against the glazing compound and tap the glazier's points halfway into the sash, 4 to 6 inches apart.

3. Form the glazing compound into a rope about ⅜ inch in diameter, and press the rope into the groove along the glass.

4. Holding the putty knife at an angle, draw it over the glazing compound to form a neat triangular strip.

5. Allow the compound to dry for about a week. Then paint it, overlapping the glass 1/16 inch as a seal against moisture.

If ocean spray has deposited salt on your windows, remove the spots with denatured alcohol.

Has paint sealed a window sash to the frame? Insert a wide putty knife (never a screwdriver) between the sash and the frame and work the knife around the edge of the sash to break the bond. You may have to tap the handle with a hammer to coax the blade in.

Tap lightly

To remove dried paint from rough-textured glass, use paint stripper. Make sure the stripper doesn't drip on window sills or sashes. Clean up residue immediately.

If a double-hung window moves but doesn't slide easily, clean out the sash channels with steel wool. Then vacuum the area and lubricate the channels with hard soap, paraffin, or silicone spray.

WINDOW SCREENS

To wash window screens, lay them flat on a smooth, cloth-covered surface, such as an old sheet on a picnic table. Scrub them gently, rinse with a hose, and shake off excess water.

ELIMINATING SASH CORDS IN DOUBLE-HUNG WINDOWS

Avoid replacing sash cords—install vinyl or aluminum friction sash channels. They come in kits at home and building supply centers.

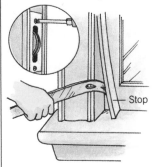
Stop

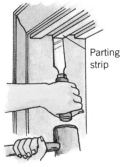
Parting strip

Tape

1. Pry off and save inner stops. Remove lower sash and the sash pockets; take out weights and cords (or let them drop inside jambs). Pry off side parting strips; remove upper sash and pulleys (inset). Fill hollow with insulation.

2. From top parting strip chisel off ½ in. If new channels are too high, cut at bottom in line with sill's slant, using tin snips and a fine-tooth hacksaw. Scrape, sand, and prime the old side jambs.

3. Place sashes in channels with lower sash toward indoors. Tape sashes and channels together. Grasp sashes as shown; feed lower end out of window; fit tops of the channels into jambs, and swing lower end into position.

87

Dirty screens not only block out sunlight but cause spots on windows whenever it rains. Without removing screens, brush or vacuum them periodically.

If you find a tiny hole in a screen, there's no need to patch it. Just dab some rubber cement or clear nail polish on the opening to keep out bugs. (For other screen repair tips, see pp. 173–174.)

MAKING WINDOWS ENERGY-EFFICIENT

When the weather turns cold, allow as much sunshine as possible into the house. Remove and store window screens. On sunny days, open blinds, shutters, and shades and tie back curtains. Trim trees and shrubs that shade windows.

Light colored curtains will keep a room warmer than dark colored ones because the former reflect sunlight back into the room. Line the curtains with an acetate or acrylic fabric so that warm air doesn't pass through the curtains and out the window.

Cap curtains with an air seal by tacking or stapling a piece of fabric to the window frame, several inches above the curtain rod.

STICKING DOORS

Before trying to fix a sticking door, wait until cool, dry weather arrives. The problem may last only as long as the humidity.

If a door sticks year-round, check the screws in the hinges and the strike plate. They may need to be tightened or reinforced (p. 190).

Before repainting a door, sand its edges. This helps to prevent paint buildup, which is one of the most common causes of sticking doors.

When planing a door, always work with the grain. Plane the top or bottom of the door from the outer edge toward the center. When you finish, lay a straightedge along the surface and sand any irregularities you find.

SLIDING DOORS

Buy sliding glass doors with thermal-break aluminum frames. This type prevents cold from being conducted into the house.

If a sliding door rattles, check the bottom door guides. Replace them if they're faulty or missing.

FIXING A DOOR THAT BINDS

A door may stick because of loose or improperly mounted hinges, swelling of the wood, or even settling of the house. You can locate the points where the door binds by sliding a thin sheet of stiff cardboard between the edges of the door and the jamb while the door is closed. As a temporary measure, rub wet soap on those spots where the door sticks.

To fix an improperly mounted hinge, place a wedge under the outer edge of the door to hold it steady. If the door binds at the top, remove the screws from the jamb leaf of the bottom hinge, insert a cardboard shim under the leaf, and replace the screws. If the door binds at the bottom, remove the screws from the jamb leaf of the top hinge, insert a shim under the leaf, and replace the screws.

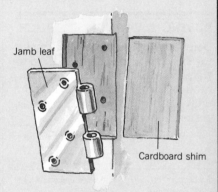

Jamb leaf

Cardboard shim

If the door still binds slightly near the top or bottom edge after either hinge has been shimmed, sand or plane a small amount of wood from the point of friction (the spot rubbed bare of its paint). If that doesn't correct the problem, your best bet is to plane an entire edge of the door.

With a hard pencil, scribe a line on the door face ⅛ inch in from the side that's binding. If the door binds near the top or along the upper edge, use a wedge to hold the door open while you plane to the line. If the door binds near the bottom or along the lower edge, remove the door from its hinges and plane to the line. In either case, prime and paint the newly bared wood to prevent the door from absorbing moisture and swelling.

Does your sliding closet door drag because it hangs crooked? Loosen the adjusting screw on the back of the roller. Then raise or lower one end of the door until it's parallel with the floor.

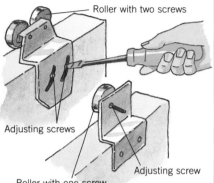

Roller with two screws

Adjusting screws

Roller with one screw

Adjusting screw

To clean sliding-door tracks, spray household cleaner on a terry cloth rag, wrap the rag around the tip of an old screwdriver, and move the padded tip along the track.

Use powdered graphite or silicone spray to lubricate the tracks of sliding glass doors. Oil attracts dirt, which makes matters worse.

SPECIAL DOOR PROBLEMS

To straighten out a door that's slightly bowed in the center, lay it on supports and place weights on top of the bulged side. Leave the weights on until the door returns to its proper shape.

To remove loose pins from their hinges, pry them up with a screwdriver and tap gently with a hammer. Remove the pin from the bottom hinge first. If a pin is rusted, apply penetrating oil.

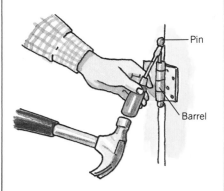

Pin

Barrel

Is that squeaky door getting on your nerves? Remove the pin from the noisy hinge, lubricate the barrel with household oil or silicone spray, and replace the pin. Move the door back and forth several times to work in the lubricant.

Here's how to fix a slightly warped door without taking it off its hinges. Add a third hinge at the spot where the door is bowed. Over time, pressure will straighten out the curve.

BUYING A VACUUM CLEANER

Before shopping for a vacuum, list the items you need to clean (carpets, hard floors, upholstered furniture, draperies). Select a model with as many appropriate accessories as possible (p. 93).

CHOOSING A VACUUM CLEANER

Type	Uses	Advantages	Disadvantages
Tank/canister	Above-floor cleaning; bare floors; low-pile carpets	Provides best suction for above-floor cleaning; includes variety of attachments	Lacks agitating brush for carpet cleaning
Tank/canister with power nozzle	Above-floor cleaning; cleaning embedded dirt from carpets	Combines best suction for above-floor cleaning with carpet-cleaning ability	Attachments must be changed to suit tasks
Upright with attachments	Cleaning large carpeted areas or sturdy rugs; minor above-floor cleaning	Combines best agitation for carpet cleaning with above-floor cleaning ability; adjusts to different carpet heights	Attachments must be changed to suit tasks
Central (built-in) system	Cleaning carpets; above-floor cleaning	Quiet; no heavy equipment to carry	High-cost installation; may lack agitating brush for carpet cleaning
Wet-dry	Cleaning carpets; above-floor cleaning; cleaning liquids from leaks or spills	Versatile; includes special attachments for difficult chores	Tank must be emptied, washed, and dried after each use
Hand-held	Cleaning small, lightly soiled surfaces quickly; cleaning hard-to-reach areas	Convenient to use and store; available in cordless models	Not suitable for large surfaces or embedded dirt; cordless models require recharging after each use

To test a vacuum's efficiency, see how well it picks up a granular substance, such as sand or salt, from a carpet. Check below the carpet's pile to make sure the grains have been picked up, not just pushed down.

The more convenience features your vacuum has, the more time and effort you'll save on cleaning day. Look for a lightweight machine with a lengthy cord and easy-to-use controls, accessories, and bag-changing procedures.

Suction alone won't remove dirt that's deeply embedded in carpets; only a vacuum with rotating brushes will do the job properly.

VACUUM MAINTENANCE AND REPAIR

A full dust bag reduces a vacuum's suction power. Change or empty the bag before it's full.

Lint, hair, or thread that collects on bristles can interfere with the cleaning action of the brushes. Use the vacuum's hose to remove lint or hair. To remove threads, clip them off or unravel them after disconnecting the plug.

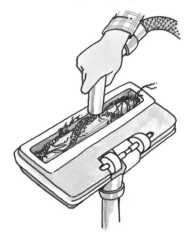

To patch a hole in a vacuum hose, wrap duct tape around the area. Make sure the seal is tight.

VACUUM CLEANER PROBLEMS: WHAT TO CHECK BEFORE TAKING IT IN FOR REPAIRS

Caution: Before cleaning or repairing any parts, unplug the vacuum cleaner.

Problem	Possible cause	Solution	Problem	Possible cause	Solution
Motor doesn't run	Plug not secure	Insert plug firmly into outlet	**Motor runs but suction is poor (cont.)**	Obstruction in hose, wand, or attachment	Remove the obstruction
	Power off at outlet	Replace fuse or reset circuit breaker		Leak in hose, wand, or attachment	Repair leak with duct tape or replace part
	On-Off switch broken	Replace switch		Fan obstructed	Remove the obstruction
	Power cord broken	Replace power cord (p.160)	**Vacuum blows fuses**	Too many appliances on circuit	Turn off other appliances on circuit
	Handle cord (from switch to motor) broken	Replace handle cord		Short circuit in power cord or plug	Replace power cord (p.160)
	Fan obstructed	Remove the obstruction		Short circuit in handle cord	Replace handle cord
Motor runs but suction is poor	Dust bag filled	Empty or replace dust bag	**Vacuum makes excessive noise**	Power brush loose or imbalanced	Adjust or replace parts
	Filter dirty	Clean or replace filter			
	Hose improperly connected to cleaner	Secure hose to cleaner	**Vacuum shocks user**	Power cord frayed	Replace power cord (p.160)

Bending a vacuum hose to roll it up for storage could damage its wire frame or woven shell. Instead, drape the hose over two clothing hooks in a utility closet.

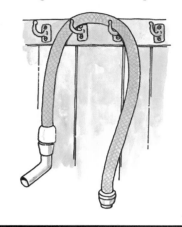

BEFORE YOU VACUUM

Pick up any small, hard objects, such as pins, buttons, coins, or plaster chips. They can easily clog the hose and filter or, even worse, damage the fan and motor.

Take chairs, footrests, and wastebaskets out of the room or set them on larger furniture to minimize furniture moving while you vacuum.

Adjust the nozzle of your upright vacuum so that it rides in close contact with the carpet's pile. If the nozzle is too low, it will make the vacuum hard to push. If the nozzle is too high, air will enter the vacuum above the carpet instead of being pulled through the carpet. Also, the brushes won't reach dirt that's embedded in the pile.

VACUUMING CARPETS

The old custom of hanging a carpet on a clothesline and beating the dirt out can break the carpet's backing. Use a vacuum instead.

Vacuum carpets at least once a week. Clean heavy-traffic areas daily with a lightweight vacuum.

To remove as much dirt as possible, move the vacuum over the carpet slowly and make several passes over each area. Work in overlapping parallel strokes.

Pay special attention to areas in front of couches and chairs. People tend to shift their feet around as they sit, loosening soil particles from their shoes and grinding them into the carpet.

VACUUM CLEANER ATTACHMENTS

No more climbing to reach ceiling dust! Use your vacuum's brush attachment and extension wands. This method gobbles up spider webs (and spiders) with no mess.

The crevice tool of your vacuum is ideal for cleaning around the legs of chairs and the bases of hard-to-move furniture.

For indoor-outdoor carpets and others with low pile, use the bare-floor brush. It's also good for sewn or braided rugs, which can be damaged by the harsh, rotating brushes of a power nozzle.

DEEP CLEANING

Save a remnant of each wall-to-wall carpet you install. When the carpet looks darker than the remnant, it's time for a deep cleaning.

If you have several dirty carpets, consider renting a steam cleaner (p.94) from your local hardware store or supermarket. It'll work better than any home vacuum and it's less expensive than a professional carpet cleaner. Prepare rooms thoroughly in advance so that you can finish the job and return the equipment in one day.

If your baby still crawls, don't deep-clean carpets until the child starts walking. Carpet-cleaning chemicals can be irritating or toxic to young children.

Wet shampoo can stain the surface of a shag or delicate carpet; use dry shampoo instead.

Some professional carpet cleaners offer discounts of up to 20 percent if you're willing to move your own furniture out of the room.

Here's how to brighten a carpet that's not made of wool without shampooing it. First, vacuum the carpet. Mix ½ cup clear ammonia and 1 pint water; then test the solution on an inconspicuous part of the carpet. If there's no color change, dip a sponge mop into the solution, wring it almost dry, and run it over the surface of the carpet lightly.

If you must replace furniture on a freshly cleaned carpet before it has dried completely, place coasters under the legs to prevent stains and indentations.

VACUUM CLEANER ATTACHMENTS

Attachment	Uses	Comments
Rug-cleaning tool	Worn or low-pile carpets	Should swivel to reach under and around furniture
Bare-floor brush	Hard floors, masonry surfaces, wooden decks	Replace if worn (to prevent scratching hardwood floors)
Upholstery tool	Upholstered furniture, draperies, clothing, mattresses, automobile interiors, carpeted stairs, walls	Cover with a soft, clean cloth to dust delicate surfaces
Dusting brush	Furniture crevices, lighting fixtures, baseboards, blinds and shutters, pictures, bookcases	Cover with a soft, clean cloth to dust delicate surfaces
Crevice tool	Radiator fins, carpet edges, cushion crevices, window tracks, refrigerator grilles	Wipe clean after each use
Power nozzle	Carpets, sturdy rugs	Rotating brushes should extend to both ends of roller

SHAMPOOING CARPETS

If a carpet is small or lightly soiled, the easiest way to clean it is with an aerosol spray foam, available in supermarkets.

First, do the following: Open windows to ventilate the room and speed up drying. Remove all furniture; if a piece can't be moved, wrap aluminum foil around its legs. Vacuum the carpet thoroughly. You may need to pretreat some stains; read instructions carefully.

Shake the can vigorously and apply a small amount of foam on an inconspicuous part of the carpet. If there's no color change, hold the can upside down and spray a thin, even layer of foam over the entire surface of the carpet. Let the foam dry thoroughly. Vacuum the carpet at top suction, using an empty dust bag.

DEEP-CLEANING METHODS FOR CARPETS

Each of the following methods has its advantages and drawbacks. The information below can help you decide which is best for a particular job. In each case, you'll have to rent equipment or buy an appropriate cleaning compound. Always vacuum before deep-cleaning, preferably with a power nozzle.

Method	Procedure	Comments
Rotary shampooing	Move unit continuously while releasing shampoo into carpet; let carpet dry for several hours; vacuum to remove released soil and shampoo residue	Rotary brushes can damage wool, cotton, or acrylic carpets and rag or braided rugs; overwetting can cause shrinkage or discoloration
Dry cleaning	Sprinkle absorbent cleaning compound on carpet and brush into fibers; wait 1 hour; vacuum thoroughly, using strong suction	Most effective on greasy soil; least effective on dry, gritty soil; easiest to use
Steam cleaning	Move unit continuously in a W pattern, releasing steam on push strokes and removing moisture on pull strokes; for heavy soil, repeat steps in opposite direction	Most effective on wool, shag, and heavily soiled carpets; water over 150° F can shrink wool fibers; overwetting can damage floors and promote mildew

SEASONAL CLEANING

Rugs will be easier to carry outdoors for an airing if you roll them up first. Delicate rugs should be rolled right side out to avoid crushing the pile; sturdy rugs can be rolled with the pile inside.

Air rugs on a flat surface, such as a wooden deck or driveway, to prevent them from being distorted. Choose a shady spot; direct sunlight could cause fading.

At least twice a year, vacuum the padding and the floor beneath an area rug. Because this can't be done under a wall-to-wall carpet, you should clean its surface frequently and thoroughly.

PRESERVING CARPETS

Turn rugs around periodically so that they wear and soil evenly.

Chemicals in some furniture polishes can destroy red carpet dyes, causing a blue or green discoloration. Before polishing furniture, cover carpet areas around legs and bases with newspaper.

Want to prevent carpet seams and edges from fraying? Brush them with a liquid resin that locks the yarns in place as it dries. It's sold at most fabric and craft shops.

The outermost braid of a braided rug usually wears out first. Save the rug from this fate by sewing a strip of bias binding around the edges of the rug.

Here's how to prolong the life of your stair carpet. When the carpet is installed, fold an extra foot of length under and against one or two risers at the top of the stairs. Periodically lift the entire carpet and shift it downward an inch or two at a time. As the excess carpet moves to the foot of the stairs, fold it under or against the lowest riser, or trim it off.

SPECIAL CARPET PROBLEMS

Always save the manufacturer's label from a new carpet. Knowing the carpet's brand name, pattern number, grade, and fiber content will help answer questions that may not arise until some time after the purchase.

The key to preventing spills from staining carpets is to act fast. Blot the spill quickly with paper towels or a clean, white towel. Scrape away any sediment with a spoon. Cover the area with a clean, white towel and place a sheet of plastic or aluminum foil over the towel. Lay books on top. If the area is still moist the next day, repeat the process with fresh towels.

If a spill causes carpet discoloration, dip a clean white towel into a solution of 1 tablespoon liquid hand dishwashing detergent or ½ cup white vinegar and ½ cup warm water. Alternately dab the spot and blot it with a clean white towel. Repeat until all of the spot's color transfers to the towel. Then cover the area with a clean white towel until it's dry. (If this method fails, you may want to seek professional advice.)

A lingering odor with no visible stain on the carpet may be an indication that your pet has left an unwelcome surprise under a piece of furniture. Check under chairs, sofas, and beds.

Scented carpet deodorizers serve a dual purpose: the rug smells better and so does the vacuum.

Repair snags and pills by holding scissors parallel to the rug's surface and snipping them off. Pulling on fibers could damage the rug's weave.

PATCHING A HOLE OR WORN SPOT IN A CARPET

1. Remove the entire damaged area by cutting out a square or rectangle with a utility knife. Make each cut with one pass of the knife, keeping the edges clean and straight. Cut through the carpet backing, but avoid cutting the padding or floor.

2. Using the damaged section as a pattern, cut a patch identical in size, design, and pile direction. (If no remnant is available, purchase one from the store where you bought the carpet.) Check the patch for fit, and trim it if necessary.

3. Spread a thin layer of carpet adhesive under the patch and the edges of both the surrounding carpet and the patch. Press the patch into place, then brush the pile with your fingertips to hide the seams. Let dry for several hours before vacuuming.

To remove deep indentations left in your carpet by furniture, lay a damp bath towel over the depression and press lightly with an iron. When the towel area is dry, the indentation will be gone.

Wrinkles in wall-to-wall carpeting have several causes. If faulty installation is to blame, ask the dealer to make adjustments. If furniture has been dragged across the carpet, lift the furniture and shift the carpet slightly from the wrinkled area to the flat area. If a carpet has been overwetted during cleaning, dampen the wrinkled area slightly and place a flat, heavy object on top of it.

A carpet treated with an antistatic agent may attract dirt easily. A better way to reduce static electricity during cold months is to place a humidifier in the room.

To prevent accidents, secure carpets and area rugs to the floor. Apply double-face carpet tape under seams and edges.

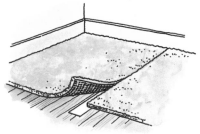

Instead of placing lamp cords under carpets, where they pose a safety hazard, run them along the wall. Hide them with electrical cord covers, available at electrical supply shops.

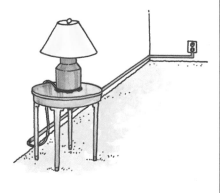

REPAIRING A CARPET BURN

1. Trim away the burned fibers with scissors, then dab rubber cement into the hole with a toothpick.

2. Cut matching tufts of carpet from an unseen area, dab their ends with rubber cement, and insert them in the hole.

3. Work the tufts upright with a pin. When dry, use the pin to blend them with the surrounding pile.

Although a vacuum with rotating brushes can be a bit unwieldy for cleaning a carpeted staircase, it's the best kind to remove ground-in dirt on the center of steps. For the corners, which don't get nearly as dirty, use the upholstery tool, a hand-held vacuum, or a sponge moistened with cleaning solution.

When vacuuming the fringes of delicate rugs, use light suction and the upholstery tool. A hand-held vacuum is even better because it's more gentle.

Here's how to straighten an area rug if no one is around to help you. Working from the center of the width, roll it up evenly with your hands as far apart as possible. Make sure the pad is smooth,

straight, and in the proper position. Lift and drop the rug, one end at a time so that its edges match those of the pad. Unroll the rug partially and weigh down the corners that are in the right position. Unroll the rest of the rug slowly. Remove the weights.

ORIENTAL RUGS

If your Oriental rug needs cleaning, don't try to do the job yourself. Instead, take the rug to a professional carpet cleaner.

Trimming the untidy fringes of an Oriental rug could cause the entire rug to unravel. Instead, tie a few strands together in a single loose knot. Then tighten the knots, lining them up as you go so that they form a straight row.

Before storing a valuable rug, make sure that it's clean and dry. Then roll it up and wrap it in brown paper. Store the rug in a dark, well-ventilated place where the temperature stays between 40° F and 60° F. Otherwise, put it in professional storage.

BEGINNING TO CLEAN A ROOM

To clear out a room before you begin cleaning, carry a plastic trash bag with you to catch the contents of ashtrays and waste-baskets. Follow up with a laundry basket or carton for out-of-place items you can sort after you've finished cleaning.

Begin with dust-raising cleaning and proceed in the following order: ceiling, walls, windows, doors, blinds, draperies, lamps, radiators, shelves, upholstery, furniture surfaces, floors, carpets.

FURNITURE CARE

Arm yourself with plenty of clean, soft cloths, such as old sheets or cheesecloth, when it's time to dust your wood furniture. A dirty cloth can scratch surfaces; so turn it frequently. To hold dust on the cloth, spray it with a commercial dust-control substance.

For extra protection, wipe your wooden furniture with this finishing polish: 10 drops lemon extract mixed into 1 quart mineral oil. Apply this homemade mixture sparingly and then finish the job by polishing with a soft cloth.

Plastic furniture covers are not only cold, uncomfortable, and un-sightly, they attract and show dirt much more readily than uphol-stery does. Protect your furniture with a spray-on chemical soil re-tardant instead.

Attach casters or wide-based glides to furniture legs so that you can easily move furniture to clean un-der it. This also prevents marring of floor coverings.

LIGHT FIXTURES

A lamp base needs only dusting or wiping with a damp sponge. Clean metal parts with the appro-priate polish. Never submerge the lamp base in water—it will damage the wiring.

Wipe off light bulbs occasionally with a damp sponge to maintain maximum light. But first be sure that the bulbs are cool and that the lamp is disconnected.

To clean a glass ceiling fixture, first check that it's cool, then loosen the screws. Let the globe or lens (the glass or plastic translucent part) soak in a sink full of hot soapy water (or ammonia and water for greasy kitchen fixtures). Rinse with hot wa-ter, air-dry, and replace.

If chandelier bulbs flicker, a build-up of grime may be interfering with the flow of electricity. Turn off the power to the fixture (p. 163), remove the bulbs, and, with fine sandpaper, gently sand all con-tacting surfaces.

CLEANING SPECIAL OBJECTS

Before you vacuum a room, use a hand-held hair dryer (on *Low*) to blow the dust off silk or dried flowers. Use a clean, soft artist's brush to flick away stubborn dust.

Spray glazed figurines and ceramic lamps with window cleaner. Dry with paper or lintless cloth towels.

Take the risk out of vacuuming bric-a-brac. Place the foot of an old nylon stocking over the end of the dusting brush—this way, only the dust will be sucked in.

Want an easy way to clean a lot of little glass and china knickknacks? Place them in the kitchen sink and spray them thoroughly with window cleaner. Move them to a towel to air-dry.

Dusting typewriter keys, louvered doors, carved furniture, or anything with nooks and crannies is easier with a clean, soft, ever so slightly dampened paintbrush.

Ashtrays—pottery, brass, or china (not glass)—are easier to keep clean if they're rubbed with liquid furniture polish before use.

PIANO CARE

To remove fingerprints from pianos and other wood surfaces with a high shine, clean with a dampened chamois. Polish dry with a second, dry chamois.

When a piano is not in use, close its top, but expose the keyboard to light. Ivory turns yellow if continuously kept from the light.

Whiten yellowed piano keys by rubbing them with a soft cloth and a tiny amount of one of the following pastes: toothpaste; 2 parts salt and 1 part lemon juice; or baking soda and water. Being careful not to get paste into the cracks between the keys, wipe off with a damp cloth, then buff with a dry cloth.

FIREPLACE CARE

Clean the fireplace and hearth at least once a week during the months that you use it. Vacuum or brush up ashes, then wipe down the hearth with a damp cloth or sponge.

The walls of the firebox (where the fire is laid) should be cleaned with a dry bristle brush or the dusting attachment of the vacuum cleaner. (Be sure to wash and dry the attachment before using it on any other surface.) Don't scrub the firebrick or cement block with water; it may reduce heat retention.

Clean the fireplace chimney flue once a year (more often if you use it frequently). If you're adept at scaling roofs, you can do it yourself with chimney rods and brushes (available at hardware or fireplace equipment stores). Otherwise, call in a professional chimney sweep to do the job.

Dust brass and iron fireplace tools and fire screens regularly. Wash brass tools occasionally with warm sudsy water, rinse, and dry. If iron tools feel sticky, rub them with a cloth moistened with kerosene. Be sure to dry them thoroughly before placing them near the fire.

Before removing ashes, sprinkle damp tea leaves over them to keep down the dust.

Make your slate hearth gleam. Every 6 weeks or so, wash and dry it and then coat it with lemon oil.

HOME ENTERTAINMENT SYSTEMS

Unplug your TV, stereo, VCR, or home computer before cleaning it. Except for the TV screen, avoid using spray cleaners directly on the appliance—you may damage the wiring or clog the ventilation or sound-projecting holes. Instead, spray the cleaner onto your cleaning cloth.

TV, stereo, and speaker cabinets are usually made of plastic or wood veneer. Clean plastic exteriors with mild soap and warm water, using a cloth wrung nearly dry to prevent drips. Dust wood-veneer cabinets frequently with a soft, clean, slightly damp cloth.

To clean metal cabinets, chrome, or any other shiny trim on home entertainment equipment, use a soft cloth moistened with a bit of rubbing alcohol, white vinegar, or window cleaner.

ANTENNA PROBLEMS

If you have a roof antenna and your TV reception is poor, check out the problem by hooking up a set of indoor rabbit ears for comparison. If this improves reception, you'll know the roof antenna is the problem.

The lead-in wire, which connects the antenna to the TV, may be the cause of poor reception. Check connections at the TV, the signal splitter (if you have your FM radio connected to the antenna), and the antenna.

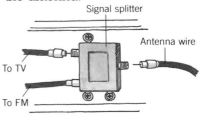

When the lead-in wire flaps in the wind, the TV picture flip-flops and color fades in and out. Make sure that this wire is fitted snugly to the house along its entire length.

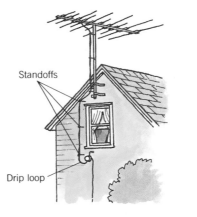

SOUND SYSTEMS

Keep your sound system looking good and operating coolly by vacuuming the ventilation louvers and speaker grilles periodically to prevent dust buildup, which can cause overheating. Cover the system when it's not in use.

When installing a stereo component system, keep all connecting wires short, direct, and neatly arranged between parts. This prevents hum and makes it easy to check connections in case there's a problem.

Staple speaker wires to the wall to prevent people from tripping over them. If you must place the speakers at a distance from the receiver, use a wire with lower resistance (14- instead of 16- or 18-gauge) for better sound.

If you don't want your sound system to bother your neighbors, place the speakers in a room with lots of padded and textile-covered surfaces. Or get a sound-dampening pad at a stereophonic equipment store.

VIDEOCASSETTE RECORDERS

VCR heads need periodic cleaning. You'll know the time has come when you can't eliminate interference on the screen with either fine tuning or VCR tracking. Refer to your owner's manual for the proper method of cleaning.

Store videocassettes away from direct sunlight, excessive heat, moisture, and the strong magnetic field that's present on top of the TV or stereo speaker.

THE DINING ROOM

To keep dining table pads clean, wipe the tops with a clean cloth soaked in warm sudsy water and wrung nearly dry. Vacuum the felt backs with the dusting or upholstery attachment, or go over them with a soft-bristle brush or a lintless cloth.

When a guest spills something on your tablecloth during a dinner party, blot up the substance as quickly as possible. As soon as your guests leave, deal with the specific stain, following the recommended method.

TELEPHONES: WHAT TO DO BEFORE CALLING FOR SERVICE

If you're having a problem with your home telephone, you may be able to locate the source of your difficulty with the following checklist.

1. Disconnect any telephone accessories, such as an answering machine, from your line. Now check to see if the cord from the phone to the wall as well as the cord from the phone to the handset are in good condition and tightly in place.
2. If you have an extension phone, try to make a call on it. If you succeed, the problem is in the other phone, not in the wire or the line.
3. If you can unplug your phone, move it to another outlet. If the phone works in the second outlet, the problem is probably in the inside wire of the first outlet.

4. If you can unplug your phone but don't have another outlet, test the phone in a neighbor's outlet. If it works there, the problem could be with the inside wire or the line.
5. If you rent your phone and the problem is in the phone or in the cord from the phone to the wall, contact the supplier. If you own your phone, check the warranty or contact the place where you bought the phone.
6. If the problem is in the line or the inside wire, contact your local telephone company's repair service.
7. If you've made all these checks and you still can't locate the trouble or you can't unplug your phone to do the tests, contact your local telephone company's repair service.

CLEANING A CHANDELIER

When you don't want to take a crystal chandelier apart, here's an easy, no-mess way to clean it. First, put a few towels on the floor under the chandelier and spread several thicknesses of newspaper over the towels. Next, to prevent any moisture from getting into the sockets, cover each bulb with a small plastic bag and secure it with a twist tie. Now, spray enough window cleaner on each pendant so that the dirt runs off onto the newspaper. The pendants can then drip-dry, or you can polish them with a soft cloth for more shine.

CANDLELIGHT DINING

Remove hardened wax from candlesticks the easy way. Place them in the freezer for an hour or so; then peel off the frozen wax, wash the candlesticks, and dry them.

If you can't wait for the wax to freeze, run the candlesticks under very hot water; then cover your finger with a soft cloth and push the wax off.

Did the candles drip onto your good wood dining table? Scrape up as much as you can with a fingernail or a plastic spatula. Rub the remaining wax into the wood with a soft, clean cloth.

When candle wax drips onto the tablecloth, rub the wax with an ice cube to harden it and then scrape off the wax with a spatula. Cover any remaining wax with paper towels under and on top of the tablecloth, and press with a warm iron, changing paper towels as the wax is absorbed. Sponge off the residue with dry-cleaning solvent, then rub gently with heavy-duty liquid detergent. Launder the tablecloth as soon as possible.

ARRANGING FLOWERS

Instead of that spongy green substance that florists use to arrange flowers, put a bunch of glass marbles into a net bag and set the bag in the bottom of a vase or bowl to hold flowers.

When arranging long-stemmed flowers in a wide-mouthed vase, crisscross strips of cellophane tape just inside the top of the vase and insert the stems into the spaces between the tape.

Anchor your flower arrangements with plastic hair rollers. Bind several together with a rubber band and place them at the bottom of an opaque, not transparent, vase.

KEEPING CUT FLOWERS FRESH LONGER

Pick flowers in the early morning or early evening. Wrap damp paper towels around their stems until you get them indoors or plunge them immediately into a container of water.

Once inside, cut the stems at an angle and put them in a pail of tepid water. (Use a sharp knife; scissors will compress the stems, keeping out the water.) Hold off arranging the flowers until the water has reached room temperature.

As you arrange the flowers in a clean container or vase, remove all leaves that will be under water.

To prevent dehydration, keep the finished arrangement away from drafts, including fans or air conditioners, and out of direct sunlight. (Sometimes wilted blooms will revive if you immerse their stems in warm water.)

HAPPY HOUSEPLANTS

Repot your root-bound plants. You can tell it's time by tapping the plant out of the pot and inspecting the root ball to see if the roots are thickly encircling it.

When repotting, transfer the plant to a clean pot only one size larger than the old one. Any larger size pot encourages overwatering and premature death.

Going on vacation? To keep a plant healthy for up to a month, water it well, then enclose it completely in a clear plastic bag, tying it securely at the top and bottom. Place the plant in northern light. When you return, untie the top and let the plant adjust to room air for a day before completely removing the covering.

If your hanging plant doesn't have a saucer, put a plastic shower cap across the bottom of the basket or pot while watering it to catch the drips and protect your floor.

To keep smooth, heavy-textured leaves clean, bathe them with a dishwashing detergent solution.

If a houseplant is badly infested with bugs (p.104), your best bet is to throw it away before any other plants are affected.

103

HOUSEPLANT PESTS   (not shown life-size)

Pest	Description	Controls	Pest	Description	Controls
Aphid	Green, black, or red $\frac{1}{16}$-inch-long insect with tiny pear-shaped body and long legs	Insecticidal soap; pyrethrum, acephate, resmethrin or tetramethrin spray; spray off with water	**Scale insect**	White, brown, or black $\frac{1}{8}$-inch-long stationary insect protected by hard covering	Resmethrin or acephate spray
Fungus gnat	Black $\frac{1}{18}$-inch-long fly Larva	Pyrethrum spray Scour pot, rinse soil from roots, repot in sterile soil. Use Bt/H-14	**Slug**	Yellow, orange, gray, brown, or black shell-less snail from $\frac{1}{2}$ inch to 5 inches long	Remove by hand
Mealybug	Slow-moving $\frac{1}{4}$-inch-long insect covered with white fuzz	Insecticidal soap; acephate, pyrethrins plus rotenone, or resmethrin spray; remove by hand or with cotton swab saturated with alcohol	**Spider mite**	Barely visible black, white, or red spiderlike creature	Insecticidal soap, acephate, dicofol, or tetramethrin spray
			Whitefly	Flying white $\frac{1}{16}$-inch-long insect	Insecticidal soap, tetramethrin, pyrethrins plus rotenone, or acephate spray

BEDROOM UPKEEP

Here's a way to keep your bedspread clean. When you make the bed, pull up the spread halfway and fold it over on itself. This way, you'll protect the spread from daily dirt and wear, and it will look neat enough for every day. (You can make up the bed properly when company's coming.)

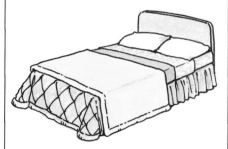

To freshen bedspreads, blankets, and pillows, place them in the dryer with a sheet of fabric softener or a washcloth that's been soaked in a solution of water and liquid fabric softener and wrung nearly dry. Tumble on the air-only setting for about 20 minutes.

MATTRESS CARE

If a mattress or box spring becomes dirty or stained, clean it with foaming upholstery shampoo. Let it dry completely before making up the bed.

Do a good turn for your mattress. Every week or so, flip it over—side to side one time, end to end the next. This distributes wear and sag evenly.

To remove accumulated dust, go over all the mattresses in your home every now and then with the upholstery attachment of your vacuum cleaner. An occasional airing in the sun will also help keep them fresh and clean.

BED LINENS

Put linens just back from the laundry on the bottom of the pile in the linen closet. This way, as you take fresh linens from the top, sheets and pillowcases will rotate uniformly in use and wear.

Many people prefer the lightness of a thermal blanket, which, when used with a top covering, traps heat in the fabric's open spaces. However, this arrangement may not be as warm as a conventional blanket with a top covering.

A good way to increase the loft of a down comforter is to tumble it with a pair of clean sneakers in the dryer (on *Low*).

PILLOW TALK

Choose pillows for the purpose they'll serve. For reading in bed, select a pillow with firm support; the pillow you sleep on should be much softer.

As a general rule, a pillow should be just thick enough to hold your head in the same relation to your shoulders and spine as when you are standing. Side sleepers need a thick pillow; stomach sleepers, a thin one.

Allergy sufferers may find relief with polyester fiberfill pillows. Available in varying degrees of softness, they're not as fluffy or resilient as feather or down pillows, but they're less irritating.

To revive a down or feather pillow, machine-wash it on the gentle cycle, using warm water and mild detergent (half as much as for a normal load); dry on the *Low* setting. Then shake the filling to one end, open the seam on the other end, and insert new feathers or down a bit at a time. Stitch the opening closed.

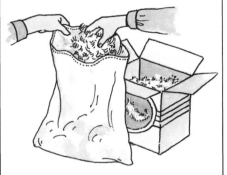

KITCHEN CLEANING BASICS

Soak-and-dissolve is still the easiest way, but a plastic windshield ice scraper is good for prying loose dried-on foods from the floor, table, and counter if you're the impatient type.

Keep sponges, plastic scrubbers, and dishmops clean and fresh smelling; every now and then, run them through a dishwasher load in the top rack.

KITCHEN SAFETY

Place a smoke detector on the same level as your kitchen, but not too near your appliances—everyday cooking can easily set it off.

Never turn off a smoke detector because you're cooking something that will cause it to sound off. It's too easy to forget to turn it back on again.

Don't panic if a fat fire starts in your frying pan. Just turn off the heat, stand back, and toss generous handfuls of dry baking soda at the base of the flames.

Caution: Don't try this with deep fat, however, as it could spatter the grease and spread the fire. Instead, cover the pan with a large metal lid.

If you have small children, store items that are *not* appealing to them in the cabinets over the range. Every year hundreds of children get burned as a result of climbing onto the range to reach treats, such as candy and cookies.

Choose flexible, round pot holders for lifting hot lids and handles; mits or casserole holders (one long piece with a pocket at each end) for removing pans from the oven. Square, stiff pot holders are unsafe because, when folded diagonally, they can get into the flame.

KITCHEN APPLIANCES

To keep appliances shiny, wipe them with a cloth or sponge wrung out in lukewarm sudsy water; rinse and wipe dry with a soft cloth to remove water spots. To protect the finish, apply a creamy appliance wax every now and then.

Give the chrome trim on your appliances a quick shine with a soft cloth moistened with rubbing alcohol.

Here's a remarkably easy way to remove rust from kitchen chrome. Wrap aluminum foil around your finger, shiny side out, and rub the rust until it disappears. Then wipe the surface with a damp cloth.

To clean under and behind an appliance, take your car's snow brush and whisk the dirt out in a flash. Be sure to unplug the appliance before poking around behind it.

RANGE MAINTENANCE

It's a lot easier to wipe away cooking spills and spattered grease on the range top while the cooking surface is still warm. Use warm sudsy water and a cloth or sponge.

Heating coils on top of an electric range usually don't need washing. Instead, turn them on *High* to burn off spills. If a spill is massive, wipe up as much as possible after the coil has cooled and let the rest burn off the next time you use the unit.

If you don't have a continuous-cleaning oven, you can still prevent grease buildup by wiping out the inside with a sudsy sponge or paper towels. Otherwise, the grease will harden and burn each time you turn on the oven.

CLEANING AN EXHAUST FAN

Covered with grease and dust, a kitchen exhaust fan may appear daunting, but it's really not difficult to tackle. For a cleaner and safer kitchen, clean your fan every 6 months or so, using the instructions that came with your fan. If you can't find yours, follow the steps below.

1. Turn the power off at the service entrance or fuse box. If the grille is removable, detach and soak it in a mild dishwashing detergent solution. If not, sponge it clean with the solution.

2. Unplug and remove the fan-and-motor unit and lay it on an old newspaper. Wipe off the heavy grease with a soft, dry cloth. (Do *not* immerse metal and electrical parts in water.)

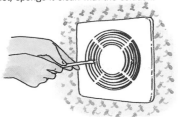

3. Wipe out and clean the fan opening with a soft, dry cloth (do not use water), then replace the clean fan-and-motor unit and plug it in. Dry and replace the grille if you've removed it. Turn on the power.

4. If you can't remove the fan-and-motor unit—for example, in a vented range-hood exhaust—remove the grease filters. Soak them in a detergent solution. Clean the fan with the crevice tool of your vacuum. Wipe the hood with the solution before replacing the filter.

Apple pie spilled on the oven floor? Soak up the spill with a wet sponge or paper towels. Or let it cool and dry, then scrape it off with a single-edge razor blade set in a holder, being careful not to harm the surface of the oven.

Clean oven racks by placing them on an old bath towel in the bathtub and soaking them in a solution of ammonia and hot water.

Wipe off a self-cleaning oven's frame and the part of the door liner that's outside the oven seal *before* the cleaning cycle. These areas aren't reached during automatic cleaning, but they do get enough heat to bake on soil, making it harder to remove later.

To clean under an electric range that has a storage drawer at the bottom, remove the drawer to get at the floor easily. For a gas range with a broiler below the oven, remove the broiler drawer.

CLEANING THE BROILER AND GRILL

For easy broiler cleaning, put a few cups of water in the bottom of the pan before broiling.

To clean the broiler pan, remove it from the oven while it's still hot and pour any drippings into a grease can. Invert the grid over the pan and pour in dishwashing detergent. Then fill the pan with hot water and let it stand. Scrub later with a steel-wool soap pad.

Before your next cookout, clean the grill with a wire brush dipped in warm sudsy water or a baking-soda solution. Rinse, dry, and coat the grill with cooking oil to keep food from sticking to it.

MICROWAVE OVENS

Wipe off all spills as soon as possible, using wet paper towels to saturate dried or cooked-on food. Do not use metal tools to scrape up food because they seriously damage the interior of the microwave.

Deodorize and clean your microwave every now and then. When the oven is turned off and cold, wash its inside surfaces with a solution of 4 tablespoons baking soda per 1 quart warm water.

Two microwave cleaning don'ts: Don't use commercial oven cleaners in a microwave. Don't ever remove the cover in the top of the oven for cleaning.

REFRIGERATORS

Sticky, greasy dust on top of the refrigerator? Get after it with a heavy-duty all-purpose cleaner or a solution of 1 part ammonia to 10 parts water. Let the solution stand to break down the grease, then wipe it off with paper towels. Finish up with an application of appliance wax to make cleaning easier the next time.

Remove odors and spills inside the refrigerator with a cloth wrung out in a solution of 1 tablespoon baking soda to 1 quart warm water. Rinse and wipe dry.

If your artistic youngster uses your refrigerator door as a canvas for his permanent marker, try a little lighter fluid to remove the artwork. Then wash the door with soap and water and rinse completely.

SMALL APPLIANCES

If you use a drip coffee machine daily, you should clean it thoroughly at least once a month. Pour a solution of equal parts water and distilled vinegar into the water reservoir and run it through the brew cycle. Rinse your machine by running clean water through the cycle.

If there are any sticky crumbs left after you've shaken the toaster gently, blow compressed air (available in cans in photography supply stores) inside the appliance.

An easy way to clean your blender is to partly fill it with a solution of warm water and hand-dishwashing detergent, then cover and run it for a few seconds. Empty the blender, rinse, and air-dry.

CLEAN KITCHEN COUNTERS

Rub countertop stains, such as mustard, tea, or fruit juice, with baking soda and a damp cloth or sponge. If the stain persists, wipe it with a cloth moistened with a little chlorine bleach.

Erase those pesky purple price marks that transfer from containers onto countertops. Rubbing alcohol gets rid of them easily.

Every few days (or immediately after cutting meat or poultry), wipe down food preparation surfaces with hot soapy water to discourage bacteria. Rinse thoroughly and wipe dry.

WOOD SURFACES

To keep a butcher block countertop clean and fresh, scrape off all waste after each use; rub it with salt or a baking soda paste every now and then.

After cutting onions or garlic on a wood surface, rub it with a slice of freshly cut lemon. Rinse well and wipe dry.

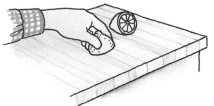

Tiny knife marks are sometimes considered attractive on wood surfaces. But deep scratches should be sanded with fine sandpaper and then reoiled.

SINK CARE

To remove stains from a porcelain sink, fill it with lukewarm water, add a few ounces of chlorine bleach, and let stand for an hour or so. If stains are stubborn, line the sink with paper towels saturated with chlorine bleach and let stand 8 to 10 hours.

Do not use chlorine bleach on old, porous, or cracked porcelain surfaces. The bleach can penetrate to the iron base and cause further discoloration by rusting.

Avoid abrasive cleaners when cleaning a stainless steel sink. Instead, simply wash it with hot sudsy water and dry it (to remove finger marks and water spots).

To give a stainless steel sink extra sparkle, clean and polish it occasionally with glass cleaner or a baking soda paste.

Has your stainless steel sink become scratched or slightly pitted? Rub it gently with very fine steel wool, then buff to a sheen with a soft cloth.

HANDLING GARBAGE

Good garbage pail hygiene prevents odors. Line the pail with a plastic bag; drain all garbage before throwing it in the bag. Wash the pail frequently with disinfectant cleaner or hot sudsy water with a little chlorine bleach or ammonia added (do not use both). Dry in fresh air.

Eliminate odor from your garbage disposer by grinding cutup orange, grapefruit, or lemon rinds while flushing the disposer with hot water.

DEALING WITH DRAINS

Keep a drain odor-free by running very hot tap water through it after each use. About once a week, throw in a handful of baking soda, followed by hot water. Or pour in 1 cup of vinegar, let it stand for 30 minutes, then run very hot water through the drain.

It's easier to avoid a clogged drain than to clear one. Pour cooking grease into an empty can or a milk carton—never into the sink. The same applies to coffee grounds and other bits of garbage.

UNCLOGGING A DRAIN

1. Remove the sink stopper or strainer. Clean out any material stuck in the top of the drain or on the stopper. Test water flow. If there is an overflow opening, block it with a wet cloth; fill the sink about half full.

2. Place a plunger over the drain and rapidly pump it up and down 10 times, abruptly lifting it from the water on the last stroke. If the water rushes out, you've unclogged the drain. Otherwise, try several more times before giving up.

3. If the plunger fails, you'll have to get into the trap under the sink. Place a bucket beneath the trap, unscrew the plug on the bottom of the trap with a wrench, and let the water run out.

4. If there's no plug, remove the trap itself by unscrewing the two coupling nuts, beginning with the higher one. Clear the stoppage by hand or with a wire. Replace the plug or the trap.

5. If you still can't reach the clog, you'll need a snake (available at hardware stores). Twist the handle of the snake clockwise, pushing into and pulling out of the drain, until you reach the obstruction and clear it.

6. Call a plumber if all of these steps fail to clear the drain. Do not, under any circumstances, use chemical drain cleaner; it could cause serious burns to your skin and create a problem for the plumber.

To retrieve hairpins or cutlery that have fallen down the drain, go fishing. Use a magnet attached to a length of stiff twine. If the expedition fails, use a multipurpose grabber (available at hardware stores) or open the trap (p. 110).

Before using a commercial drain cleaner, try clearing a sluggish drain with a plunger. If that fails, but there is some flow of water, you can try drain cleaner. But be aware that drain cleaners are caustic and poisonous; it's important to follow the manufacturer's instructions to the letter.

DOING THE DISHES

A dishwasher is self-cleaning, except near the rim of the door opening. Be sure that you wipe this area clean before you start the machine; that way, spills here won't become baked on.

Washing dishes by hand may not save hot water if you run the water continuously. Always use a sink stopper or a dishpan and run the hot water as little as possible. Rinse the dishes in cold water.

Wash the following by hand: fine decorated china; colored anodized aluminum; wooden items; hollow-handled knives; pewter; cast iron; milk glass; some plastic vessels and utensils.

Remove eggs, cooked cereal, and other dried-on foods from dishes by soaking them immediately in cold water. If you don't remember to do this until later, put them in a solution of dishwasher detergent and water instead. Let the dishes stand overnight, then lift off the food with a rubber scraper.

Ugly stains on your plastic dishes or utensils? Combine ¾ cup chlorine bleach and ¾ cup baking soda and let the mixture remain on the stained utensil for 5 minutes. Wash and rinse thoroughly.

VACUUM BOTTLES

Hand-wash—but don't immerse—glass-lined vacuum bottles in dishwashing detergent and warm water. Use a bottle brush if necessary. Rinse and invert to dry.

Before filling a vacuum bottle that has absorbed beverage odors or been stored for a while, freshen it with 1 tablespoon of baking soda and warm water. Let stand 20 minutes, scrub out, rinse, and air-dry.

POTS AND PANS

Store cast-iron cooking pots in a dry place between paper towels, leaving lids off to prevent mustiness, moisture, and rusting.

When stirring and turning food in nonstick cookware, use only wooden or plastic utensils; avoid temperatures over 450° F.

To brighten darkened aluminum, cook an acidic substance, such as tomatoes, rhubarb, apples, or vinegar, in the pan. Try removing stains or discoloration by boiling 2 tablespoons cream of tartar in 1 quart water in the pan.

Check the manufacturer's care instructions before washing enamel cookware in the dishwasher. Use only nonabrasive cleaners to remove cooked-on food on enamel. Soak stained white enamel pans in warm water and a small amount of chlorine bleach.

Remove coffee and tea stains from glass or ceramic pots by soaking them in a solution of 2 tablespoons chlorine bleach per 1 cup water. Another method is to soak the stained cookware overnight in a solution of 2 tablespoons automatic dishwasher detergent to 1 pot warm water.

Remove stains from a pan with a nonstick surface by boiling a solution of 1 cup water and 2 tablespoons baking soda in it. Wipe the surface lightly with cooking oil or shortening before using again.

KNIFE CARE

If you have a good set of knives, don't stir hot food with them; heat damages some blades.

Unless the manufacturer specifies that cutlery is dishwasher safe, wash all good cutlery by hand immediately after using it. Avoid soaking it in water, which can damage and loosen wooden handles. Always dry thoroughly.

Knives with serrated edges depend upon notches for their cutting ability. They should be sharpened only by professionals—or not at all.

SHARPENING KNIVES

The most effective way to get a good cutting edge on a knife is to use a whetstone with a coarse and a fine side. Before using a whetstone, saturate it with vegetable oil. Sharpen a very dull knife first on the coarse side, then on the fine side; with a blade that is slightly dull, sharpen on the fine side only. Afterward, clean the stone thoroughly and wrap it in a cloth to store it.

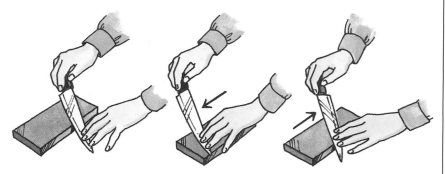

1. Holding the knife firmly, place the blade at an angle to the stone, as shown.

2. Slide the knife firmly across the stone *away from you* from its heel to its tip. Repeat four times.

3. Turn the knife over and reverse the procedure, working *toward you.* Repeat four times.

REPAIRING A FAUCET'S LEAKING SPOUT

If your stem faucet drips when it's turned off, the washer, valve seat, or both probably need replacing. Before you begin: Turn off the stop valve under the sink; turn on the faucet; protect chrome surfaces with electrician's tape.

(If your faucet has a one-piece ball, cartridge, or valve, get replacement parts from a home center, plumbing supply store, or hardware store. Or contact the manufacturer.)

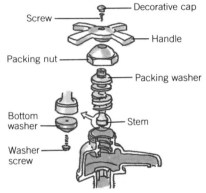

Decorative cap
Screw
Handle
Packing nut
Packing washer
Bottom washer
Stem
Washer screw

1. Pry the decorative cap from the handle, then, after removing the handle screw, lift off the handle. With an adjustable wrench, remove the packing nut. Pull out the stem, and replace the stem's bottom washer.

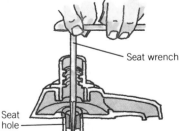

Seat wrench
Seat hole

2. Run your little finger around the valve seat to see if it's chipped or worn. If you feel any roughness, remove the seat with a seat wrench, using the taper that matches the seat's hole (hexagonal or square). Replace it with a new valve seat.

3. Before putting the faucet back together, coat all interior parts with heatproof, waterproof grease. In addition to its intended purpose, it makes for easy reassembly and a good seal.

BATHROOM SAFETY

If you must have a lock on the bathroom door, install a doorknob with an outside lock release. This will prevent children from getting locked inside accidentally.

Prevent bathroom falls by laying scatter rugs with nonskid backings and by providing tubs and showers with suction-backed rubber mats or adhesive decals.

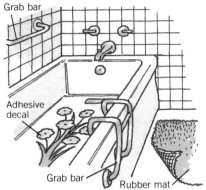

Grab bar
Adhesive decal
Grab bar
Rubber mat

Grab bars in the bathtub or shower and next to the toilet are a help for all and a must for the elderly. Fasten the bars to wall studs.

Avoid using electric appliances, such as space heaters, hair dryers, or radios near water. All bathroom outlets should be equipped with GFI's (ground fault interrupters) to prevent the possibility of fatal shock. Even then, you should take the precautions mentioned.

To prevent hot-water burns when you take a shower or bath, always turn on the cold water first and turn off the hot water first.

Does your shower scald you when another cold water tap is turned on or a toilet is flushed? Correct this with a temperature-control or pressure-balanced mixing valve. The latter maintains even pressure as well as temperature.

Mixing valve

KEEPING BATHROOMS CLEAN

Keep your bathroom sparkling clean in just 4½ minutes a day. Armed with a spray bottle of disinfectant cleaner, a sponge, and a paper towel, wipe down all bathroom surfaces. Work from the cleanest (mirror) to the dirtiest (floor), covering the sink, tub, and toilet along the way.

If you can't get around to cleaning the bathroom every day, sponge down the tub, shower, and sink with a liquid disinfectant cleaner at least once a week.

Use a cloth moistened with vinegar to rub away hard-water spots and soap scum from chrome faucet handles and drains. Dry and polish with a soft cloth.

Prevention is the best method for eliminating mildew. After showering, keep the shower curtain extended (not bunched) so it can dry thoroughly. Clean your bathroom regularly with disinfectant and keep it as dry and well ventilated as possible.

Exhaust fans (vented to the outside) and built-in heaters (in the ceiling where they won't cause burns) do a good job of removing excess moisture from the bathroom. When it's dry outside, leave the window and curtain open.

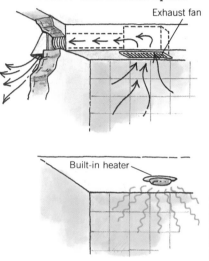

Exhaust fan

Built-in heater

Machine-wash (gentle cycle) colorfast plastic shower and window curtains in warm water. Add water conditioner to remove soap curd. Hang to dry. If the curtains are mildewed, add ¾ cup chlorine bleach to the wash cycle.

TUB AND TILE CARE

Remove mildew and stains from tub and tiles by wetting the surfaces with water and then spraying them with a solution of 1 cup bleach to 1 quart water. Make sure that the room is well ventilated while you do the job and that bath towels and fabric shower curtains are out of spray range.

Stained tub or sink surfaces come clean with a cream of tartar-hydrogen peroxide paste. Spread the paste over the stain and scrub lightly with a brush. Let the paste dry and then wipe or rinse it off.

Wipe away soap spots or film from tile with a solution of water and water conditioner or a solution of 1 part vinegar to 4 parts water. Rinse, then dry with a soft cloth.

Clean grungy looking tile grout with full-strength vinegar instead of bathroom or kitchen cleaner.

The best time for bathroom cleaning? Right after taking a shower or bath, when steam has loosened the dirt. Just wipe off the damp surfaces with a paper towel.

Fiberglass tub tough to clean? Use a water conditioner, such as Calgon, or a commercial bathroom cleaner containing EDTA (ethylene diamine tetraacetate).

After grout has set, seal it with a commercial silicone preparation (available in hardware stores).

When caulking a crack between a bathtub and a wall, use a silicone caulking compound, which is flexible and won't crack from the water's weight when the tub is in use.

If you're tired of cleaning around nonskid decals in your porcelain tub or shower, scrape them off with a straight-edge razor blade (in a holder) dipped in soapy water. Remove adhesive residue with acetone or nail-polish remover.

Bathroom floors covered in dull, old resilient tile may need especially strong cleaning measures. Scrub with a solution of 1 part ammonia to 4 parts water, then dry with a towel. Apply a thin coat of wax, following the directions on the container.

SHOWER MAINTENANCE

A quick way to defog the bathroom mirror after a shower is to turn your hand-held hair dryer on it, using the *Low* setting. The warm air will clear the mirror.

When glass shower doors turn dull and filmy, wipe them down with a soft cloth saturated with distilled white vinegar or water softener solution, then shine with a dry cloth.

Mineral deposits frequently clog shower heads. To remedy this problem, unscrew the head, take the pieces apart, and soak them in a bowl of vinegar; brush out any stubborn sediment. Reassemble the shower head and reattach.

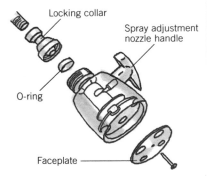

Locking collar

Spray adjustment nozzle handle

O-ring

Faceplate

Installing an inexpensive water restrictor or a water-saving shower head can cut water use in half. Follow the manufacturer's instructions; you'll need only a wrench or pliers to do the job yourself.

While you're at it, why not install a "telephone shower" for shampooing? You simply add a diverter valve between the pipe and the shower head and a hook to hold the "telephone" on the wall.

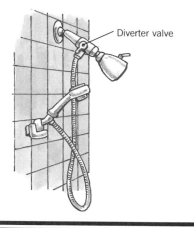

— Diverter valve

TOILET TIPS

Put petroleum jelly on the lip of your plunger. It will help to stabilize its position on the drain hole.

Remember to clean under the inside rim of the toilet bowl. The holes in the rim can get clogged with lime deposits from the water; this affects the flush. Unclog each hole with the end of a coat hanger that's been bent for the job.

Undiluted chlorine bleach, allowed to stand just a few minutes, will frequently do just as good a job as commercial toilet-bowl cleaners. It will also remove mildew and surface stains (except rust) from porcelain bathroom fixtures. Use a toilet-bowl cleaner to remove rust.

Retard stain buildup and remove discoloration by scrubbing briskly inside the toilet bowl with a bowl brush for a few seconds daily.

To remove old mineral buildup in the toilet, sprinkle ½ cup of water softener around the bowl (above the waterline), immediately after flushing. Really tough, old rings may require pumice or a little wet-dry sandpaper.

UNCLOGGING A TOILET

If, when you flush the toilet, the bowl fills up but won't drain, then your toilet is clogged. If the bowl is full to the brim, bail out half of it in order to prevent splashing while you work to unclog the toilet.

Place the cone of your plunger securely over the bowl's drain hole and pump the plunger up and down vigorously about a dozen times. If this doesn't dislodge the obstruction, wait for about an hour and then give it another try.

If plunging fails, aim the bent end of a closet (toilet) auger into the drain hole. Crank the auger's handle clockwise to feed its snake into the hole until it meets the obstruction. Crank the auger's handle just a bit more, then pull the auger out as you continue cranking clockwise.

If neither method works, the problem may be in the main drain; you may have to have the toilet bowl removed. The best thing to do is call a plumber.

The first rule of toilet repair: Carefully remove the breakable ceramic tank cover and set it on the floor on top of a towel, carpet remnant, or layers of newspaper before you go to work.

Here's a quick way to check for stopper-ball or stopper-valve leaks: Put a few drops of food coloring into the tank and, without flushing, see if the colored water comes into the bowl. If it does, you can assume there's a leak.

TOILET PROBLEMS: WHAT TO FIX

Water won't stop running: Float ball or arm; float valve

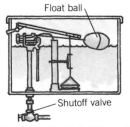

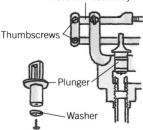

1. Lift the float ball. If the water shuts off, unscrew the ball from the float arm and shake the ball. If there's water in it, replace the float ball with a new one.

2. If there's no water in the float ball, bend the float arm slightly so that after you flush again, the water level rises no farther than ¾ inch below the top of the overflow tube.

3. Problem persists? Close shut-off valve under tank; remove float arm assembly (turn thumb-screws) and plunger. Replace washer and, if worn, valve seat. Or replace entire system with a plastic ball-cock assembly.

Sluggish or incomplete flush: Stopper ball

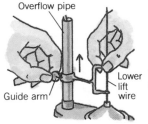

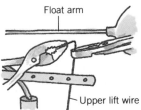

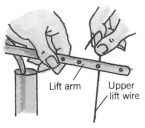

1. The stopper ball may be falling too quickly on the valve seat. Loosen the thumbscrew(s) on the guide arm. Raise the guide arm about ½ inch on the overflow tube so that the stopper ball will float longer.

2. To make the stopper ball rise higher, shorten the upper lift wire slightly by unhooking it from the lift arm, bending it slightly, and then rehooking it in the same hole in the lift arm.

3. If the flush is still unsatisfactory, try unhooking the upper lift wire from its hole on the lift arm and hooking it in another hole on the arm.

Gurgling, partially filled tank: Outlet valve seat

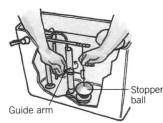

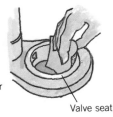

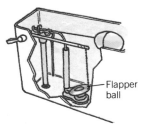

1. Check the stopper ball. If it isn't centered on the valve seat, turn off the main water valve and flush the toilet empty. Loosen the screw on the lift wire's guide arm. Move the guide arm until the stopper ball is seated properly. Then tighten the screw.

2. Inspect the valve seat with your fingertips. If it feels rough or pitted from corrosion, scour it with wet-dry sandpaper.

3. If the tank still doesn't fill and the gurgling sound persists, your best bet is to replace the stopper ball with a flapper ball, available at hardware or plumbing supply stores. Installation instructions are included.

ATTICS

For an attic with a small entrance, install a disappearing stairway. Made to fit an opening as small as 22½ by 54¾ inches, it folds into three sections for stowing above its door.

If there are any openings around ducts or pipes where they enter the attic floor, seal them with sheet metal or stuff them with steel wool or fireproof insulation. This will help prevent a fire from spreading upward through the house.

Good attic ventilation is the key to protecting a well-insulated home from winter moisture problems and summer heat buildup. If you have only gable vents, add vents to the roof or soffits. (For hints on attic insulation, see p.178.)

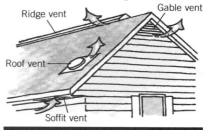

Ridge vent

Gable vent

Roof vent

Soffit vent

BASEMENTS

If you have small children, install vertical rails along the basement staircase to prevent falls. At each step, bolt one end of a 2 x 4 to the stair stringer and nail the other end to the handrail.

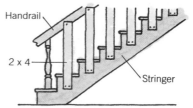

Handrail

2 x 4

Stringer

CONTROLLING DAMPNESS IN BASEMENTS

Left unchecked, dampness in a basement can rot wood, peel paint, and promote rust and mildew. Here's a simple test to determine if dampness is caused by seepage or excessive humidity. Cut several 12-inch squares of aluminum foil. Tape them to various spots on the floor and walls; seal the perimeters tightly. If moisture collects between the foil and the surface after several days, waterproof the interior walls. If moisture forms on the foil's surface, take steps as follows:

Close windows on humid days.

Install a window exhaust fan.

Vent your clothes dryer to the outdoors.

Wrap cold-water pipes with fiberglass insulation or foam plastic sleeves.

Clear clogged drains and roof gutters.

Use a dehumidifier, especially during the summer months.

Treat walls with epoxy-base waterproofing paint or epoxy masonry sealer.

Cover a dirt or gravel floor with a 4-inch layer of concrete poured on top of a plastic vapor retarder.

Install a drainage system or a sump pump to combat chronic flooding.

Regrade around the house so that water will flow away from the foundation.

Keep boxes and valuables on high shelves or on 2 x 4's set on concrete blocks. The former prevents damage from floods; the latter provides ventilation around the boxes.

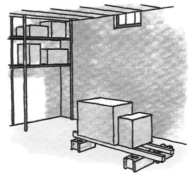

Store flammable substances, such as oil-base paint and turpentine, in metal containers well away from the heating system, the hot-water heater, or other sources of heat.

If a musty odor persists even after you have done all you can to ventilate the basement, stitch bags of sturdy cloth, fill them with calcium chloride, and hang them from the ceiling. They will absorb moisture, cause of mildew—and mustiness.

HELP! THE BASEMENT IS FLOODED

Remove water from a flooded basement as quickly as possible. If the flood was caused by a ruptured pipe, shut off the water supply. If the water is an inch or two deep, bail it out with buckets or soak it up with mops or a wet-dry vacuum.

Deeper water must be pumped out by a plumber, a waterproofing contractor, or the fire department. If no one is available, rent a submersible electric pump from a plumbing supply store. Connect the pump to a garden hose and run the hose outdoors to a storm sewer or to a spot where the runoff will flow away from the house. Then lower the pump until it rests on the basement floor. Using an extra-long heavy-duty extension cord, connect the pump to a neighbor's outlet. Keep debris away from the pump's intake.

Caution: Because water conducts electricity, have the power company turn off the electricity to your house. If you must enter a deeply flooded basement, wear high, heavy rubber boots and thick, dry rubber gloves. Standing on a wooden chair or ladder, turn off the power. Use a dry piece of wood, such as a broom handle, to flip the main switch or pull out the main fuse block. Don't touch a wall or anything else until the power is off (p. 163).

PATCHING AN INACTIVE CRACK IN A BASEMENT WALL

An active wall crack (one that continues to enlarge) may indicate a serious structural problem. Have it examined promptly by an expert. Inactive cracks (those caused by settling) can be repaired easily. To determine whether a crack is active or inactive, see p. 167.

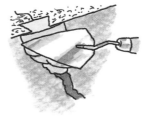

1. Using a chisel and a sledge-hammer, enlarge the inactive crack to a wedge that's wider at the rear than the front. Brush out any debris, vacuum the area thoroughly, then dampen it.

2. For a large crack that won't leak during repair, use a mixture of 1 part portland cement to 3 parts fine sand. For smaller cracks, use a two-part epoxy within ½ hour after mixing.

3. Apply the mortar or epoxy mix with a trowel, forcing it well into the rear of the crack. Smooth and level the mortar immediately; wait ½ hour before smoothing the epoxy with a wet trowel.

LEAKS AND SEEPAGE

Clean leaves and debris out of basement window wells periodically. If allowed to accumulate, they can cause seepage or flooding. Lay gravel at the bottom of wells to improve drainage.

If your basement floods frequently, have a plumber install an interior drainage system of pipes connected to a sump pump. The sump pit should be 1½ to 2 feet in diameter to collect sufficient water and prevent the pump from turning on and off too frequently.

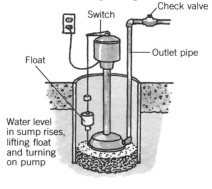

Switch

Check valve

Outlet pipe

Float

Water level in sump rises, lifting float and turning on pump

Sealing the exterior of basement walls against leaks is far more effective than sealing the interior, but it's much more costly because it requires excavating around the foundation. Use this method only as a last resort.

PLUMBING

Before making any plumbing repair, shut off the water supply at either the main valve or the valve nearest the fixture. In homes supplied by a municipal system, the main valve is the one nearest the water meter; in homes with their own wells, the main valve is near the water-storage tank.

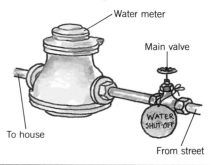

Water meter

Main valve

WATER SHUT-OFF

To house

From street

QUICK FIXES FOR LEAKY PIPES

Because dripping water can cause damage and create an electrical hazard, even minor leaks should be repaired promptly by a professional plumber. Until then, use one of the following methods to repair the leak temporarily. First, shut off the water supply to the pipe. Then remove any rust from the pipe with steel wool, and wipe the area clean and dry.

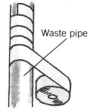

Waste pipe

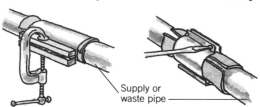

Supply or waste pipe

To seal a small crack or puncture in a waste pipe, wrap layers of electrical tape around the pipe from one side of the leak to the other.

For a small leak, wrap a rubber pad around the leak and cover it with a hose clamp. Or cut a tin can along its seam, wrap it around the rubber pad, and secure it with a C-clamp and two blocks of wood.

For a large leak, wrap a rubber pad around the leak, cover it with a pipe clamp, and bolt or screw the clamp. Make sure the clamp is centered directly over the leak.

Hang a tag on the main shutoff valve so that family members will be able to identify it quickly and easily during an emergency.

If you hear a loud bang when a faucet is turned off abruptly, it's probably the result of pressure built up from the water flow. Because this vibration can damage pipes, install a shock-absorbing air chamber to the pipe that leads to the fixture. This hammering sound may return once the chamber becomes filled with water. If so, draining the plumbing system will readmit air to the chamber.

THAWING FROZEN PIPES

Before attempting to thaw a pipe, shut off the main water valve. This will prevent water from gushing out as soon as the pipe is thawed. Also, open the taps supplied by the pipes to reduce steam pressure, which can cause pipes to burst. Close the taps when the pipes have thawed.

If water isn't running anywhere in the house, a pipe near the water meter may be frozen. To confirm this, touch the meter and the exposed pipes adjacent to it. If they feel extremely cold, a nearby pipe probably needs thawing.

When water runs in only one part of the house, a pipe in an outside wall or uninsulated crawl space may be frozen. Turn up the heating system, then open the kitchen and bathroom sink cabinets to let in the warm air. Or heat the pipes where they emerge from the wall.

If a pipe is partly frozen, open the affected faucet all the way. Then open other hot-water faucets in the house to raise the temperature of the nearly frozen pipe. Once hot water is flowing from all the faucets, close them to a trickle. Don't turn them off completely until water is flowing freely from the affected faucet.

Once you've pinpointed the frozen section of a pipe, heat it slowly with a hand-held hair dryer or a heat lamp to a temperature your hand can tolerate. Work backwards from the faucet toward the frozen area.

Boiling water, propane torches, or open flames of any kind should not be used for thawing. Pipes can explode if they're heated excessively or too suddenly.

PREVENTING FROZEN PIPES

Wrap thermostat-controlled heat tape or cable around exposed pipes that tend to freeze. When the ambient temperature approaches freezing, the pipes will warm up automatically.

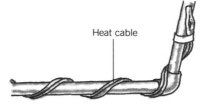

Heat cable

Taking a long winter vacation? Ask a plumber about draining the plumbing system to prevent frozen pipes and water damage.

ENERGY CONSERVATION

Want to cut your heating bills by 7 to 12 percent a year? Install an automatic setback thermostat. It can be programmed to lower the heat or cool the air while everyone's out during the day or when they're snug in bed at night; it turns the system on just before you get home or at daybreak.

Want a cheap heat reflector to insert behind radiators and baseboard convectors? Tape heavy-duty aluminum foil to a panel of insulation board.

Aluminum-foil-covered insulation board

Radiators or baseboard convectors not delivering heat efficiently? Dust and dirt buildup may be inhibiting heat flow. Every couple of months, turn the radiators or convectors off, let them cool down, then vacuum them with a crevice attachment and wipe them clean with a damp cloth.

Save energy dollars by wrapping insulation around the pipes leading to radiators and convectors.

Opening windows to cool rooms overheated by steam radiators wastes heat and money. Have your plumber install radiator thermostats; they maintain a set temperature. The cost varies widely; shop around for the best price.

WARM-AIR HEATING SYSTEMS

Floor-length draperies "robbing" rooms of heat from convectors or warm-air registers? Install air deflectors over them to prevent this.

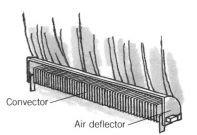

Convector

Air deflector

Cut down the amount of dust that a forced warm-air heating or central air-conditioning system brings into your rooms. Take out the grates monthly for a scrubbing in a mild detergent solution; vacuum inside the registers as far as your extension tool will reach.

How often should you change the filter to your warm-air heating system? To devise a schedule suited to your system, install a new filter and then check it every 4 weeks for dirt accumulation by holding it up to a bare light bulb. When the light shining through the filter is diffused, it's time for a new filter.

OIL BURNER MAINTENANCE

Oil bill too high? Your oil burner could be the cause. Have a service technician check its combustion efficiency by measuring the carbon dioxide (CO_2) level in the flue. If it's 10 to 13 percent, your oil burner is functioning very well; an 8 to 10 percent CO_2 level is acceptable; if the CO_2 level is less than 8 percent, the serviceperson should examine the burner's combustion chamber for air leaks, insufficient or excessive draft, and an out-of-balance air-to-fuel ratio.

WHAT TO CHECK WHEN HEAT WON'T OPERATE

At the thermostat. Set the thermostat more than 5° F above room temperature and see whether the heat goes on.

If you have an automatic day-night thermostat, make sure that the cycle hasn't been reversed.

If your thermostat's contact points are exposed to air, they may need an occasional cleaning. First, turn off the power (p.163), then carefully remove the cover. Lower the setting to open the contact points, then run a business card between them. Raise the setting to close the points, then repeat the cleaning procedure. Replace the cover and restore power.

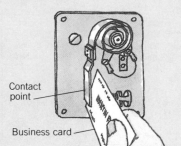

Contact point

Business card

To clean the contact points of certain round thermostats, first turn off the power, then remove the temparature-setting dial. Wipe the points with a cotton swab dipped in a 50-50 vinegar-water solution.

Contact point

Switch lever

On your way to the furnace or boiler. Check for a blown fuse or a tripped circuit breaker (see p.163).

If you have a remote emergency switch, make sure it isn't turned off.

If you have an oil burner, check the fuel gauge on the oil tank; if there's no gauge, remove the cap of the tank-filler pipe and check the oil level with a stick.

At the furnace or boiler. Check the emergency switch to make sure it isn't off.

If you have an oil burner, press the overload reset button on the motor housing; then push the stack-control relay switch (located on the flue or on the burner housing).

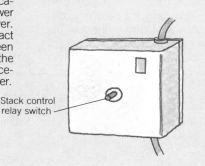

Stack control relay switch

If your oil burner is controlled by a photoelectric cell, this "seeing eye" cell could be dirty, preventing the unit from operating. First turn off the emergency switch, then unscrew the transformer from the fan housing and flip it over. You'll find the photoelectric cell on the underside of the transformer or on the housing. Gently wipe it with a clean cloth.

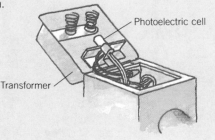

Photoelectric cell

Transformer

If you have a gas burner, make sure the pilot light is on. If it isn't, relight it according to instructions in the owner's manual or on the plate mounted on the unit. If the pilot light won't stay lit, have a serviceman check the thermocouple. If your system runs but delivers inadequate heat, see p. 124.

Some oil-burner motors need their bearings lubricated; check your owner's manual. If your burner runs a warm-air system, the blower motor may need the same maintenance. Look for lube points on the motor housing.

The filter to your oil burner should be replaced twice a year—once during the annual maintenance and again midway in the heating season. Ask your oil supplier to show you how.

ATTIC AND ROOM FANS

Winter winds sneaking into your home through closed attic-fan louvers? Tape an interior (plastic) storm window over the louvers. Or cover with rigid board insulation. Both are available at hardware stores and home centers.

Run your whole-house fan efficiently: Open only the windows and doors of rooms in use while the fan is running.

HEATING SYSTEM RUNS BUT HEAT IS INADEQUATE

Hot-water system. If the water circulator pump has a reset button on it, press it.

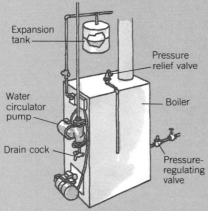

Expansion tank

Pressure relief valve

Water circulator pump

Boiler

Drain cock

Pressure-regulating valve

If your system has a pressure-regulating valve to automatically maintain the correct water pressure, check the gauge on the boiler. If pressure is below the minimum mark, call for service.

If the expansion tank feels hot all over and water spurts from the pressure relief valve, the tank needs recharging with air. See owner's manual or call for service.

If some of your radiators fail to heat, they have air trapped inside. Open the valve on the end of the radiator. When water spurts out (it will be very hot), quickly close the valve.

Steam system. Is the water at the half mark in the boiler's sight glass? If not and your boiler lacks an automatic water-feed valve, fill it using the manual water-feed—after the boiler has cooled (cold water could cause a hot boiler to crack). Open the try cocks; steam should issue from the top one, water from the bottom.

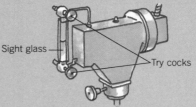

Sight glass

Try cocks

Sediment can interfere with the boiler's operation. If you haven't drained the low-water cutoff valve recently, put a pail under the drain, and open the valve. Careful, the water will be hot! Fill the pail; then refill the boiler. If the water remains dirty, add a boiler-cleaning compound.

If the boiler cycles on and off frequently and you've checked that the water level is correct, add an antisurge compound.

Warm-air system. The dust filter may be clogged, decreasing warm-air flow. Feel the ducts leading to and from the furnace; the filter is located in the one that returns cool house air. Open the panel covering the filter; if it's fiberglass, replace it; wash a plastic or aluminum filter.

CENTRAL AIR CONDITIONERS

Before buying a central air conditioner, get a SEER list of makes and models from your contractor. SEER stands for Seasonal Energy Efficiency Rating. The higher the SEER number, the more efficient the unit.

Before going on summer vacation, set your central air conditioner thermostat at 78° F and put the unit on an automatic timer. Running the air conditioner just several hours a day will usually keep mildew at bay.

AIR-CONDITIONING SENSE

Stop cold air leaks through floor-level openings. Close heating-system registers; tape sheets of plastic over them. Weatherstrip undersides of doors to the outside and basement.

Keep your room air conditioner working efficiently. Remove the front panel monthly and wash the filter in tepid water and mild detergent; allow it to dry thoroughly before reinstalling it. While it's out, vacuum all accessible surfaces.

Bent aluminum evaporator fins in room air conditioners obstruct efficient air transfer. Remove the front panel and filter, then straighten the fins with a plastic spatula.

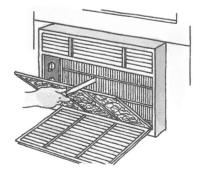

NOISE-BUSTING A ROOM AIR CONDITIONER

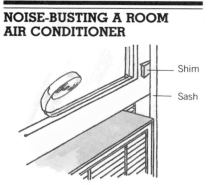

Shim

Sash

1. The unit's vibration may be the cause of noisy windows. With the unit on, press your palm against the window sash and then the glass. If the noise changes pitch in the first case, insert thin wood shims between the sash and the window frame. If the glass is the culprit, stick cellophane insulating tape tightly between the edge of the glass and the frame or reputty.

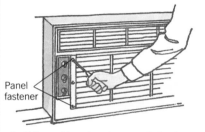

Panel fastener

2. If the unit's noise changes pitch when you press both your palms against the front panel, tighten the panel fasteners. If this doesn't work, seal the panel to the cabinet with duct tape.

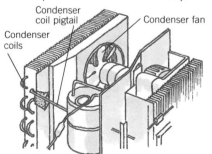

Condenser coil pigtail

Condenser fan

Condenser coils

3. Unplug the air conditioner and slide the chassis partway forward out of the housing; rest it on a stool to keep it level. If your model can be unhoused only when it's entirely out of the sleeve, have someone help you move it onto a work surface. Spin the fan blades by hand to see if their position is uniform. If a bent blade is striking the condenser fins, straighten it. Jiggle the chassis; if the condenser coil's pigtail is striking the fan's housing, insert a foam rubber wedge between them.

PEST CONTROL

The key to keeping pests away is to deny them food, water, and shelter. Store food in tightly sealed glass or plastic containers. Clean up crumbs and spills immediately. Keep counters and cabinets spotless. Keep sink areas dry. Clean garbage cans regularly and secure their lids. Fill cracks and crevices. Repair torn screens. Cover chimney and flue openings with spark-arresting screening.

Electric bug zappers are ineffective on most stinging and biting insects, such as bees, wasps, and mosquitoes. However, they do draw other flying insects away from pool, patio, and picnic areas at night.

A chemically treated pest strip should not be placed in a room with an infant, a pet, or someone who is ill or elderly. Also, avoid hanging a pest strip in an area where food is prepared or where people stay for prolonged periods.

COMMON HOUSEHOLD PESTS (not shown life-size) See pesticide precautions, p.128.

Pest	Habitat	Comments	Controls
Carpenter ant	Nests in moist or decaying wood	Can cause severe structural damage	Treat nest area with a household formulation of bendiocarb, boric acid, chlorpyrifos, diazinon, or propoxur
Household ant	Attracted by sweet or greasy food	Can be found by following ants' path from food supply to nest	Over the counter bait stations should be placed directly in the path of ant trails; seal gaps and cracks where ants are entering with caulk; keep kitchen counters and pet food areas clean
Bedbug	Mattresses, box springs, floor and wall cracks, furniture, wallpaper	Feeds on human blood; appears flat and brown when empty, round and red when full; nocturnal	Treat with a household formulation of pyrethrum labeled safe for bedding; let bedding dry completely before replacing sheets; for serious infestations, call an exterminator
Book louse	Warm, humid areas	Feeds on microscopic molds that form on moist surfaces; transparent	Ventilate and dry infested areas; remove food packages and utensils; treat shelves with a household formulation of propoxur; replace shelf paper
Carpet beetle	Carpets, feathers, furs, hair, silk, upholstery, wool	Feeds on lint and dead insects	Treat carpet edges and empty clothes closets with a household formulation of diazinon or tetramethrin labeled safe for carpet, upholstery, and fabric; vacuum dust- and lint-prone areas often (empty infested contents immediately); remove dead insects; repel with mothballs or moth crystals as per label directions
Cockroach	Lives in cracks and crevices; moist, warm, dark areas	Feeds on anything organic; nocturnal	Use over-the-counter baits in discs or syringe tubes. Place baits in or next to cracks and corners, under stove and refrigerator and in drawers; eliminate paper bag storage; take garbage out at night; correct moisture problems; seal gaps, cracks and crevices; for serious infestations, call an exterminator

To stop ants from invading the house, sprinkle a few crumbled bay leaves on windowsills. If ants flock to your flour and sugar bins, place a couple of bay leaves inside. Replace them every month.

Avoid using so-called all-purpose pesticides. They sometimes lack the one ingredient needed to kill a specific insect. For advice on how to select the right pesticide, consult your local Cooperative Extension Service.

If there's no bug spray on hand when a flying insect attacks, use hair spray as a substitute. It immobilizes the bug's wings, making the target easier to swat.

COMMON HOUSEHOLD PESTS (not shown life-size) See pesticide precautions, p.128.

Pest	Habitat	Comments	Controls
Flour beetle and flour moth Larvae (wormlike)	Flour, grain, bird seed, pet food	Throw away all infested foods; store fresh supplies in tightly closed plastic or metal containers	Clean shelves thoroughly; remove food packages and utensils, brush or spray corners and crevices with a household formulation of diazinon, propoxur, resmethrin, or tetramethrin
Housefly	Food, garbage, and decaying organic matter, such as manure or cut grass	Spreads disease by contaminating food	Use fly swatter; screen doors and windows; seal garbage containers; old-fashioned sticky traps should be hung near windows or lights and thrown away when full. If needed, treat with space spray containing allethrin, pyrethrum, resmethrin, or tetramethrin
Mosquito	Stagnant water	Adult females feed on human and animal blood; some types transmit disease	Screen windows and doors, drain stagnant water, use a fly swatter, apply insect repellent to clothing, treat with space spray containing allethrin, pyrethrins, pyrethrum, resmethrin, or tetramethrin
Silverfish	Cool, damp areas, such as basements	Feeds on starches, including glue and paste; nocturnal	Improve ventilation, correct moisture problems. Treat cracks and openings around wall pipes with a household formulation of bendiocarb, chlorpyrifos, diazinon, propoxur, or silica gel plus pyrethrum
Spider	Spins webs in corners and crevices	Feeds on insects; harmless, except for black widow and brown recluse varieties	Remove webs and spiders with broom or vacuum with a dusting brush attachment; treat with a household formulation of diazinon, chlorpyrifos, propoxur, pyrethrins, resmethrin, or tetramethrin
Wasp, hornet	Attics, porch ceilings, roof overhangs, trees; mud tubes on siding; holes in ground	Hazardous to humans allergic to their sting	Treat outdoor nests at night during cool weather with a commercial wasp and hornet formulation which has a long distance spray. Early in season knock down nests as they are being built

Ticks can easily fall off your pet and hide in the crevices and baseboards of your house. If you suspect this has happened, spray the area with a household formulation of malathion or diazinon.

To discourage bats from entering the house, screen all openings larger than ¼ inch in diameter and sprinkle naphthalene flakes in confined areas. If a bat has entered a room, open the windows and any doors to the outside just before dark; then turn out all the house lights. Once the bat exits, close windows and doors.

WHEN USING PESTICIDES

DO'S

Do read and follow package directions and warnings carefully.

Do mix pesticides in a well-ventilated area.

Do wear rubber gloves.

Do keep pesticides in original containers that are tightly closed and clearly labeled.

Do store pesticides in a locked, well-ventilated area, away from heat and direct sunlight.

Do wrap empty containers in thick layers of newspaper before discarding them.

Do exhaust all gas from pressurized cans before disposing of them.

Do remove food, utensils, pets, and their dishes before spraying indoors.

DONT'S

Don't use pesticides near children or pets.

Don't smoke, eat, drink, or chew gum.

Don't inhale sprays, dusts, or vapors.

Don't store pesticides near food.

Don't dump pesticides in places where they could endanger fish or wildlife or contaminate water.

Don't reenter a treated room for ½ hour after it has been sprayed.

If a chipmunk or squirrel strays into the house, set up a live-animal trap baited with dry peanuts. Release the captured animal into the woods.

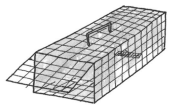

To keep mice from becoming trap shy, bait unset traps for 2 or 3 days, using bacon fat, peanut butter, raisins, or cheese. Secure them with thread or wire. Then, to avoid catching your fingers, use a pencil to move the set, freshly baited traps near the wall.

SECURING YOUR HOME

The view afforded by your door's peephole should be as wide as possible. Install a model with a 180-degree fish-eye lens. Or attach a curved mirror to a wall or tree opposite the peephole.

Locks are only as strong as the material they're attached to. Replace hollow exterior doors with solid-core or metal doors. When installing locks to window frames, use screws long enough to penetrate the studs behind the frames.

Because basement windows are often obscured by shrubbery and because they lead to an area of the house that's seldom occupied, they're a favorite access point for burglars. Keep these windows locked whenever possible.

Burglaries committed in occupied homes are not as rare as you might expect. Keep your doors locked even when you're home.

For greater security and convenience, equip each exterior door with one or two high-quality, pick-resistant locks rather than a row of standard or inexpensive ones.

All doors, including those leading to the basement, cellar, garage, and storage rooms, should be secured with a dead bolt lock rather than a latch lock. The dead bolt should be 1 inch thick and have a throw of 1 inch.

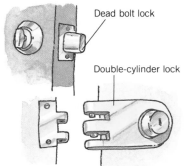

Dead bolt lock

Double-cylinder lock

For doors with a window or a mail slot, use a double-cylinder lock that requires a key to unlock the door from either side.

The lock on the outside door of your garage or porch should be as sturdy as the one on your front door. If a burglar gains access to either one of these areas, he'll be well out of view, and free to take his time breaking into the house.

To prevent sliding glass doors from being lifted out, insert spacers or protruding screwheads in the top grooves. Place a length of pipe or a cut broom handle in the inside bottom track to prevent the door from being moved sideways.

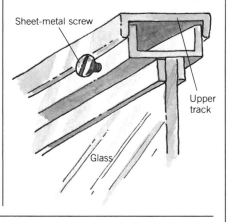

Sheet-metal screw

Upper track

Glass

SORTING OUT SECURITY SYSTEMS AND ALARMS

Even the most sophisticated electronic security system can give a false alarm, be bypassed by an expert burglar, or become worthless in a home where other precautions aren't taken. Yet of all the security measures you can take, installing an alarm system is the most effective. To determine which system is best suited for your home, ask your local police department to conduct a free survey of your property.

Type	How it works	Advantages	Disadvantages
System			
Perimeter (protects boundaries)	Alarm is activated by a break in an electric circuit that connects all windows and doors	Inexpensive; easy to install; visible deterrent	Easily penetrated by an expert burglar
Motion detectors (protects interior)	Alarm is activated by motion registered by infrared beams, ultrasonic waves, sensitive microphones, or pressure-sensitive mats	Difficult to spot and elude	Easily activated by pets, children, or air conditioners
Alarm			
Local	On-site alarm and flashing lights are activated	Sudden, conspicuous noise and light deter intruder	Ineffective if no one is nearby; often goes off when no intruder is present
Central	Switchboard operator is alerted to call home, office, or police	Reduces false alarms	Provides extended time for intruder to act and escape
Police hookup	Police switchboard operator is alerted to dispatch unit	Provides fast assistance	Frequent false alarms may incur fines

Here's how to make a double-hung window extra-secure. With the window closed tightly, drill a hole through the top of the lower sash into the bottom of the upper sash. Insert a nail whose shank is long enough to penetrate the entire thickness, but narrow enough to remove easily when you wish to open the window.

TAKING PRECAUTIONS

Before you move into a new house or apartment, have the cylinders of each door lock changed.

Overgrown shrubbery and high hedges provide as much privacy for burglars as they do for you. Trim foliage often so that it can't camouflage a burglar's activities.

Prune tree branches and remove trellises if they provide access to second-floor windows.

In an apartment building, lock any windows or doors that lead to balconies, fire escapes, or roof-tops. If you live on the first or second floor, lock all windows when you're not home.

Make your valuables harder for thieves to sell, and easier for police to find, by engraving your Social Security number on them. You can borrow an engraving tool from a local police department.

Engraving tool

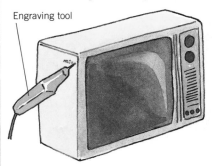

If you have a telephone answering machine, don't reveal your name, whereabouts, or any other personal information on the recorded message. Say simply that you can't come to the phone right now, but will return the call as soon as possible.

A family dog is one of the best burglar alarms you can have. The sound of loud, frantic barking is often all that's needed to discourage a would-be intruder and alert family members and neighbors.

Whether you're planning an evening out or an extended vacation, invest in an automatic timer to create the illusion that someone is home. Use it to activate those items that will make the house appear occupied, such as lamps, TV's, and radios.

When leaving town for an extended absence, ask a friend, neighbor, or relative to park a car in the driveway, mow the grass, shovel snow, and put out garbage on pickup days. Also, arrange to have mail and newspaper deliveries halted until you return.

Those Wonderful Appliances

SELECTING A REFRIGERATOR OR FREEZER

How large should your refrigerator be? Plan on 8 cubic feet for two people plus 1 cubic foot for each additional person in your household. Add 2 more cubic feet if you do a lot of entertaining.

A refrigerator with a freezer and main compartment that are side by side usually provides more freezer space than a unit with a freezer at the top. But a side-by-side's narrow shelves can be a problem if you have to store large or bulky items. Also, it uses about 15 to 20 percent more energy.

Confused by the various defrosting claims? With cycle defrosting, the refrigerator compartment defrosts itself, but you have to defrost the freezer. On a frost-free model, both compartments defrost themselves. However, these units, also called no-frost, frostless, or fully automatic, use from 10 to 20 percent more electricity.

Consider a refrigerator with casters. You'll find that rolling it rather than pushing it to clean underneath is easier on you and the floor. But don't get casters if you have a soft vinyl floor covering; they'll leave imprints in the vinyl.

Which freezer style is best? Depends on your needs. A chest uses less energy because its cold air, which is heavier than warm air, stays inside when you open the top. But an upright takes up less floor space. And since its contents are easier to reach, you probably won't keep the door open as long when you look for food.

HOW LONG WILL YOU HAVE AN APPLIANCE?

Knowing how many years you're likely to keep an appliance helps you to compare models more accurately than if you base your purchasing decision on just the initial cost. With a major appliance, first find the estimated yearly cost on the appliance's energy guide label, then multiply that yearly cost by the appliance's estimated life. Add the result to the purchase price and you will have a good approximation of the appliance's true cost.

Average first-use life of appliance in years

Blender	8	Dishwasher	11	Mixer	9
Broiler oven	9	Food processor	8	Range (electric or gas)	15
Clothes dryer (electric)	13	Freezer	15	Refrigerator	13
Clothes dryer (gas)	14	Garbage disposer	10	Toaster	8
Clothes washer	12	Humidifier	8	Trash compactor	10
Coffee maker (drip)	3	Iron	9	Water heater (electric)	12
Coffee maker (percolator)	6	Microwave oven	11	Water heater (gas)	10

For a guide to the operating costs of various models, send for the *Consumer Selection Guide to Refrigerators and Freezers* from the Association of Home Appliance Manufacturers, 20 North Wacker Drive, Chicago, IL 60606. It's published yearly; the cost is nominal.

INSTALLING AND MOVING A REFRIGERATOR OR FREEZER

Locate your refrigerator or freezer away from direct sunlight or from a heat source, such as a range, dishwasher, or heating vent.

Don't put your refrigerator in an unheated space either. At room temperatures below 60° F a unit won't run often enough to keep food properly cold.

Don't blow a fuse or trip a circuit breaker and end up with spoiled food. Always plug a refrigerator or freezer into a 15-ampere circuit with nothing else on it. The outlet should accept a grounded three-prong plug. If you must use an extension cord, it should be a heavy-duty three-wire cord.

Lay a carpenter's level on top of a a new or relocated unit to make sure that it's level. If it isn't, tilt the unit back and prop it with a wood block. Then screw the leveling legs in or out a few turns, remove the block, and check again. Consult your owner's manual to adjust casters or a different type of legs.

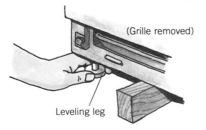

(Grille removed)

Leveling leg

When you open a refrigerator door to a 45-degree angle and let go, it should shut itself. If it doesn't, adjust its legs so that the refrigerator tilts back slightly.

Before transporting a refrigerator or a freezer, turn it off for a day. Take out all removable parts. Secure the doors with rope. Move it upright; not on its side or back.

To move a refrigerator without casters, tilt it and slip pieces of carpet scrap, pile side down, under the front and back legs.

Carpet scrap

If your refrigerator has an automatic ice maker, the water tube attached to it limits how far you can pull the unit from the wall.

When discarding an old refrigerator or freezer, remove the doors to prevent a child from crawling in and getting trapped.

When storing a freezer or refrigerator, secure the door with strong tape or rope. To prevent mildew, however, use a wood block to keep the door open a crack.

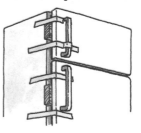

GET THE MOST FROM YOUR REFRIGERATOR AND FREEZER

A refrigerator or freezer operates most efficiently when fully loaded, but be sure to leave enough space between items for air to circulate. In a refrigerator's freezer compartment, take care not to cover any vents that send cold air to the refrigerator compartment.

Keep a refrigerator between 34° F and 40° F. Keep a freezer close to 0° F. To check a refrigerator's setting, leave a refrigerator-freezer thermometer in a glass of water overnight. To check a freezer, stick the thermometer in ice cream or between frozen-food packages.

Refrigerator-freezer thermometer

Here's a more casual way to check the temperature: Your milk is cold without crystals and ice cream is firmly solid but not brick-hard.

Is sweat forming on the outside of your freezer? You may have set the unit at an unnecessarily low temperature; 0° F is adequate. If conditions are humid, try blowing a small fan across the surface. If the problem occurs in a chronically damp place, such as a basement, a dehumidifier will help.

A power-saver switch on a refrigerator saves energy when it's off. It controls small electric heaters that keep the outside of the cabinet from sweating. Turn it on during humid periods, but keep it on *Off* during dry weather.

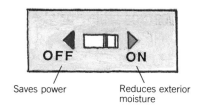

Saves power   Reduces exterior moisture

STORING FOOD CORRECTLY

Control refrigerator odor! To prevent odors from spreading, make sure all food is wrapped, covered, or bagged in plastic. The only exception is the fruits and vegetables stored in crisper drawers. And in a frost-free, bag those too; otherwise they'll dry out.

Before refrigerating any liquid, put it in a tightly sealed container. Moisture that evaporates inside a refrigerator just makes the unit work harder.

To cool food quickly before freezing (and to reduce energy costs), set hot pans in ice water. Wrap the food and freeze it at once.

When stocking an empty freezer, add 3 pounds or less of unfrozen food per cubic foot of space each day until the freezer is full. This will allow the food to freeze quickly and thoroughly, retarding the growth of bacteria.

Keep an inventory of the foods stored in your freezer. Such a list cuts the time you keep the freezer door open looking for food and helps you use older items first.

DEFROSTING

Defrost a refrigerator or a freezer when the frost is ¼ inch thick.

Scraping frost with a sharp utensil can cause serious damage. Use a dull plastic scraper instead and don't scrape against metal parts.

After defrosting, dip a cloth in glycerin and wipe the freezer coils with it. The frost will come off more easily next defrosting.

To free a stuck ice-cube tray, apply a towel soaked in hot water to its edges for a few seconds.

REFRIGERATOR TROUBLES

Is your door's gasket tight? To check, put a 150-watt outdoor flood lamp inside and aim the light at one side at a time with the cord coming out the other. With the kitchen lights off, close the door and look for light leaks.

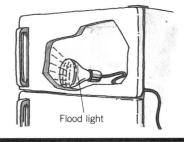

Flood light

REPLACING A REFRIGERATOR DOOR GASKET

If the rubber gasket on a refrigerator door is torn or badly worn and doesn't seal tightly, you should replace it. This can be tricky because the screws that hold the gasket also hold the door's inner panel and insulation in place. To avoid having the door come apart, work on one section at a time and loosen the screws only partway. If the door does becomes misaligned, you may have to repeat Step 3 below a few times to straighten it.

Get a new gasket that fits your door's exact size from an appliance dealer. Or get replacement gaskets in L-shaped sections at a hardware store; you cut these to size and install the magnet strips from the old gasket in them. Soak the gasket in hot tap water for a few minutes to make it pliable and to remove the crimps.

The gasket shown is the most common type. If yours differs, consult your dealer about the replacement procedure. Most gaskets are held on by hex-head screws that you remove with a nut driver of the appropriate size.

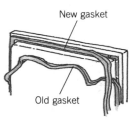

New gasket

Old gasket

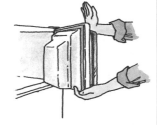

1. Starting at a top corner, fold out the old gasket and loosen the screws along half of the top and half of the side. Loosen the screws only as much as you need to pull the gasket from under the metal retainer strip.

2. Pull the old gasket out of the way. Then attach the new one by pushing its lip under the metal retainer and retightening the screws. Replace the other top corner section and then each bottom one in the same way.

3. Close the door. Check for gaps between the gasket and the frame, indicating door warp. If necessary, reloosen screws and straighten the door by pushing at the top and pulling at the bottom, or vice versa.

A poor gasket seal can often be corrected by simply adjusting the refrigerator's leveling legs (p. 132).

Are there black specks in the cubes made by an automatic ice maker? They indicate that the coating on the tray that molds the cubes is disintegrating and needs to be replaced. Hard water is probably the culprit.

If you find discolored water in your frost-free's drain pan, don't worry. A spill was probably washed into the pan by defrost water.

To fix a sagging door, loosen the hinge screws at the top of the door, using a nut driver. Then lift the door into position and retighten the hinge screws.

REFRIGERATORS: WHAT TO CHECK BEFORE CALLING FOR SERVICE

Problem	Possible cause	Possible solution
Unit doesn't run; light inside is off	Power cord disconnected	Plug in cord
	Tripped circuit breaker or blown fuse	Check that no other appliance is operating on same circuit. Then reset circuit breaker or replace fuse (p.163)
	Faulty power cord	Unplug. Remove back panel and check all of cord. If needed, remove screws holding cord and test it (Step 2, p.160). If faulty, install an exact replacement. Be sure to connect grounding wire
Unit doesn't run; light inside goes on	Temperature control turned off	Check control and reset it
Noisy operation	Loose shelf; touching food containers hitting one another	Open door and wait for unit to turn on. Listen and look for noisy items
	Rattling defrost drain pan	Remove base grille. Reglue any felt pads that have fallen off. Make sure pan rests securely on its tracks
	Refrigerator not level	Test with a level; adjust legs (p.132)
	Paper caught in condenser fan blade	Disconnect power and remove paper
Unit runs longer than usual	Hot, humid weather; large amounts of warm food in unit	It's normal for a unit to run longer under these conditions
	Door opened frequently	Plan ahead; open door once to remove all the items for a meal
	Condenser coils under refrigerator clogged with dust	Vacuum the coils
	Door gasket not sealing	Replace gasket (see facing page)
	Light stays on when door is shut	Open door and press door switch. If light stays on, remove bulb until you can get switch replaced
Unit not cold enough	Temperature control not set properly	Reset. Consult instructions on unit or in owner's manual
	Not enough air circulating to coils on back of unit	Make sure unit is 4 inches from wall; remove any paper or other items caught in coils

NOTE: Any cause that makes a unit run longer can also keep it from cooling properly

If water puddles under your frost-free's vegetable and meat drawers, the drain may be clogged. If there's a drain cup, remove and wash it. Then use a meat baster to shoot hot water through the drain tube into the drain pan.

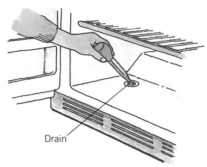

Drain

Frost in your frost-free? Check the defrost timer behind the grille. With the refrigerator running, use a screwdriver to turn the slotted knob slowly clockwise until you hear a click and the refrigerator goes off. Wait 5 minutes for defrost water to appear in the drain pan. If the frost doesn't melt or if the problem recurs, call for service.

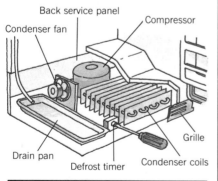

Back service panel
Condenser fan
Compressor
Drain pan
Defrost timer
Condenser coils
Grille

SELECTING A RANGE

Gas or electric? Generally a gas range costs less to operate, has fewer breakdowns, and allows faster control of the top burners' heat. An electric range usually operates more cleanly and efficiently, giving off less waste heat.

A freestanding range or built-ins? A model that stands alone is cheaper to install and easier to move. A separate built-in cooktop and oven allow greater flexibility in planning a kitchen, but require all new cabinetry.

Look for features that will avoid or aid cleanups. Among them are a lipped cooktop that stops spills from running down the front and sides of the range, and a lift-up or removable top that allows below-surface access for easy cleaning.

Depending on whether you use them or not, some features may be an added convenience or an unnecessary expense. These include a clock, extra indicator lights, oven window, and griddle, grill, and rotisserie accessories.

Whenever possible, get a range hood with a multispeed fan that blows fumes and other cooking odors outdoors through a vent. If you can only have a nonvented hood, get one with a charcoal filter. Replace the filter each year.

Ever heard of a downdraft cooktop? It has a built-in venting system that draws smoke downward before expelling it outdoors. It's a wise choice for a kitchen where you can't easily install a hood.

CONTINUOUS-CLEANING OR SELF-CLEANING OVEN?

Both of these automatic oven-cleaning systems can relieve you of a thankless, messy task on either a gas or electric range, but each does it in a different way. A continuous-cleaning (catalytic) oven has a special rough-textured porcelain lining. Spills and splatters spread over this material and gradually burn off as you use the oven. The lining's speckled appearance helps hide the soil while it burns off, but the oven may not always look as clean as you would like.

A continuous-cleaning oven costs only slightly more to buy than a regular oven. And because it cleans while you use the oven, it costs nothing more to operate. It consumes extra energy only when heavy baked-on deposits must be burned off at 400° F or more with the oven empty. But you can often eliminate this by always wiping up large spills as soon as the oven cools. Starchy and sugary spills especially need to be wiped up; the system doesn't remove them as well as it does greasy soil. Because scrubbing the spe-

cial lining or applying oven cleaner to it will damage it, many ranges have a standard porcelain finish on the oven floor and door so that such spills can be cleaned in the normal fashion.

A self-cleaning (pyrolytic) oven has a special cleaning cycle. It lasts about 1½ hours and raises the temperature to nearly 900° F, incinerating spills and splatters. Before next using the oven, you just run a damp cloth over the oven floor to collect the fine gray ash that remains. On some models you can also put the reflector or burner bowls from the cooktop in the oven and clean them too.

Surprisingly, an oven that self-cleans doesn't use a lot of energy, because it's heavily insulated. Indeed, a cleaning cycle costs less than the chemical oven cleaner that you'd need for a standard oven. The insulation saves energy during cooking and lets you bake or roast without overheating the kitchen, but it does reduce oven size. You can't use an oven during the self-cleaning process.

GAS RANGE CONSIDERATIONS

A pilotless electric ignition system uses a spark or a red-hot coil to ignite the gas when you turn on a burner. It uses 30 percent less energy than a pilot light.

If you're moving to an area without natural gas, bear in mind that a service technician can convert almost any gas range to burn LPG (liquefied petroleum gas).

When you're shopping for a gas range, check whether the oven floor is removable. It'll be a lot easier to clean if it is.

If you make soups and stews often, look for a thermostatically controlled burner. It controls the flame precisely for a perfect simmer.

ELECTRIC RANGE CONSIDERATIONS

On an electric range, check that the cooktop elements plug in (so that you can remove them for cleaning) and that the bake element in the oven bottom lifts up (so that you can wipe up spills).

Do you do a lot of baking and need a steady temperature? Consider an electronic temperature control. It keeps an oven within 5° F of the setting; a regular thermostat may allow up to 25° F variation.

For the most even baking, get a convection oven. It has a fan that circulates heated air, which eliminates any hot and cold spots. This usually speeds up cooking too, so be sure to follow the baking times given in the owner's guide.

SAVING ENERGY ON YOUR COOKTOP

Adjust a gas burner's flame so that it just touches or is lower than a pot's bottom. A flame that curls around a pot wastes energy.

On an electric range, put a pan on a cooking element that's the same size or slightly smaller than the utensil's bottom. Make sure the bottom is absolutely flat so that it's in full contact with the element.

Put your burner or element control on a high setting when you begin cooking a dish; then turn it lower to finish. In fact, turn off an electric element a minute or two before the food is done and let the residual heat complete the cooking.

On an electric range, the oven vent is usually under a burner. Use that burner to keep a dish warm when the oven is on. You can locate the vent by the heat it gives off when the oven is hot.

Use a pressure cooker. It cuts cooking time on the stove top by almost two-thirds, and it beats a microwave at cooking tough cuts of meat and large quantities of food. It's especially good if you live at a high altitude and have to extend cooking times to make up for lower boiling temperatures.

SAVING ENERGY IN AN OVEN

Arrange racks in an oven before you turn it on. It not only saves heat; it's a whole lot safer.

If a roast or a casserole will cook for more than an hour, start it in a cold oven and cook it for the prescribed time. If the time is under an hour, extend it slightly. Reserve preheating for baking.

Cook small quantities of food in a microwave oven rather than in an electric oven. A microwave can use one-third to one-half as much energy as an electric oven. But always use a range oven for large quantities of food.

ADJUSTING YOUR OVEN'S TEMPERATURE CONTROL

To test your oven, place an oven thermometer in its center, set the oven for 350° F, and run it for 20 minutes. To get the most accurate readings, use an oven thermometer with a mercury-filled column. They are stocked by kitchen specialty shops and are great baking aids too.

To adjust the thermostat on many ovens, pull off the temperature control knob and look on its underside. Loosen any screws (or clips) and adjust the disc. A notch usually represents 10 degrees. If you have to move more than two notches, have the thermostat replaced.

For other ovens, pull off the temperature control knob and turn the screw inside the knob's hollow shaft. Turning it clockwise lowers the setting; counterclockwise raises it. If it requires an adjustment of more than 25 degrees, about an eighth of a turn, have the thermostat replaced.

Put as many dishes in an oven at once as you can. If their recipe temperatures differ, just adjust their times. If you have three dishes that require 325° F, 350° F, and 375° F, set the oven for 350° F. Then cut a few minutes from the 325° F dish and add a few minutes to the 375° F dish. Leave 1 or 2 inches of space around each dish.

If you have dishes, such as several sheets of cookies, that you can't bake at the same time, do them in quick succession.

Keep track of cooking time with a timer. Don't keep peeking into an oven. Each peek can cost as much as 25° F; it can also affect browning and baking.

If possible, start the self-cleaning cycle of an oven while it's still warm from cooking.

COOKING SAFELY

Use only dry pot holders. A damp pot holder transmits heat. Also avoid using dish towels. They're not thick enough to protect you.

Dress safely when you cook. A loose sleeve could hook a pot handle, or a dangling scarf could brush a burner. Wear close-fitting clothes or an apron.

Turn pot and pan handles so that they are over the center or sides of the range. Don't place handles over an adjacent burner where they can get hot and burn you or over the front where someone can bump into them.

IF YOU SMELL GAS

If you smell a heavy gas odor, immediately turn off any flames, open the windows and doors, and get everyone out of the house. If your range's shutoff valve isn't within easy reach, turn off your home's main gas shutoff valve at the meter or liquefied petroleum gas tank. Do not touch a light switch, pick up a telephone, or make any electrical connection that could create a spark. If you need light, use a flashlight. Report the leak to your gas company or your gas supplier from a neighbor's telephone.

The shutoff valve on a gas range or oven is located near the point where the gas line enters—usually under the cooktop. If yours isn't there, consult your owner's manual or call your appliance dealer. On some models it's under the broiler drawer.

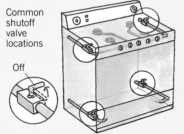

Common shutoff valve locations

Off

If you notice a faint scent of gas, check for a burner flame or a pilot light that has blown out. Check the oven also. If you're not cooking, probably a pilot light has gone out. Turn off any flames and air out the room. Relight the burner or pilot only after all gas odor is gone. If any odor persists after you've aired out the room, turn off the gas at your home's main shutoff valve and call the gas company.

When ventilating a room, keep in mind that natural gas is lighter than air and collects in the upper part of the room; liquefied petroleum gas sinks to the floor.

For your kitchen, get a dry chemical or foam fire extinguisher approved for fires ranked Class B (grease and other flammable liquids) and Class C (electrical).

RANGE PROBLEMS

Before making a repair to an electric range, turn off the power at the fuse box or circuit breaker (p. 163).

To remove a cooktop element, lift the edge just enough to clear the reflector. Then pull it straight out.

Always open and close an electric range's lift-up cooktop carefully to avoid pulling or crimping wires that carry current to the elements.

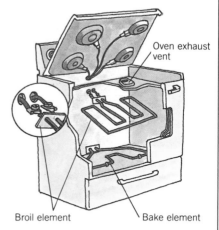

Oven exhaust vent

Broil element   Bake element

To replace a broil or bake element, turn off the power (p. 163), and remove the screws holding its front and rear brackets. (For some bake elements you needn't detach the front bracket.) Then carefully pull the element forward and unscrew the wires leading to it.

ELECTRIC RANGES: WHAT TO CHECK BEFORE CALLING FOR SERVICE

Caution: Before making any repair to a range, shut off the power to it by removing the fuse or turning off the circuit breaker (p. 163). Let a heat element cool completely before touching it.

Problem	Possible cause	Possible solution
No cooktop or oven elements will go on; lights and timers are out	No power to range	Check for a blown fuse or a tripped circuit breaker (p. 163)
One cooktop element won't go on	Burned-out element	Before replacing element, try it in receptacle for a same-size element or have repair shop test it
	Faulty receptacle for element	Remove element; clean contacts if dark and corroded. Check receptacle with a flashlight; if blackened and corroded, have it replaced
One oven element goes on; the other doesn't	Burned-out element	Remove element (see above); have a repair shop test it
Oven won't go on	Oven set to come on automatically at a specific time	Switch the automatic-manual control to *Manual*
Oven dishes are burned or undercooked	Temperature control set too high or low	Recheck recipe temperatures and times
	Temperature control incorrect	Readjust temperature control (p. 138)
	Food dishes blocking air circulation	Space dishes at least 1 in. apart

GAS RANGES: WHAT TO CHECK BEFORE CALLING FOR SERVICE

Problem	Possible cause	Possible solution
Cooktop burner won't light	Pilot light out	Relight pilot (see below); stop any drafts that may have blown it out
	Gas supply off	If other burners and gas appliances won't light, call your utility company
	Dirty spark igniter	Clean igniter (see owner's manual)
Burner flames are uneven	Clogged burner	Clean holes in burner (see below)
Yellow burner flame, soot on pot bottoms	Not enough air in gas-air mixture	Open the air shutter as needed (see below)
High, hissing burner flame	Too much air in gas-air mixture	Close the air shutter as needed (see below)
Oven won't light; top burners work	Pilot light out	Relight pilot following directions in owner's manual
	Electric ignition not working	Make sure power to range is on
	Oven set to come on automatically at a specific time	Switch automatic-manual control to *Manual*

If a spot on a electric cooktop element glows brighter than the rest of it, the element may be failing. Replace it before overheating at the bright spot damages your pots. The same is true of a broil or bake element in the oven.

If the holes in a gas burner become clogged, clean them with a straight pin or pipe cleaner. Avoid toothpicks, which may break off and plug the hole.

If a power failure knocks out your gas range's electric igniter, start a burner by holding a match to it and turning the control to *High*.

If a knob won't pull off, just slip a piece of cloth under the bottom edge and pull.

Does oil collect on one side of the frying pan? Do cakes rise unevenly? Your range is probably not level. Check it with a spirit level. You can level an electric range as you would a refrigerator (p.132), but a gas range should be leveled by a service technician.

FLAME ADJUSTMENT ON A GAS RANGE

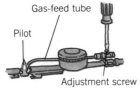

Gas-feed tube
Pilot
Adjustment screw

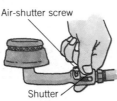

Air-shutter screw
Shutter

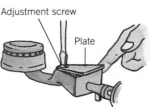

Adjustment screw
Plate

To relight a pilot, turn the screw on its gas-feed tube counterclockwise slightly. Hold a match to the pilot, and turn the screw clockwise until the flame is ¼ inch high. A pilot that's too high can damage the cooktop.

To regulate a burner on a range that has a barrel-shaped chamber for mixing air with the gas going to the burner, loosen the air-shutter screw. Then open or close the shutter by rotating it. Retighten the screw.

On other ranges the mixing chamber is triangular shaped and covered by a flat plate. To regulate the burner, loosen the screw holding the plate and pivot the plate from side to side. Then retighten the screw.

SELECTING A DISHWASHER

If buying and installing a built-in dishwasher is too expensive, consider a portable. It can be almost as easy to use, especially if you have a convenient place to store it between uses. And like all portable appliances, it can go with you if you move.

Are you delaying purchasing a dishwasher until you remodel or move? Get a convertible model, which you can use as a portable now and later have built in.

To save energy, get a dishwasher with a booster heater that automatically heats hot water from your water heater to the temperature required to clean dishes. It saves energy by letting you keep the water heater at a lower temperature. It's also your best bet if you live in an apartment and can't control water temperature.

LOADING A DISHWASHER

Don't bother to rinse dishes before loading them. The machine's water system pulverizes and flushes away food particles. But it's not a waste disposer; scrape off bones and large quantities of food. Just empty glasses and cups.

Put pots and baking dishes with heavy or encrusted residue in the lower rack facing down toward the spray arm. Make sure pot handles are secure and can't drop down and block the spray arm.

Put large platters or cookie sheets in the back or on the sides. In the front, they can keep water from reaching the detergent dispenser and the silverware basket.

A dishwasher can't clean everything. If a pot has burned-on or charred food, the only way to get it clean is to wash it by hand.

Use the top rack for smaller and lighter items, including plastics rated dishwasher-safe. Put cups and glasses between or over the prongs; don't let them hang loosely on prongs. Never wash glasses or fragile glassware in the bottom.

To keep lightweight items, such as plastic cups, from flipping over, put them in the top rack's corners where the water spray is weakest. Sometimes you can anchor them between heavier objects or fit them snugly over two prongs.

Silverware cleans best when you put it in the basket with the handles downward. But for safety point sharp knives down. Just be careful not to let a thin knife stick through the basket bottom and stop the spray arm.

SAVING ENERGY WITH YOUR DISHWASHER

Always wash full loads. A dishwasher uses the same amount of hot water and energy whether it's half-filled or fully loaded. Use the rinse-and-hold cycle when you don't have a full load.

Let your dishes air-dry. If your machine doesn't have an *Energy Saver* switch to stop heated drying, just wait for the final rinse to end, then release the door latch and turn the control knob to *Off*. Wait a few minutes for the steam inside to subside, then open the door and pull the top rack out partway to hold it open.

GETTING THE MOST FROM DISHWASHER DETERGENT

Fill a detergent dispenser just before washing. Left standing, detergent absorbs moisture, cakes, and loses its cleaning power.

Are you wasting dishwasher detergent? You may want to experiment to determine just how much you really need to get dishes clean. Try filling the dispenser only halfway if you live in a soft-water area and three-quarters in an area with moderately hard water. Use a full dispenser only in a hard-water region.

DISHES NOT GETTING CLEAN?

Make sure your water is hot. Put a glass in the sink and run hot water into it for a few minutes. Then put a candy or meat thermometer in it. If the temperature is not between 140° F and 160° F, adjust your water heater.

If your water heater is not near your kitchen, run the hot-water tap in the sink until the water is hot before starting the dishwasher.

Do your dishes seem less clean only in cold weather? The water temperature may be dropping as it flows from the water heater. Insulate exposed pipes and turn up the water heater in winter.

Taking a shower, running a load of clothes, or watering the lawn while using the dishwasher can also result in uncleaned dishes. When the water pressure drops too low, the dishwasher doesn't get enough water during the time allotted to filling.

SPOTS AND STAINS

Black marks on china are probably the result of metal utensils rubbing on the china. Separate metal items from china. Secure lightweight aluminum pans between heavier pans so that they can't bounce around.

Is there a film on your dishes? Check that the water is hot. Also try using more detergent or a new brand. To remove the film, open the dishwasher after the rinse phase, remove all metal items, and set a bowl containing 2 cups of white vinegar on the bottom rack. Then wash and rinse again.

If your glassware has become etched with a film that you can't rub off, the damage is permanent. To avoid the etching of other glasses, try using less detergent and loading fewer dishes. Another possible cause is low water pressure, which prevents the machine from filling completely.

To prevent pitting on silverware, rinse it before you put it in the machine whenever you're going to delay washing. Don't sprinkle detergent on silver.

Find water spots on your dishes? Use a rinse agent. It causes water to flow off the dishes in sheets. If your unit doesn't have a dispenser for liquid rinse agent, get a rinse agent in a solid bar that hooks onto the upper rack.

A DISHWASHER IN DISTRESS

Yellow or brown stains on your machine's interior (and on dishes) indicate iron in the water. To remove stains, stop the machine after it fills for the wash and add ½ cup citric acid crystals. Or try a compound that appliance dealers sell to remove rust from a water softener's resin and follow directions. To stop staining, install an iron filter in your water supply.

DISHWASHERS: WHAT TO CHECK BEFORE CALLING FOR SERVICE

Problem	Possible cause	Possible solution
Dishwasher won't run	No power to unit	Check for blown fuse or tripped circuit breaker (p.163); check that portable unit is plugged in
	Door not latched	Make sure door is fully latched
	Jammed or stiff door latch is not engaging door switch	Try opening and closing door a few times
	Cycle-selecting button not depressed	Push button all the way in
Dishwasher doesn't fill	Water cutoff valve closed	Open the valve located under sink on the water line going to the dishwasher
	Float switch stuck in up position	Clear obstructions under the float switch
Dishwasher doesn't drain	Clogged filter screen	Clean filter screen (p.145)
Dishes aren't completely clean	Water not hot enough	Test water temperature (p.143) and reset water heater's thermostat
	Clogged spray arm or filter screen	Clean spray arm and filter screen (p.145)
	Detergent dispenser not dumping	Move any dish or pan obstructing dispenser operation. Open front panel of door (see owner's manual) and check dispenser mechanism for a broken spring or lever or for corrosion
Dishes don't dry	Water not hot enough	Test water temperature (p.143) and reset water heater's thermostat
	Water not draining	Check for a clogged filter screen (p.145)
Dishwasher leaks from door vent	Improperly loaded dishes deflecting water through vent	Reload dishes following instructions in owner's manual
Dishwasher leaks from bottom of door	Oversudsing	Don't use a nondishwasher detergent. Don't prerinse dishes in liquid detergent
	Door gasket is worn or cracked	Replace gasket; some pop in, others are held by screws or clips (see owner's manual)
Dishwasher is noisy	Spray arm hitting dishes	Reload so that spray arm can rotate freely; check loading guidelines in owner's manual
	Low water pressure prevents machine from filling completely	Don't use house water supply while dishwasher is filling
	Silverware or broken dishware in bottom of tub	Remove piece; let heating element cool completely before reaching in tub
	Dishes bouncing around	When loading dishes, make sure lightweight items are held firmly in place

Is there a chalky deposit in your dishwasher? Start the machine without dishes or detergent on a rinse-and-hold cycle. During the fill, add 1 cup white vinegar and let the machine finish the cycle. Then add detergent and run the empty machine through a cycle.

If a dish rack sticks, its rollers may be jammed. Turn them by hand to loosen them. If they are worn and no longer round, replace them. Some can be removed by taking out screws; most simply pull off.

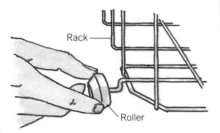

If a rack sticks because it's bent, replace it. On many machines, you lift out a rack simply by pulling and tilting it. On others, you have to take out the pins that hold it to its slides.

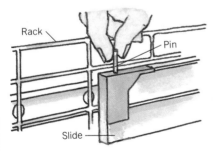

Are the prongs on a rack chipped? Appliance parts dealers stock repair kits containing rubber tips that glue over the damaged ends.

To tell whether a spray arm is rotating, note its position and start the washer. Then stop the machine and see if it has moved.

To clean a spray arm, remove the racks, unscrew the hub cap holding the arm, and lift it off. Unclog the holes with stiff wire. Flush out the arm under a running faucet.

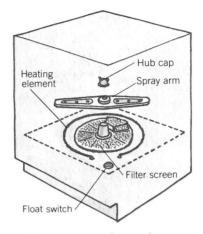

If a filter screen is clogged, remove the spray arm and any clips securing the screen. Then wash the screen under running water with a stiff brush.

GETTING A NEW CLOTHES WASHER

If you don't have space for a washer and dryer next to each other, buy units that stack or get a combination machine, which does both washing and drying.

A front-loading washer is a space saver; its top is free for work space. Also, instead of agitating, a front-loader tumbles clothes like a dryer, making it gentler on clothes and less wobbly when spinning. But most models have less capacity than a top-loader and can't clean ground-in dirt as well.

Give your washer room to vibrate. Make sure the space where you plan to put it is an inch wider all around than the machine.

If your washer's power cord won't reach an outlet, have the outlet moved or have a longer power cord installed. Don't use an extension cord. If water touches the connection between it and the power cord, you could be electrocuted.

Don't install a washer in an unheated garage or utility room. It can be damaged if water trapped inside freezes. A washer in an unheated vacation home should be drained completely by a service technician at summer's end.

KEEPING YOUR WASHER PROPERLY CONNECTED

A burst washer hose can flood your house. Always turn off the faucets when you finish washing. If household members tend to forget, put up a sign to remind them. Leaving the house while a washer is running invites a disaster.

Every month or so, turn the water on and run your hand over the washer hoses. Replace both hoses if you feel a bulge in either.

Hoses made by a washer's manufacturer usually resist pressure and heat better than brandless bargain replacements.

The screens that filter water going into a washer need cleaning occasionally. On some washers, just unscrew the hoses from the faucets and take them out. On others, unscrew the hoses from the washer and use a screwdriver or long-nose pliers to take them out of the washer's inlet ports. Scrub them with a toothbrush under a faucet.

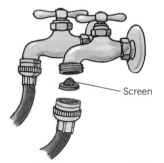

Screen

When replacing a washer's drain hose, you'll find it easier to put on the new hose if you replace the spring hose clamps with worm-drive hose clamps. Just be careful not to overtighten the new clamp.

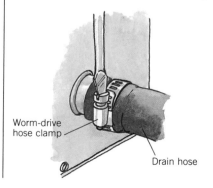

Worm-drive hose clamp

Drain hose

CONTROLLING WASHER NOISE AND VIBRATION

Does your washer wobble excessively when spinning? The cause may be an unevenly distributed load, often a large item that has wadded up to one side. Just stop the washer and redistribute the clothes for better balance.

Ordinary washer vibration can cause a machine to move and become unlevel and noisy. Periodically stop the water while the machine is filling and see if the water is even with a row of holes around the tub diameter. You can level most washers as you do refrigerators (p. 132).

If a washer that's level produces excess vibration and noise, open the top of washer and check the snubber assembly, a device that absorbs vibration. Look for a loose or broken spring. Clean and lightly sand the friction pad if the snubber sticks to the pad's surface. If necessary, replace the pad.
Caution: Unplug your washer before attempting to make any repair. Disconnect hoses if you have to move the washer.

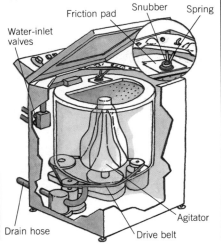

Water-inlet valves — Friction pad — Snubber — Spring — Agitator — Drain hose — Drive belt

To open the top on most washers, cover a putty knife blade with masking tape and slide it into the joint between the top and the cabinet about 2½ inches in from the edge. Then push to release a clip. Repeat at the other corner and raise the hinged top.

Clip

When opening the top of a washer, be sure to release any hoses that are attached to the top.

OTHER WASHER PROBLEMS

Agitation or spinning problems may be caused by a loose drive belt. To test a drive belt, remove the washer's rear access panel and press the belt in. If it bends in more than ¾ inch, tighten it. If it's worn, have it replaced.

To tighten a loose belt on a top-loading washer, simply loosen the motor's mounting nut and move the motor along the slotted opening, increasing tension on the belt. Then retighten the nut.

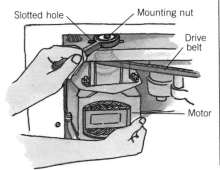

Slotted hole — Mounting nut — Drive belt — Motor

147

If your machine leaks, check first to see if it's a simple hose problem you can fix yourself. Run the unloaded washer through a cycle. Look for a damaged inlet hose during the fill and for a loose drain hose during the spin.

If tears or snags appear in clothes after washing, wrap an old nylon stocking around your hand and slowly rub it around the washer tub and agitator to find any sharp edges or rough spots. Smooth them with fine sandpaper.

Did you find a cracked or broken vane on an agitator? Replace the agitator or it'll tear your clothes. A loose or worn agitator can also rip or tear your clothes.

To remove a washer's agitator, take off any softener dispenser and unscrew the agitator cap. If the agitator won't lift off easily, fill the tub with hot water. If it still won't come off, place a block of wood next to it and tap it gently with a hammer to loosen it.

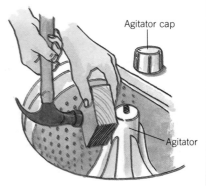

Agitator cap

Agitator

CLOTHES WASHERS: WHAT TO CHECK BEFORE CALLING FOR SERVICE

Problem	Possible cause	Possible solution
Machine won't turn on	No power to machine	Check for unplugged power cord, blown fuse, or tripped circuit breaker (p.163)
	Overload has tripped automatic safety switch	Reduce load; then reset switch (see owner's manual)
Machine won't fill or fills slowly	Water faucets closed	Turn on faucets
	Clogged filter screens on water hoses	Clean filter screens (p.146)
	Kinked or pinched water hoses	Straighten hoses; replace hoses if kinks have hardened
Water isn't hot	Hot-water faucet off	Turn on faucet
	Inlet hoses are reversed	Check hose connections; correct if necessary
	Clogged filter screen on hot-water inlet hose	Clean filter screen (p.146)
	Hot-water supply exhausted or water heater set too low	Check water heater; set thermostat higher if necessary
Motor runs but machine doesn't agitate	Loose drive belt	Tighten drive belt (p.147)
Machine spins but clothes remain wet	Oversudsing is slowing spin	Add cold water to reduce suds. Use less detergent in future
	Clogged or kinked drain hose	Clear obstruction or straighten hose; replace hose if kink has hardened
Machine doesn't spin or spins slowly	Overload or unbalanced load has tripped automatic safety switch	Reduce or redistribute load; reset switch (see owner's manual)
	Overload or unbalanced load keeps basket from reaching proper speed	Reduce or redistribute load
	Loose drive belt	Tighten drive belt (p.147)

SAVING ON WATER-HEATING BILLS

Except for heating and cooling units, the water heater is your home's largest energy user. Unless you need a higher temperature for a dishwasher (p.143), set your unit for 120° F. Turn it off when you go away for more than a few days.

If you have an electric unit, find out if your power company offers off-peak rates. Schedule bathing, laundering, and dishwashing for these periods, or just prior to them. You need to have a special meter installed. It's usually on a circuit with a timer set to run the water heater during off-peak hours.

Does your water heater feel warm when you touch it? It's losing heat. Wrap it with an insulating fiberglass blanket available as a kit. Take care not to cover a gas unit's top or to block the air flow to the gas burner at bottom.

If you're buying a new water heater, get a superinsulated energy-saving model. Putting extra insulation on one won't save much.

WATER-HEATER UPKEEP

If your plumbing is noisy only when the hot water is running, the water temperature may be too high, creating steam in the pipes. Try lowering the temperature.

Is your hot water dirty? Does it take a long time to reheat after the tank is exhausted? Both indicate sediment in your water heater's tank.

To clear sediment from a tank, turn off the gas or power and the cold-water inlet valve. Open an upstairs hot-water faucet. Then attach a garden hose to the drain valve and drain the tank through the hose into a floor drain. This may take a few hours. Reopen the cold-water valve and let water run through the empty tank until the water drains clear.

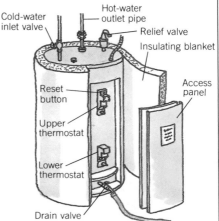

It's easy to prevent a sediment buildup. Drain the tank into a pail (or through a hose) until the water is clear two to four times a year, or monthly for very hard water.

No hot water from your electric water heater? If a tripped circuit breaker or a blown fuse isn't the cause (p.163), turn off power, remove the access panel, and press the reset button on the upper thermostat. Replace the access panel; then restore power and test.

If your heater runs out of hot water often, you may be doing tasks that consume lots of hot water too close together. One tub bath can exhaust a typical 40-gallon tank and it can take up to an hour to reheat.

To find out how quickly your water heater recovers, look for a plate on it that notes how many gallons it can heat in an hour.

SETTING UP A NEW DRYER

Plan to locate a dryer in a place where the surrounding temperature stays above 45° F; the higher the better to cut drying time.

Before buying a dryer, check the location of its exhaust hole. Then check the spot where you plan to put the dryer to make sure that you can run a vent hose from the exhaust hole to the outdoors. Depending on the dryer, you may be able to vent out to the back, to either side, or through the floor.

Don't vent a dryer into a chimney, crawl space, or attic. Lint from the dryer is highly combustible.

Plastic vinyl hose is not very effective for venting. Get either rigid or flexible metal ducting instead. Exterior vent hoods that open a full 4 inches are more efficient than ones that open less.

If a dryer's vent hose is too long, it will greatly increase your clothes' drying time. Keep the length from the dryer to the outside vent hood to 25 feet or less. Deduct 5 feet from this length for each elbow, except for the elbow at the dryer.

FOR DRYER EFFICIENCY:

Clean the lint filter after each use.

Dry light and heavy fabrics separately.

Avoid overloading and underloading a dryer; both waste energy.

Don't add wet items to a load that's already partly dry.

When drying more than one load, dry them one immediately after another to utilize the heat in the dryer from the previous load.

DRYER MAINTENANCE

Is a lint-clogged venting system keeping your clothes from drying completely? Go outside and hold your hand under the vent hood while the dryer is running. If it's venting properly, you should feel a strong flow of air.

To prevent a lint buildup in your dryer's vent duct, clean it once a year. Remove the duct and shake it out. If necessary, run a wadded cloth through it. Be sure to reseal joints with fresh duct tape.

Outdoors, clean the damper and its hinge by inserting a length of straightened coat hanger into the vent hood.

Make sure that your vent duct is straight. Dips and kinks collect water and lint, blocking air flow. If the duct runs through an unheated area such as a crawl space, cold can aggravate the problem.

To shut off all the power to an electric dryer, you have to remove two fuses or flip two circuit breakers in your home's main electric service panel (p. 163). Both together control the power to the heating element and one also controls the power to the motor.

Is your dryer making unusual noises? Rotate the drum by hand. A slow thump that varies with the speed that you turn the drum probably indicates a worn drive belt that needs replacing.

If you hear many thumps each time you rotate the drum, it indicates a worn support roller. To replace it, consult your service manual or have a service technician make the repair.

Is a leaky door seal the cause of long drying times? Check for moisture on the door. Also move a piece of tissue paper around the door's edge while the dryer is running. If the paper is drawn in, the seal needs to be replaced.

If a door seal is just glued to the door or jamb, you can replace it by pulling off the old seal and gluing on a new one. Get a special nonflammable adhesive at the appliance parts store when you buy the new seal. Have a seal that mounts between the cabinet and drum opening serviced.

Seal

DRYERS: WHAT TO CHECK BEFORE CALLING FOR SERVICE

Problem	Possible cause	Possible solution
Dryer won't run	No power to dryer	Check for unplugged power cord, blown fuse, or tripped circuit breaker (p.163)
	Dryer door is not fully closed	Shut door firmly
	Drying cycle selector may not be set	Set control to a drying cycle
	Start button has not been pressed	Press start button
Clothes take too long to dry	Dryer is overloaded	Reduce amount of clothing
	Incorrect drying cycle selected	Consult owner's manual to determine correct cycle
	Dryer venting system is clogged	Clean the lint filter, vent duct, and vent hood (facing page)
	Final washing machine rinses are being done with cold water	Expect longer drying times than when using warm rinses
	Clothes were too wet when put in	Make sure washing machine isn't being overloaded and is draining and spinning properly
	Leaky door seal	Test door seal (see above); if necessary, replace or have serviced
Dryer doesn't produce heat	One of the fuses or circuit breakers that controls heating element on electric dryer is blown	Replace fuse or reset breaker (p.163)
	Temperature selector set for air cycle rather than heat cycle	Reset control
Dryer makes noise	Foreign object is stuck in drum hole	Use a flashlight to look for nail, screw, curtain hook caught in a drum hole; remove object with pliers if necessary
	Hard objects on clothes such as buttons and zippers are hitting drum	Noise is normal
	Loose trim and exterior panels rattling	Tighten all visible screws

If you have a dryer that turns off automatically when the clothes reach the desired degree of dryness, use fabric softeners labeled safe for this type of dryer. Some softeners can coat the moisture sensors and prevent them from turning the dryer off.

If you suspect that your dryer's moisture sensors are coated with softener, wash them with warm, soapy water. (The sensors are just inside the door or on the drum's baffles; see your owner's manual).

TOASTERS AND TOASTER OVENS

Toast always getting stuck? Get wooden toast tongs from a kitchen speciality shop. When faced with a slice that's reluctant to leave the toaster, unplug the toaster, gently work the tongs around the bread, and pull it out. Be careful not to damage the heat elements.

A toaster oven has no equal in toasting split muffins or bagels. But a toaster produces better toast; in a toaster oven slices of bread tend to dry out before they brown. If you like to toast thick-sliced bread, consider a toaster with an extra wide opening.

Want a warm dish? While the food cooks, put your plate on top of the toaster oven—but not a toaster.

Keeping your toaster oven sparkling clean inside and out will extend its life. But cleaning the heat elements can cause them to fail prematurely. They self-clean by burning off spills.

Is the door of your toaster oven or broiler oven difficult to open? Unplug the unit and wash the pivots and hinge rods with a cotton swab dipped in water mixed with liquid dishwashing detergent. When the parts dry, use another swab to apply a light coating of a heat-resistant silicone lubricant. Then open and close the door a few times to spread the lubricant.

TOASTING SAFELY

Get yourself and your family in the habit of unplugging a toaster oven or broiler oven after each use. This will decrease the odds that someone may accidentally leave the switch on after baking or broiling, causing the appliance to overheat and start a fire.

Be careful not to let a metal pan or an aluminum container touch a top heating element in a toaster oven. This can create a short and burn out the element. If you are touching the metal, you could get shocked or even electrocuted.

WHAT TO LOOK FOR IN A MICROWAVE OVEN

Programmable electronic controls let you set a series of different power levels for different lengths of time. For example, you can set the controls to defrost and cook a dish, then keep it warm. It's also handy to have a turntable that rotates food for even cooking and a door release that you can operate with an elbow.

Another useful microwave feature is a temperature probe. You insert it into the food as you would a meat thermometer. When your food reaches the desired temperature, the oven sounds a signal. Some models automatically shut off but still keep the food warm.

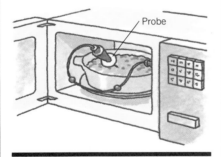
Probe

MAKING ROOM FOR A MICROWAVE

What's the best height for a wall-mounted microwave? Position the oven so that it's at the chest level of the shortest person who's going to be using it.

Want to build your microwave into a cabinet or mount it beneath? To make sure it's safe, check the model number with your dealer or the manufacturer. Also ask about a kit for trimming your model's edges (if you build it in) or a bracket for under-cabinet mounting. Be careful not to block any vents.

Putting a microwave above your range isn't a good idea because of the heat, grease, and steam a range produces and because you have to reach over a hot surface. If you have no other convenient place to put a microwave, get a special over-range unit with a range hood on the bottom.

USING THAT MIRACULOUS MICROWAVE

For the best results, follow the cooking times in the recipe book that comes with your microwave. The times in most cookbooks and magazines are for an average 600- to 700-watt microwave. To produce the desired result, a compact 400-watt microwave will take more time, and a large 1,000-watt one will take less. Also, the various power-level ratings, such as *High* or *Medium*, are not standardized.

Even if you have a turntable to rotate food in your microwave, it's a good idea to stir such dishes as stews and vegetables to ensure that all ingredients get fully and evenly heated.

Sparks or flashes in a microwave indicate a dish containing metal, which shouldn't be used for microwave cooking. Remove the dish, and transfer the food to a container that's microwave-safe.

Avoid using brown paper bags and overcooking popcorn in a microwave. And keep an eye on dishes with lots of sugar. All are common causes of flare-ups.

If a fire develops in a microwave, keep the door closed and unplug the unit. Let the fire extinguish itself before opening the door.

MICROWAVE COOKWARE

Not sure if a dish is suitable for the microwave? Put the empty dish and a glass measuring cup half filled with water in the oven and set it on full power for 1 minute. Then gingerly touch the dish and the water. If the water is hot and the dish cool, the dish is OK to use.

Some surprising items can be used as microwave cookware. Try warming leftovers on a paper plate, cooking bacon on paper towels, and heating rolls wrapped in a napkin in a straw basket.

In a microwave, food in a round dish cooks more evenly. A shallow dish also cooks more evenly than a deep one. And any dish cooks slower in the center than at the edges. Give preference to dishes with straight rather than sloping sides.

Before putting food in the microwave, cover it with plastic wrap or a glass lid. The food will heat faster and more evenly. It will also retain more moisture.

Don't rush out to buy special cookware for your new microwave. Most of your present ceramic and glass casserole and baking dishes are microwave-safe.

Save the microwave-safe plastic containers that some frozen foods come in. They're great for heating individual portions of any food in the microwave, and you can put them in the dishwasher.

Select plastic microwave cookware that can also be used for freezer storage so that precooked portions can go directly from the freezer into the microwave.

MIXER MASTERY

If you use a mixer just for whipping cream and beating eggs, a hand-held model is fine. But if you plan to do demanding tasks such as kneading dough, consider a heavy-duty pedestal model, preferably with a set of metal bowls.

Are the beaters on your mixer difficult to remove? Try putting a drop of light household oil into each beater's sleeve.

To straighten a bent beater blade, lay the damaged portion on a cutting board and press on it with the bottom of a teaspoon.

Is your pedestal mixer's bowl not turning? Swing up or lift off the top housing and adjust the beater height by turning the screw on the pedestal's top (or housing's bottom). The beaters should just clear the bowl. But if one beater has a plastic disc on the bottom, the disc should touch the bowl.

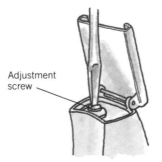

Adjustment screw

KEEPING YOUR BLENDER WHIRLING

How many speeds should your new blender have? Four or five will probably fill your needs nicely; any more will just raise the appliance's cost unnecessarily.

A switch that lets you "pulse" a blender on and off is a handy feature. Pulsing promotes even blending because the food redistributes itself between pulses. If your blender doesn't have a *Pulse* switch, you can get the same effect by just alternately pressing one of the speed-control buttons and the *Off* button.

If a blender push button doesn't work, get a can of electrical contact cleaner (often called tuner cleaner) from an appliance parts store. With the unit unplugged, spray a little on each side of the button. After it seeps in, press the button on and off several times.

If a blender's motor labors while you're processing a heavy mixture, try switching to the next higher speed. Or blend the food in smaller quantities.

Let very hot liquids cool for a while before putting them in the blender. Otherwise, trapped steam and moisture may erupt when you open the blender while processing the food.

THAT FABULOUS FOOD PROCESSOR

Look for a food processor with a built-in circuit breaker that will shut off the motor if the load is too heavy or if food gets jammed. Any food processor with a motor that's guaranteed for as long as you own the appliance is likely to have this feature.

If your food processor stops suddenly, an overload may have tripped its built-in circuit breaker. Turn the machine off and correct the problem. Wait 5 minutes before starting it again.

Does the noise that your food processor makes drive you crazy? Put the unit on a thick pad of rubbery plastic, sold in large stationery shops for keeping office machines quiet. It's a good idea to test the noise level of a food processor in the store before buying it.

Ever wondered about the large holes on your food processor's discs? They let you pick up the discs without touching the sharp edges that cut and grate.

155

CLOGGED COFFEE MAKERS

You pour 2 cups of water in your gravity-feed drip coffee maker but only 1 cup comes out! Check the drain hole in the water tank. If it's clogged, poke it open with a thin wire. If the bimetallic bar under the drain hole is corroded or broken, replace the water tank with a duplicate from the manufacturer.

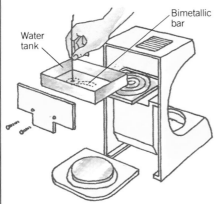

Water tank

Bimetallic bar

Spout clean and still no drip from your pump valve coffee maker? Mineral deposits may be clogging the valve. Unplug the machine, unscrew the baseplate, and remove the rubber elbow from the reservoir. Remove the valve and scrub it in detergent and warm water. Replace it; it should now move up and down freely. (For a thorough cleaning, see p.108.)

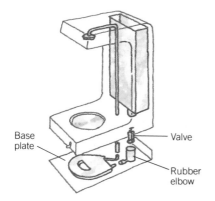

Base plate

Valve

Rubber elbow

PERCOLATORS AND URNS

If you get hot water, not coffee, from a percolator, check that the tube is firmly seated in the center well. Try brewing another potful. If you again get only hot water, replace the tube with a duplicate from an appliance dealer.

Water leaking from around the faucet of a large coffee urn? Remove the nut holding the faucet, pull the faucet out of the hole, reverse the washer, and replace it on the faucet. Reinstall the faucet and tighten the nut. If reversing the washer doesn't stop the leak, you'll have to replace the washer.

STEAM IRONS

If your iron doesn't steam as it should, minerals are clogging the steam ports. Try reaming them out with the end of a straightened paper clip, after the unplugged iron has cooled.

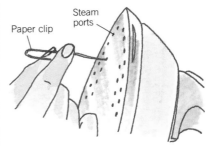

Paper clip

Steam ports

If the above doesn't help, fill the tank with a solution of half white vinegar, half water. Turn the iron on to the steam setting and, holding it horizontal, operate the spray and let it steam until the liquid is gone. More than one treatment may be necessary.

Although some makers say that it's OK to use tap water in a steam iron, why chance it? Catch rain water in a clean glass jar and mark it *"For ironing only."* Or melt frost from your freezer to get distilled water. Or run tap water through a special water filter, available in hardware stores.

CARE AND REPAIR

Does your iron stick to your clothes and stain them? Unplug the iron and let it cool. Clean the soleplate with a cloth dampened with rubbing alcohol, buff it with extra fine steel wool, and wipe it with a soft cloth. If, however, your iron is coated with a nonstick substance, rub wadded wax paper over the soleplate (warm) or buff it very gently with extra fine steel wool.

You can replace a steam iron's frayed power cord if there's a screw-on cover over the terminal housing. Disconnect the iron, remove the screw and housing cover, and detach the faulty power cord from its terminals. Install a duplicate cord, tighten the terminals well, and reattach the cover.

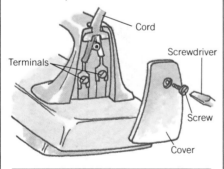

Cord

Screwdriver

Terminals

Screw

Cover

USEFUL HUMIDITY

Do you get an electrostatic shock whenever you touch someone or something in your home? Is your skin often dry, your nasal passages parched? If so, a humidifier will benefit you, your pets, plants, and furniture.

A humidifier works best if your house's insulation has a vapor barrier (pp. 176, 178). Without one, moisture seeping into the walls can render the insulation less effective and cause wood in the walls to swell and decay. In an uninsulated house, moisture within the walls can eventually cause wood to rot.

If you have a warm-air heating system, you can eventually humidify the whole house: Attach the warm-air heating system to a self-filling humidifier that is connected to a water supply pipe. Do it yourself only if the furnace manual or your heating contractor recommends it.

Portable or movable humidifiers are the only alternative if you have baseboard heating or radiators. Ultrasonic portables are safer, quieter, and more efficient than the evaporative kind.

Buy a portable humidifier with a wide-mouth tank; they're easier to clean and refill. Daily rinsing (1 tablespoon chlorine bleach per pint of water) prevents bacteria and mold growth. These microbes can be harmful to anyone with respiratory problems or allergies.

Distribute moisture evenly: Place a humidifier as near the center of a room as possible, and direct the nozzle toward open space.

ULTRASONIC HUMIDIFIERS

The white dust from a humidifier can cause electronic equipment to malfunction. Place the humidifier as far as possible from your TV, home computer, and VCR. Or fill the tank with distilled water, available at supermarkets.

Notice a decrease in your humidifier's mist output? The nebulizer (a vibrating mist-creating disc) may be clogged with mineral deposits. Clean it with a small paint brush dipped in white vinegar or in a commercial solvent recommended by the manufacturer.

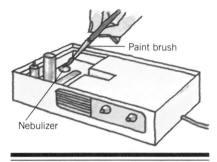

Paint brush

Nebulizer

EVAPORATIVE HUMIDIFIERS

Mineral buildup on an evaporative humidifier's belt, rollers, or padded drum reduces the machine's output. After first unplugging the humidifier, remove and clean these parts with a solution of half white vinegar, half water. Replace parts if they become difficult to clean.

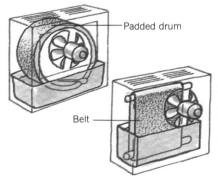

Padded drum

Belt

If after a good cleaning, your humidifier still doesn't work, check the drive belt. It should deflect ½ to ¾ inch under thumb pressure. If it doesn't, adjust it according to instructions in the owner's manual. If the belt is worn or broken, replace it.

DEHUMIDIFIERS

When purchasing a dehumidifier, check that it has automatic defrosting (to avoid frost buildup on evaporator coils), an automatic shut-off switch (to prevent water overflow), and a humidistat control (so that it runs only when the surrounding air is humid).

Your dehumidifier can do an optimum job only if you keep doors and windows closed in the area being dehumidified.

Dirt buildup can cause a dehumidifier's refrigeration system to work inefficiently. Unplug your unit each season (or oftener) and let moisture on evaporator coils dry. Then remove the dehumidifier's back cover (or the entire housing if necessary) and, with a vacuum cleaner's crevice attachment, vacuum all accessible surfaces.

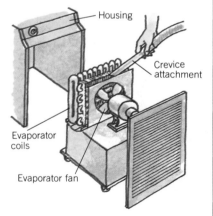

Housing

Crevice attachment

Evaporator coils

Evaporator fan

Tired of emptying your dehumidifier's condensate pan every day? If so, remove the condensate pan and place the dehumidifier right over the basement floor drain. Or run a hose from the dehumidifier's hose connection to the floor drain or into a sink (after placing the unit higher than the sink).

TRASH COMPACTORS

Avoid problems with your trash compactor: place glass bottles on their sides and don't put aerosol cans in it at all.

Even an in-compactor deodorizer can't combat the stench of tuna and sardine cans and of melon rinds. Rinse the cans well before putting them in the compactor. In addition, line the compactor's bottom with newspaper. As waste compacts, the newspaper will absorb smelly liquids (and protect the bottom from shattered glass and jagged can tops).

Trash compactor won't run? Maybe you can fix it without going to too much trouble. Open the drawer and shove it shut forcefully so that it latches; the latch should engage the switch that operates the motor. If your compactor still won't work, check it with a carpenter's level—a tilt may be preventing the drawer from latching. If neither of these helps, phone for professional assistance.

To prevent compactor odor, clean the ram weekly. Unplug the unit, and then open the drawer and lift it off its tracks. Using a scrub brush, wash the bottom of the ram with detergent and hot water. Finish the job with a disinfectant spray if you wish.

GARBAGE DISPOSERS

Thinking of buying a garbage disposer? Before you do, find out whether your municipality allows them and if the model you want can handle heavy food waste (corncobs, bones). If you have a septic tank, consider that it will need more frequent pumping out.

When a garbage disposer jams, switch off the unit, insert a dowel or the handle of a wooden spoon, and, pushing it against a flyweight, rotate the flywheel counterclockwise. If a small L- or Z-shaped wrench came with the unit, use it to clear a jam, following the owner's manual.

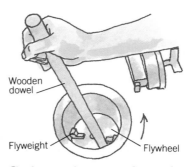

Garbage disposer clogged with greasy food? Try throwing ice cubes into the unit and running it. The ice should congeal the fat, allowing the unit to grind the fat into disposable bits.

ELECTRIC LIGHTS, PLUGS, AND CORDS

Light bulb broken off at the socket? Unplug the lamp or turn off the circuit that the light fixture is on (p. 163). Then, wearing a heavy glove, take a wad of newspaper and press down and twist counterclockwise on the top of the socket.

To replace a three-prong plug on a heavy-duty cord, trim the end and insert it in the plug; then strip off the outer and inner insulation and twist the wire strands (Steps 1, 2, and 4, facing page). Then just stick the wire ends under metal tabs or into holes and tighten the screws. Tighten the clamp screws to keep the cord from pulling out.

On flat, lightweight lamp cord, use a self-connecting, or quick wire, plug, which can be put on quickly without stripping wires. When you clamp the plug onto a cord, small points on the prongs penetrate the insulation and make contact with the wires.

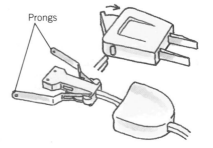

Prongs

Green screw

Prong assembly

Clamp

TESTING AND REPLACING AN APPLIANCE POWER CORD

You can often tell that a power cord is defective by just examining it for frayed insulation, a bare wire, or a damaged plug. To test a cord, buy a continuity tester, an inexpensive, battery-operated tool. If a cord passes the tests in Step 2, the appliance itself has a defect.

When replacing a cord, get an exact match from the manufactur-

er or from an appliance parts store; install it in the reverse order from which you took it off. If you must make a new cord, take the old cord to the store with you and get a cord, a plug, and connectors that match. Make sure that the cord has the same current capacity and insulation. You may also need a stripping and crimping tool.

Strain-relief fitting

Probe

Light

Connectors

Continuity tester

Clip

½"

Connectors

Crimping tool

1. To remove a cord, unplug the appliance and open it as the owner's manual directs. Then release the strain-relief fitting that secures the cord to the appliance. Use pliers to squeeze a typical fitting, rotate it a quarter turn, and pull it out. Then unscrew or unclip the cord from the appliance.

2. To test the cord, attach a continuity tester's clip to one plug prong; then touch the tester's probe to the other prong. If the tester lights, the cord has a short. Next attach the clip to one of the cord's connectors (or wires) and touch the probe to the corresponding prong. Then test the other wire. In either case, if the tester doesn't light, there's a break in the wire.

3. To make a new cord, put a round-cord or three-prong plug on one end (see above). If the old cord's bare wires were attached to terminal screws, strip and attach the new cord the same way. If wires had connectors, strip ½ inch of insulation from the wires and twist the wire strands; then attach new connectors by slipping their sleeves over the wires and squeezing them with a crimping tool.

REPLACING A PLUG ON A POWER CORD

Always replace a plug with one compatible with the cord. The steps below show how to replace the plug on a round cord, used for small appliances and medium-weight extension cords. The plug shown is a "dead-front" plug, which puts a solid barrier between you and the bare wires inside. Even when the plug you're replacing has a cardboard insulator, use this safer type of plug.

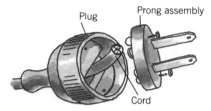

Plug   Prong assembly

Cord

1. Cut off the old plug and any damaged wire with heavy-duty scissors or wire-cutting pliers. Then unscrew and remove the prong assembly on the new plug and slip the cord through the plug.

2. Remove 1½ inches of outer covering from the cord. Use a utility knife or a sharp pocket knife to cut around the covering; then pull it off. Slit the covering lengthwise if it won't pull off easily. Be careful not to cut the wires inside. If you do, cut off the damaged section and try again.

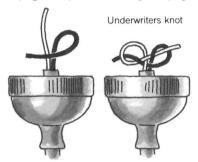

Underwriters knot

3. Tie the two wires in an Underwriters knot: Loop one wire clockwise; then loop the other wire over the first wire and pass the end through the loop in the first wire. Pull the knot tight. This keeps the cord from slipping from the terminal screws.

4. Remove ½ inch of insulation from the end of each wire. Use a wire stripping tool or cut around the insulation with a knife and pull it off. Take care not to cut off any of the wire strands. Then twist the wire strands together in a clockwise direction.

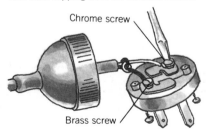

Chrome screw

Brass screw

5. Loosen the terminal screws on the prong assembly. Loop the white cord clockwise around the chrome screw. Make sure that the bare wire fits all the way around and that the insulation comes up to the screw but doesn't go under it. Then tighten the screw. Attach the other wire to the brass screw. If both screws are brass, attach the white cord to the screw for the wider prong.

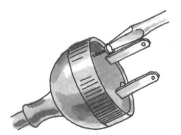

6. Pull the cord so that the knot is firmly seated in the plug. Then push the prong assembly onto the plug and screw it in place. To replace plugs on other kinds of cords, see the hints at the top of the facing page.

LIGHT SWITCHES

Do you have to grope in the dark to find a light switch? Replace the switch with an illuminated one. It has a tiny light inside the switch lever; you locate it by its glow.

If you have to feel your way out in the dark after turning off the light, put in a time-delay switch. It keeps the light on for about 45 seconds after you turn off the switch.

Do you always have your hands full when coming into or leaving the kitchen, nursery, or laundry room and can't reach the light switch? Install a switch with a large rocker lever that you can operate with your elbow.

FUSES AND CIRCUIT BREAKERS

Does an air conditioner or another appliance regularly blow a fuse when it turns on? Substitute a time-delay fuse. It withstands the temporary power surge that occurs when an appliance starts, but it'll blow if there's a short circuit or if the overload lasts longer than a few seconds.

Always replace a fuse with one of the same amperage. If you use one with a larger capacity, the circuit could become overloaded and cause a fire.

To prevent someone from installing fuses with too much capacity for the circuits, replace the fuses with Type S fuses, which fit into adapters that will accept only fuses of the correct amperage. To install them, turn off the fuse box's main disconnect, take out the old fuses, screw in the adapters; then screw in Type S fuses.

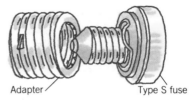

Adapter   Type S fuse

You'll never have to change a fuse again if you put screw-in circuit breakers in your fuse box. When one trips, a button pops up. After correcting the cause of the trip, you push it in to restart the power. Before installing screw-in breakers, however, make sure your local electrical code permits them.

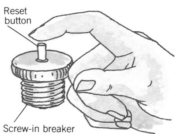

Reset button

Screw-in breaker

A close look at a fuse may reveal why it has blown. A clear fuse window with a broken metal strip inside is usually from an overload. A clouded or smudged window usually indicates a short circuit.

Overloaded fuse   Shorted fuse

SHUTTING OFF ELECTRIC POWER

Your home's main electrical service panel is usually located in the basement, the garage, or a utility room near the point where the power line enters. Four common types are shown below. When you turn off a circuit, always test to make sure that it's really off. Plug a lamp that you know works into an outlet on that circuit and make sure the light won't turn on. Flip a switch on and off to check that a light fixture it controls is really off. **Caution:** It's dangerous to touch your home's main electrical service panel when water is present. If the floor is damp, stand on a dry board. If the wiring may be wet, have the power company or an electrician turn off the electricity. In an emergency, use a dry wood pole to turn off the main switches.

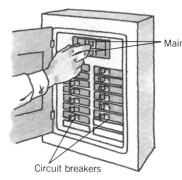

Main switches

Circuit breakers

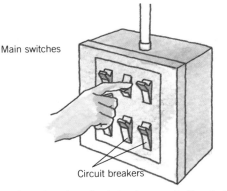

Circuit breakers

On a circuit breaker panel with one or two main switches, flip those switches to shut off all the power. To shut off power to a circuit, flip the circuit breaker that controls the circuit. When turning on a circuit breaker switch that has tripped, press it toward the *Off* side to reset it before flipping it on.

On other circuit breaker panels flip all of the switches to *Off* to shut off all the power. To shut off power to an individual circuit, flip the circuit breaker that controls that circuit. When you turn on a circuit breaker switch that has tripped, first press it toward the *Off* side to reset it; then flip it on.

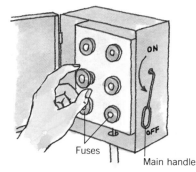

Fuses

Main handle

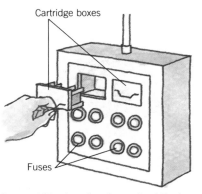

Cartridge boxes

Fuses

On a fuse box shift the handle to the *Off* position to shut off all the power. To shut off the power to a circuit, just unscrew the fuse controlling that circuit. Whenever you take out or put in a fuse, first turn off all the power with the handle.

On a cartridge-type fuse box pull out the boxes holding the cartridge fuses to shut off all power. To shut off power to a circuit, unscrew the fuse controlling that circuit. Whenever you take out or put in a fuse, pull out the cartridge boxes first.

CHAPTER THREE

OUTDOORS

Keep the exterior of your house shipshape, from rooftop to foundation. Learn how to paint like a pro. Organize your workshop so that it works for you. Tools and techniques for building and fixing. Automobile tips for emergency repairs and routine maintenance. Enhance your home with a lovely landscape. Find out how to make trees, flowers, lawn, and vegetables flourish.

The Exterior of the House
Page 165

Checking trouble spots; cleaning and repairing stucco and siding; a maintenance checklist for all seasons; spotting signs of termite activity; how to preserve porches and decks; clearing gutters; buying ladders wisely and using them safely; repairing a roof and knowing when to replace one; replacing screening in metal and wood frames; fixing storm doors; selecting the right caulk for the job and applying it properly; how to install weather stripping on doors and windows; questions and answers about home insulation; painting the house to give it a fresh face; choosing between latex and alkyd paint; creative color combinations; preparing surfaces; when, where, and how to apply paint; putting the final touches on trim.

Workshop
Page 183

Planning a workshop; a basic household tool kit; storing tools and supplies; using tools safely and effectively; preventing rust on tools; marking and measuring made easy; checking for surface irregularities; sawing a board; driving and removing nails; drilling holes in wood and metal; driving screws; how to tighten loose screws; choosing the right glue for the job; improvising clamps.

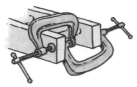

Garage & Car Maintenance
Page 193

Washing and waxing; when to service your car; rust prevention and removal; replacing an oil filter; fuel-saving tips; coping with road emergencies; replacing spark plugs; changing a tire; overheating and stalling; driving in snow, rain, or fog; frozen locks; snow tires.

Yard & Garden
Page 203

Designing a landscape for your home; getting rid of poison ivy and poison oak; planning for seasonal variety; stretching the visual boundaries of your property; protecting valuable trees while landscaping; testing your soil's pH; deciding which trees and plants are ideal for your yard; the correct way to plant young trees; providing shrubs and trees with the right amount of water and the best fertilizer; tips on pruning trees; protecting plants and shrubs from wildlife; retraining overgrown hedges; liming the lawn; lawn damage by wildlife; reseeding lawns; enriching garden soil; double-digging; how to make a compost heap; flower beds; planting bulbs; building raised beds; transplanting seedlings; roses—buying, planting, and maintaining them; increasing perennials; fruits and vegetables; choosing mulches; pest control in the garden; care and storage of garden tools and outdoor furniture.

The Exterior of the House

MAINTAINING SIDING

Before rushing to brighten dingy siding with paint, try washing it. Washing is the first step to a lasting paint job anyway.

A yearly washing helps preserve siding and its finish. For painted wood siding and aluminum siding, use a solution of 1 cup detergent and 1 quart chlorine bleach in 3 gallons of water. Use an extra-strength detergent sold by paint and hardware stores. Wear rubber gloves, safety goggles, and protective garments. Rinse the siding thoroughly.

To spruce up vinyl siding, hose it down; then sponge it with a mild liquid detergent. Rinse with spray from a hose.

Surprisingly, it's best to wash siding from bottom to top. The siding soaks up less detergent and, as a result, is less likely to streak.

WHAT TO CHECK FOR ON YOUR HOME'S EXTERIOR

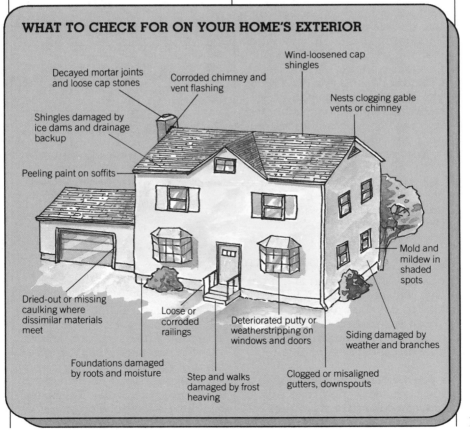

Wind-loosened cap shingles

Decayed mortar joints and loose cap stones

Corroded chimney and vent flashing

Nests clogging gable vents or chimney

Shingles damaged by ice dams and drainage backup

Peeling paint on soffits

Mold and mildew in shaded spots

Dried-out or missing caulking where dissimilar materials meet

Loose or corroded railings

Deteriorated putty or weatherstripping on windows and doors

Siding damaged by weather and branches

Foundations damaged by roots and moisture

Step and walks damaged by frost heaving

Clogged or misaligned gutters, downspouts

A great tool for washing siding is a long car-wash brush on a hose.

STAINS ON SIDING

Bleach away green copper stains with a solution of ¾ pound oxalic acid crystals in 1 gallon hot water. Sponge on and wait 5 minutes, then rub with a cloth. Repeat until the stain lightens.

Caution: Be sure to wear rubber gloves, safety goggles, and protective clothing when mixing and using solutions of oxalic acid, muriatic acid, chlorine bleach, or other stain-removing compounds.

Lighten rust stains with a solution of 1 part sodium citrate crystals to 6 parts water. Dip a cloth in it; then stick the wet cloth on the siding, covering the stain for 15 minutes.

If you're going to paint, sand rusty nailheads and surrounding stains with a medium-grit sandpaper to take off as much rust as possible. Cover a recessed nailhead with caulk (p.175). Then prime the area with a rust-inhibiting paint.

If you're not sure whether a stain is soil or mildew, dab at it with a bleach-soaked rag. If particles begin to fall off, it's mildew.

EXTERIOR MAINTENANCE CALENDAR

In most parts of the country, spring and fall are the seasons for making the majority of exterior repairs. In the spring, fix damage caused by cold weather and moisture and prepare for the coming hot season. In the fall, get the exterior in shape for winter's return.

Spring
Roofing: Repair damaged shingles and flashing

Gutters, downspouts, and drains: Clear debris and flush with water. Straighten and correct the pitch of misaligned gutters. Reset downspouts and tighten fasteners

Siding and trim: Renail loose pieces. Caulk. Touch up damaged paint. Wash all exterior surfaces

Masonry: Repair cracks and seams. Clean crumbling mortar from joints; remortar

Windows: Remove storm sashes; repair and clean before storing. Clean and unstick sashes; repair damaged putty (p.86, Steps 3–5). Install screens in windows used for ventilation and put up shading devices on south-facing windows

Ironwork: Remove rust and paint as necessary

Pests: Check foundations for termite tunnels. Check vent louvers, chimneys, and other protected nooks and crannies for bird and insect nests

Chimneys: Clean and inspect flues when seasonal use ends

Summer
Driveways: Repair holes and cracks in asphalt; protect the blacktop by applying asphalt sealant

Gutters, downspouts, and drains: Clear debris at midseason

Fall
Gutters, downspouts, and drains: Clear debris and flush with water

Outdoor water supply: In frost-prone areas, shut off supply, drain the lines, and leave valves open

Siding, trim, and foundation: Patch and seal open cracks. Seal openings where animals may take refuge. Close vents of unheated crawl spaces

Windows and doors: Put storm sashes in place. Clean and repair screens; spray with protective coating. Inspect and fortify weatherstripping. Clear debris from basement window wells

Winter
Chimneys: Clean and inspect flues in midseason if you use a wood stove or fireplace frequently

Gutters, downspouts, and drains: Keep clear of ice

If a white crusty powder, known as efflorescence, builds up on a brick or concrete surface, scrub it off with a solution of 1 part muriatic acid to 10 parts water. For heavy buildups, use a solution of up to 1 to 2 parts. Rinse thoroughly.

REPAIRING SIDING

If a siding board is warped, try inserting 2-inch wood screws to pull it in flat against the sheathing under it. Drill pilot and countersink holes (p.191) and cover the recessed screwheads with wood putty or caulking compound.

To fix siding that's split along the grain, pry open the crack and coat both edges with waterproof resorcinol glue (p.192). Then push the pieces together and nail along the siding's lower edge.

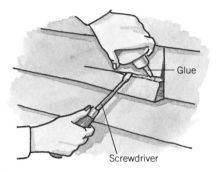

Glue

Screwdriver

When repairing siding, use hot-dipped galvanized or aluminum nails to prevent rust stains.

In stucco, fill a small crack with a latex caulk, then coat the caulk with latex paint. Chisel out all loose stucco in a larger crack and fill it with vinyl-concrete patching cement. This material adheres better than regular sand-concrete mix and doesn't have to be kept wet for days afterward.

To fix a dent in aluminum siding, drill a small hole in the dent's center. Thread in a sheet-metal screw a few turns and pull out the dent. Then remove the screw and fill the hole with plastic-aluminum filler compound. After it hardens, sand and paint the spot.

FOR FIRM FOUNDATIONS

To determine if a crack in masonry is active and indicates a structural problem, bridge over the crack's surface with a layer of plaster of Paris. Wait several months. If the plaster cracks, consult a pro.

To get from the soil to your home, termites build mud tubes. Check for them regularly on foundation walls. Look especially at the spots where pipes and conduits enter.

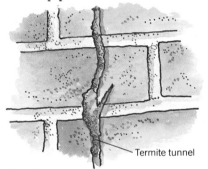

Termite tunnel

Another sign of termite activity is accumulations of translucent ½-inch wings near your foundation walls. If you spot these in early spring, call an exterminator.

If you're not sure whether winged insects are termites or ants, keep in mind that termites have thick midbodies and four wings of the same size. Ants have pinched waists and pairs of smaller and larger wings.

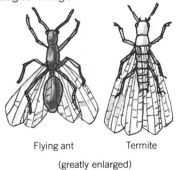

Flying ant   Termite

(greatly enlarged)

167

In some areas, carpenter ants are as much a threat to your home as termites. Get professional help if you find unexplained sawdust on the ground, wall, or floor, or spot ½-inch-long black ants, especially near wood exposed to wetness.

PORCHES AND DECKS

Most porch problems are caused by moisture from the ground below. To control moisture, cover the ground with overlapped strips of polyethylene sheeting or roofing felt. Then top this vapor barrier with 2 inches of sand.

If paint on your porch or deck is always peeling, moisture is probably entering the boards from below and causing the paint to lift off. Either install a vapor barrier or paint the underside with the same deck enamel you use on top.

If your porch is small and light, you may be able to raise a sagging joist with a support post. Establish a solid footing for the post. Then cut a 4 x 4 to fit between the footing and a joist's lower edge, adding the amount you want to raise the floor. Then force the post under the joist.

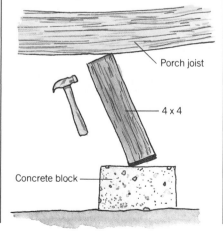

Porch joist

4 x 4

Concrete block

To reinforce a sagging, weak joist, first straighten it with a 4 x 4 post or a jack. Then nail to it a new joist of the same length and lumber size.

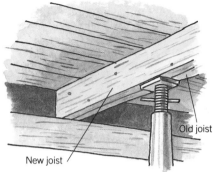

Old joist

New joist

If wooden stair treads are badly worn, carefully take them off and reattach them with their bottom sides facing upward.

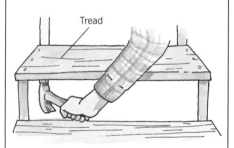

Tread

To remove a stair tread, strike the underside with a hammer. Then strike the top of the tread to drive it back down. This should pop the nailheads, making it easy to grab them with a hammer claw.

GUTTERS AND DOWNSPOUTS

A depression in the ground just under a gutter is a sure sign that the gutter isn't working properly. Clean the downspouts and check the gutter's pitch.

Icicles forming along an eave are another sign of a malfunctioning gutter that needs attention.

To check a gutter, run water from a garden hose into it. If pools of water form, look for and fix damaged hangers or brackets that allow the gutter to sag. Sight along the gutter to make sure it maintains an even downward slope.

Stablizer

Leaning a ladder on an aluminum gutter is unsafe and can damage the gutter. Instead, use a tall stepladder or add a stablizer to your extension ladder to hold it out from the wall.

When adjusting the pitch of a strap-supported gutter, you can raise areas just by twisting the straps with pliers.

If you can't unplug a downspout with water pressure from a hose, try reaming it out with a plumber's snake and flushing again.

SELECTING LADDERS

A typical house needs two ladders—a stepladder and an extension ladder. A fold-up stepladder is essential indoors and useful outdoors as well. For most homes, a 5- or 6-foot stepladder is fine. But make sure you can reach your ceiling while standing two steps down from the ladder's top.

If your house is low, you may be able to do all exterior jobs with a regular straight ladder. But most houses need an extension ladder, which has two sliding sections. Check an extension ladder's label for its "maximum working length"—its length when fully extended. This is less than its nominal length because, for safety, the two sections must overlap by 3 feet or more. Thus a 20-foot extension ladder has a 17-foot usable length. A ladder's maximum working length should be 3 to 4 feet greater than the highest level at which you'll be working.

You can get wood or aluminum ladders. An aluminum ladder is lighter in weight and less prone to decay. But a metal ladder isn't safe to use when making electrical repairs, and when on it, you should use only power tools that are double insulated and grounded. Outdoors, you must always look up to avoid touching power lines. Touching one causes a lethal shock. The same precautions apply to a wet wooden ladder.

In any ladder, look for overall sturdy construction. Check a wooden ladder for cracks, knots, and other imperfections; check an aluminum one for bends, dents, and rough edges. On a stepladder, look for grooved treads, nonslip safety shoes, and angled metal braces on the lowest tread. On a wooden one, also look for metal rods reinforcing every tread. To test a stepladder's sturdiness, open it, stand on the lowest tread, and shake it from side to side.

An extension ladder should have pivoting safety shoes, a bottom rung with braces or a reinforcing rod, and a mechanism that locks the sections together securely. A pulley and rope for extending the ladder is a great convenience. Always buy a ladder rated Type I (heavy duty) or Type II (medium duty); they're sturdier and safer than Type III (light duty).

For tips on how to use your ladders safely, see p.171.

To prevent basement dampness and damage to your foundation walls, make sure the runoff from your gutters flows away from the house. If necesssary, install splash blocks under the downspouts.

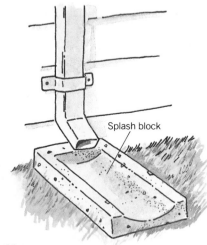

Splash block

Using wire-mesh screens to keep leaves out of gutters may seem a great idea. But they can be difficult to remove when you clear away other debris. A more practical solution is to put a leaf strainer in the top of each downspout.

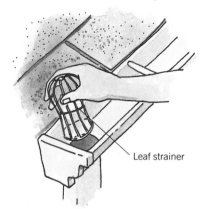

Leaf strainer

For a gutter patch that will last, get a fiberglass patching kit and apply it following directions. Make sure the area is clean and dry so that the resin will bond well.

Is a gutter leaking at the joint where two sections meet? Apply silicone sealant to the joint's inside seams. Smooth the sealer's edges so that it won't collect debris.

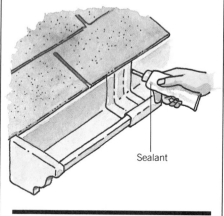

Sealant

DO YOU NEED A NEW ROOF?

Even if a roof leaks, it may not need to be replaced. If the roofing is less than 15 years old, just find the leak and patch it.

Check the condition of asphalt shingles on a warm day. Gently bend a few shingles back. If they aren't flexible or if they crumble easily, consider reroofing.

If the black mat of your asphalt shingles shows through the colored surface granules, chances are good that it's time to reroof.

If your roof's ridge isn't horizontal or if the plane of each roof section isn't flat, you've got a structural problem that needs professional evaluation—and repair.

Before reroofing with asphalt shingles, gently lift a shingle that's a couple of rows in from the edge and see if there's another layer of shingles below. If there is, you'll need to rip off all the old shingles and start from scratch.

USING A LADDER SAFELY

Inspect a ladder before climbing it; look for cracks, bends, and wobbling. Tighten the nuts on the reinforcing rods if a ladder feels shaky. Make sure an extension ladder's safety feet pivot freely. On uneven ground, put a firm, flat block under a ladder's lower foot. On soft ground, place a wide board under both of a ladder's feet.

To set up a long straight ladder, brace its feet against the wall and walk it upright, grabbing the rungs hand over hand.

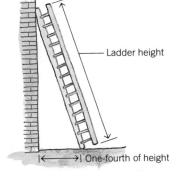

Ladder height

|←——→| One-fourth of height

Position a straight ladder so that the distance between the wall and the base of the ladder equals one-fourth of the ladder's height.

When climbing up and down, always face the ladder and use both hands. Carry tools on a belt or haul them up with a line after you're set.

When climbing onto a roof, make sure that the ladder extends 3 feet or more above the roof edge. Don't climb onto a roof from a gable end.

When working on a ladder, keep your hips within the span of the ladder's side rails. Don't lean to the side or reach out too far.

Open a stepladder fully and lock its braces. Climb no higher than the second step from the top. Standing on the top invites an accident.

FINDING ROOF LEAKS

When a roof leaks, the culprit may not be the roofing material. First, check the flashing in roof valleys and around chimneys, dormers, vent pipes, and other objects that project through the roof.

Flashing

Don't risk life and limb to inspect your roof's flashings and shingles. Get a close view with binoculars.

Leaks are rarely located directly above the water spot on the ceiling. While it's still raining, check under the roof deck for a drip trail starting at a higher point.

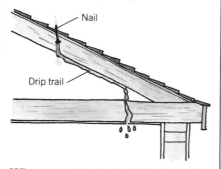

Nail

Drip trail

When you find a leak in the attic, push a nail or wire through it to help you locate it outside.

To spot roof leak sites, go to the attic on a bright day and turn off any lights. After your eyes adjust, examine the roof's undersides for telltale pinpoints of light.

On a wood shingle roof, light showing through the underside doesn't necessarily signify a leak. Wood shingles have cracks between them when they're dry, but the wood expands and seals the cracks as it absorbs moisture.

ROOF REPAIRS

You can patch any hole in roofing or flashing up to the size of a nickel by simply covering it with a layer of roof cement.

To patch an asphalt shingle, cut a rectangle of sheet copper or aluminum, coat one side with roof cement, and slip it, cement side down, under the shingle. Then put roof cement on top of the patch and press the shingle to it.

Metal patch

If a wooden roofing shingle is split but is otherwise in good shape, coat the edges of the split with roof cement, butt them tightly together, and secure them with galvanized or aluminum roofing nails. Cover the nailheads with roof cement.

Roof cement is one of the stickiest and messiest materials invented by man. When making extensive repairs with it, wear clothing and shoes that you won't mind throwing away afterward.

To clean roof cement from your skin, clothing, and tools, wipe them with a rag moistened with paint thinner. Don't use kerosene.

SCREENS AND STORM DOORS

When taking down screens or storm windows, write a number in a hidden spot on each window frame and on its screen or storm window. Put each window's hardware in a bag marked with the number. For a neat job on wooden storm windows, use small metal numbers that hammer in place.

Metal screens can last almost indefinitely. Just apply a light coat of thinned spar varnish each year. Be sure to clean the screens first (p.87); let them dry thoroughly.

To fix a hole in a screen, patch it with a square of screening. Unravel a few wires along each edge of the patch and bend the remaining wire ends at right angles. Then shove the ends through the screen and turn them down on the other side.

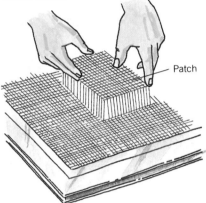

Patch

Keep the drain holes in the bottom of your storm windows clear to prevent condensation from rotting your sills. If your storm windows don't have these holes, drill them. Three 1/8-inch holes will do.

REPLACING A METAL-FRAME SCREEN

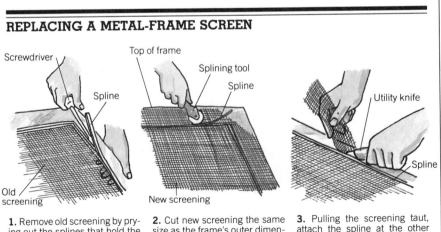

Screwdriver

Spline

Old screening

Top of frame

Splining tool

Spline

New screening

Utility knife

Spline

1. Remove old screening by prying out the splines that hold the screening in place. Start at a corner and use a screwdriver to lift each spline out of its groove. If the spline is still flexible, you can use it again. Replace metal splines or old, hardened plastic splines with new plastic splines.

2. Cut new screening the same size as the frame's outer dimensions. Trim the corners at a 45-degree angle. Then attach the screening at one end. Start at a corner and use a splining tool to force the spline in with short, firm strokes. Or put a wood block over the spline and hammer it in.

3. Pulling the screening taut, attach the spline at the other end; then attach the spline along each side. Finish by trimming off the excess screening along the edges with a utility knife.

When a screen door or storm door begins to sag, use wire cables and a turnbuckle to give it a lift. Run the support diagonally from the top corner on the hinge side to the lower outside corner, making the wires as taut as you can by hand. Then tighten the turnbuckle.

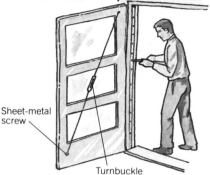

Storm-door frame

Sheet-metal screw

Turnbuckle

If your aluminum storm door won't close because it's hitting its frame, try to realign the metal frame by tightening the screws that hold it to the jamb on the hinge side.

If your storm door won't close and it's not hitting the frame, try adjusting the air-intake screw and the hold-open washer on the door's tubular pneumatic closer device. If necessary, replace it.

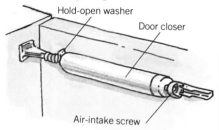

Hold-open washer

Door closer

Air-intake screw

Fix wooden screen frames when you put in new screens. After removing the old screening, reglue any corner and center joints that are loose and reinforce them with metal mending plates or long wood screws inserted from the side. Then repaint the frames.

When fixing screens, don't forget to check for loose mounting brackets on the window frame.

REPLACING A WOOD-FRAME SCREEN

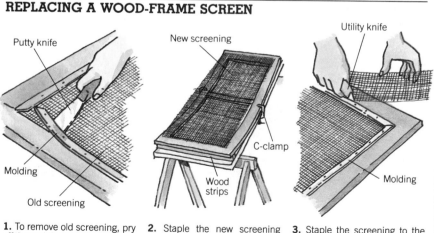

Putty knife

New screening

Utility knife

Molding

Old screening

Wood strips

C-clamp

Molding

1. To remove old screening, pry off the moldings. Then use pliers to pull out tacks or staples holding the screening. You can reuse intact molding, but if it breaks, replace it. Using strong scissors, cut new screening 2 inches larger all around than the opening.

2. Staple the new screening along the top. Then bow the frame by putting a wood strip under each end and clamping it to a work surface at the center. Pulling the screening taut, fasten it along the bottom. Remove the clamps from the frame.

3. Staple the screening to the center rail and then along each side, starting from the center and working toward the ends. Then renail the molding. With a utility knife, trim off the excess screening that's left outside the molding's edge.

Condensation on windows? If it's inside the inner windows, caulk storm windows outside and inner windows inside. Also weatherstrip cracks between sashes. If that fails, cover inside windows with plastic or interior storm windows; ventilate bathrooms and kitchens. If moisture is between storm and inner windows, weatherstrip and caulk inner windows.

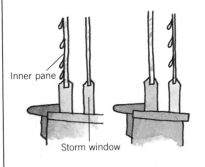

Inner pane

Storm window

SELECTING CAULK

Confused by all the caulks that are available? Silicones adhere best and last longest. Butyls bond well to metals. Latex caulks are fine for narrow cracks. Inexpensive oil-base caulks are short-lived.

Paint won't adhere to pure silicone caulk. Choose clear or a color that goes with the color of your house. If you insist on a paintable caulk and want durability, use siliconized acrylic caulk.

USING CAULK

Where should you caulk? Wherever two dissimilar building materials abut, most notably where siding meets foundation, decks, steps, pipes, chimneys, and corner, window, and door trim.

Loading a caulking gun is simple. Just pull the plunger all the way back and slip in the tube of caulk-ing. Push in the plunger and twist it to engage the ratchet. Then cut the tube's tip at a 45-degree angle and push a long nail down the spout to puncture the inner seal.

To apply caulking, squeeze the trigger slowly and draw the tip along the seam you want to fill. Work at a slow, even pace, filling the joint completely.

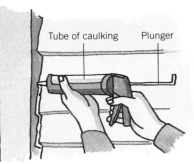

Tube of caulking   Plunger

Want to be sure a joint is filled with caulk? Push the tube along the seam instead of pulling it.

Does your caulking gun's tip leak when you pause between seams? Each time you pause, turn the gun's plunger to disengage the ratchet and relieve the pressure.

Weather affects how caulk goes on. Caulk on a mild, dry day when it's over 50° F. On a hot day, refrigerate caulk for an hour or two to keep it from running.

Keep unfinished tubes of caulk fresh. Plug the hole in the tip with a 10d common nail.

WEATHERSTRIPPING

Even in air-conditioning season, your windows should be weatherstripped and storm-sashed. Sealing windows can cut heat gain almost as much as it reduces heat loss in winter.

175

When you apply weatherstripping, lay a bead of caulking first. It acts as an adhesive and stops drafts from surface irregularities.

Tired of self-adhesive weatherstripping always peeling off? The next time you put some up, use tacks or staples for reinforcement.

It takes no time to weatherproof a door. Just tack metal-backed door weatherstrips along the stops on the jamb. Then screw a door bottom strip with a sweep onto the door. Cut both with a hacksaw. Make sure they fit snugly.

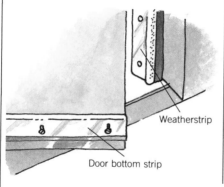

Weatherstrip

Door bottom strip

KEEPING YOUR HOME SNUGLY INSULATED

Reviewing your insulation needs? Don't overlook a wall or floor that separates your living space from an unheated garage, basement, or crawl space. Insulation at such a juncture is almost as vital as it is on ceilings and exterior walls.

Don't let condensation make your insulation wet and useless. Install it with a vapor barrier facing inward, toward the heated space.

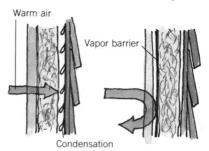

Warm air

Vapor barrier

Condensation

If you're having insulation blown into walls as a retrofit installation, coat the interior walls with a special moistureproofing paint to create a vapor barrier.

WEATHERSTRIPPING WINDOWS

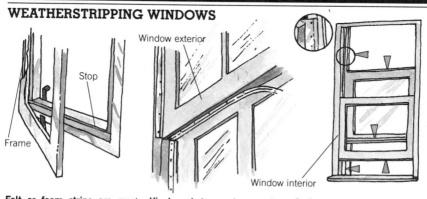

Window exterior

Stop

Frame

Window interior

Felt or foam strips are most useful on casement windows. Nail or glue them to the frame on the hinge side. Fasten them to the stop molding on the other three sides.

Vinyl gaskets are inexpensive and easy to install. Mount them on the window's exterior so that they aren't visible inside. Staple or tack vertical pieces to the stops and horizontal pieces to the window sashes as shown.

Spring-metal strips seal tightest, last longest, and show least. With the nail edge inward, install vertical strips in window channels, sliding them under the sashes' sides. Install horizontal strips on the sashes as shown.

YOUR HOME'S INSULATION NEEDS

Question: How much insulation should my house have?

Answer: The map below is a good guide. The three numbers for your climate zone are the government-recommended R-values for your house. R-values indicate the resistance to heat loss your insulation should have in ceilings, walls, and floors, respectively. For example, in the northernmost region, a ceiling should have insulation rated at R-38, exterior walls at R-19, and floors at R-22.

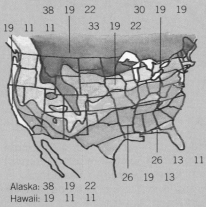

| 38 | 19 | 22 | | 30 | 19 | 19 |
| 19 | 11 | 11 | 33 | 19 | 22 | |

26 13 11
26 19 13

Alaska: 38 19 22
Hawaii: 19 11 11

Question: Why are the recommended R-values for the South so high?

Answer: The R-values also take into account the insulation needed in areas where air-conditioning loads are high.

Question: How do I determine the thickness of insulation my house needs?

Answer: An insulation's average R-value per inch is usually indicated on the package label. To determine the thickness you need, divide the insulation's R-value per inch into the R-value you want. For example, if an insulation has a value of R-3 per inch and you want R-30, you'll need 10 inches of that insulation.

Question: How do I find out how much insulation my house already has?

Answer: In an unfinished attic, simply measure the thickness of the insulation. In a floored attic, you may have to pull up a floor board. In a finished one, drill a hole in the attic's ceiling.

Question: How do I measure insulation inside the walls?

Answer: Turn off the power going to an electrical outlet or switch (p.163); then remove its cover plate and measure the insulation next to it. Cut away some of the plaster or wallboard if necessary.

Question: What about measuring my house's floor insulation?

Answer: Above an open crawl space or an unheated basement, look for blankets or batts between floor joists. In an enclosed crawl space, the insulation is usually inside the foundation walls, running from the sill to the ground. Aboveground walls in a heated basement should also have insulation.

Question: How do I convert my measurements of insulation into R-values?

Answer: Rock wool, which looks like large pieces of lint, has an average value of R-3.3 per inch in batts or blankets and R-3 as loose fill. Fiberglass, which looks like cotton candy, has the same average R-values. With other materials, consult a local building supplier or your state's energy office. Take a sample of your insulation if possible.

Question: If I insulate to twice my area's recommended R-values, will I save a lot more money?

Answer: No. The recommendations are for the most efficient levels based on installation cost and energy savings. Above these, your returns diminish. Also, an insulation's R-value per inch declines as you add more insulation.

If you live in a humid region that requires more air conditioning than heating each year, the main problem is outside moisture condensing. Reverse the standard rule and put the vapor barrier facing toward the exterior wall.

Fiberglass insulation is extremely irritating. When working with it, wear a dust mask, goggles, work gloves, and clothing with tight-fitting openings. Coat exposed skin with petroleum jelly.

For a fast, neat job, cut batts of insulation with hedge trimmers or a serrated kitchen knife.

To insulate a floor over an unheated crawl space, garage, or basement, push the batts or blankets, vapor barrier up, between the floor joists. Support them by stapling chicken wire to the joists.

ATTIC INSULATION

If snow on a roof melts in one spot before others, it's a sign of missing or damaged attic insulation.

An often overlooked source of heat loss is the attic hatch. Make sure yours is well insulated and weatherstripped.

When insulating an attic floor for the first time, lay polyethylene sheeting as a vapor barrier between the joists before installing loose wool or unfaced blankets and batts as insulation.

To add more attic insulation, just put a layer of unfaced batts or blankets on top of the insulation that's there. The second layer shouldn't have an effective vapor barrier. If it has a foil face, slash the foil diagonally every foot.

If your present attic insulation is already level with the joist tops and you want to add more, increase the value of the second layer by installing it at right angles to the joists.

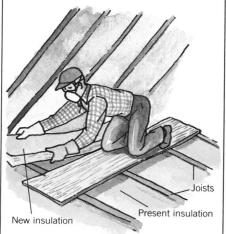

New insulation · Joists · Present insulation

In an unfinished attic, lay boards across the joists to walk and kneel on when installing insulation. A couple of 1 x 6's or some ¾-inch plywood will do.

When you install attic insulation, work from the eaves toward the center. This way you can do any cutting and fitting in the area with the most headroom.

PAINTING: GIVE YOUR HOUSE EXTERIOR A MAKE-OVER

To make a low house look more gracefully proportioned, emphasize its verticals. Paint elements such as doors, shutters, and corner trim in a color that contrasts with the siding.

Accentuate horizontals on a high house. Use a contrasting trim color on parts such as windowsills, flower boxes, foundation walls, and fascia boards and gutters at the roof edge.

COLOR COMBINATIONS TO ENLIVEN YOUR HOME'S EXTERIOR

When selecting exterior paint colors, first consider the color of the roof and coordinate with it. The roof color is the hardest to change. To accent your front door, pick a second compatible trim color.

Roof	Siding	Trim
BLACK OR GRAY	Cream-yellow	Bright red, tile red, bright yellow, dark green, gray-green, white
	Pale green	Tile red, bright yellow, green, dark green, gray-green, white
	Dark green	Pink, cream, bright yellow, light green, white
	Putty	Red-orange, tile red, dark green, gray-green, dark blue, blue-gray, brown
	Dull red	Pink, cream, light green, blue-gray, white
	Gray	Pink, bright yellow, white, all reds, all greens, all blues
	White	Pink, cream, bright yellow, all reds, all greens, all blues
GREEN	Cream-yellow	Bright red, tile red, light green, dark green, gray-green, brown, white
	Pale green	Red-orange, tile red, bright yellow, dark green, white
	Dark green	Pink, red-orange, cream, bright yellow, light green, white
	Beige	Tile red, dark green, gray-green, blue-green, dark blue, blue-gray
	Brown	Pink, cream, bright yellow, light green, white
	Dull red	Cream, light green, gray-green, white
	Gray	Red-orange, cream, bright yellow, light green, white
	White	Pink, cream, bright yellow, brown, all reds, all greens, all blues
RED	Cream-yellow	Bright red, tile red, blue-green, dark blue, blue-gray
	Pale green	Bright red, tile red, white
	Dull red	Cream, light green, gray-green, blue-green, white
	Light gray	Bright red, tile red, dark green, white
	White	Bright red, tile red, dark green, blue-gray
BROWN	Buff	Tile red, dark green, gray-green, blue-green, brown
	Pink-beige	Tile red, dark green, gray-green, brown, white
	Cream-yellow	Tile red, dark green, gray-green, blue-green, brown
	Pale green	Dark green, gray-green, brown
	Brown	Red-orange, cream, bright yellow, white
	White	Red-orange, tile red, bright yellow, dark blue, blue-gray, brown, all greens
BLUE	Cream-yellow	Red-orange, tile red, dark blue, blue-gray
	Blue	Red-orange, cream, bright yellow, light blue, white
	Gray	Red-orange, cream, light blue, dark blue, white
	White	Red-orange, tile red, bright yellow, light blue, dark blue

You can also make a house look lower by painting it a dark color, provided the roof is dark too. A light color, on the other hand, will help your house look larger.

For a coordinated look, paint your garage, toolshed, playhouse, and other outbuildings with the same color combination as your house. Use the trim color on wood fences and lampposts.

If your house is a hodgepodge of conflicting textures—vertical siding, shingles, and brick, for example—effect a peaceful reconciliation. Paint them all the same color or two related shades of the same color. Overall dark tones especially disguise architectural flaws.

Painting metal roof flashing the same color as the roof will make it less noticeable.

SELECTING HOUSE PAINT

Latex is almost everyone's first choice for exterior paint because it is easy to apply, cleans up with water, and dries quickly. On top of that, it's long-lasting.

If you don't know what you're painting over, choose alkyd paint. Alkyd will adhere to most surfaces, including chalking ones; latex is more finicky about what old paints it will bond with.

Is it always damp around your house? Choose a latex paint or stain. Porous latex breathes and lets moisture escape. Moreover, it doesn't contain vegetable oils that encourage mildew by feeding it.

Latex is also great for most masonry and can usually be applied without a primer. It bonds best when the surface is slightly damp.

For cinder blocks, get a solvent-thinned rubber-base paint. The water in latex can penetrate into the blocks, causing embedded iron particles to rust and stain your fresh paint job.

Before choosing a stain color or blend, test the color on an inconspicuous spot on your siding. Display samples can be misleading.

You can revive faded aluminum siding with any standard topcoat. But first you must sand the problem areas, wash the surface well, and coat any bare metal with a zinc-base primer.

For doors, windows, and other places where durability is a concern, pick a glossy paint. It contains more of the resins that give a paint body and hardness.

PREPARING SURFACES FOR PAINT

If your house's exterior is badly soiled, rent power washing equipment. The high-pressure jet of water it emits will blast away flaking paint as well as dirt.

Scraping off loose flaking paint is an important part of preparation. But don't overdo it. There's no need to scrape off any paint that's firmly stuck to the surface.

For heavy scraping, a pull scraper is better than a flat blade scraper. Be sure to have replacement blades for the pull scraper.

Keep a beer can opener handy when you're preparing a surface. It's perfect for scraping old paint, caulk, and putty from hard-to-reach cracks and crannies.

Areas where you've scraped off flakes and blisters will be less noticeable after the final paint job if you smooth the sharp edges of the old paint with sandpaper.

WHEN TO PAINT?

For best results, paint when the temperature is from 50° F to 90° F. With alkyd paint, pick a warm, nonhumid day to cut drying time between coats. (Latex dries in a few hours in any weather.)

Spring and fall are the best seasons for painting. Besides moderate weather, nearby leaf-bearing shrubs are usually bare.

Don't be an early bird when painting! Let the dew evaporate before starting. In the evening, stop before dampness sets in.

To prevent a sunstroke for yourself and a paint problem for your house, avoid working in direct sunlight. Do your house's west side in the morning and its east side in the afternoon. Paint the south side when it's most shaded.

When painting, try to time your breaks to occur where siding and trim meet or at some other visual transition point. This prevents lap marks and disguises subtle color differences that may occur when you start again.

PAINTING TECHNIQUES

With alkyd paint, two thin coats are better than one thick one. But with latex, apply a heavy coat, even when you plan another.

Even if you buy a standard color, ask your paint dealer to shake the cans on his automatic mixing machine. It'll reduce the amount you have to stir.

Working from a full paint can invites spills and dripping. Pour half of the paint into an extra can or bucket and use that for painting. Seal the original can until you need more paint.

Avoid paint-can mess! Punch a series of holes in the rim groove; the paint that collects there will drain back into the can. Tape or glue a drip-catching paper plate to the can's bottom.

Loop of masking tape

PAINTING SIDING

Paint a wall from the top down. Work your way across its entire width, painting areas about 3 feet wide and five boards deep. After finishing an area, skip ahead the same distance and then paint back toward the area that you've just completed. This procedure can be used with most types of sidings. If a siding has grooves or recesses, paint them first. On vertical siding, paint boards from top to bottom.

1. Paint the bottom edge of the board. Work paint into the crevice with the brush tip.

2. Apply three or four short dabs of paint across the main surface of the board.

3. Smooth the paint across with long, even strokes. Finish the other boards the same way.

For easier stirring and better mixing, drill a few ¼-inch holes in your stirring paddle.

You won't have a messy can or brush if you load the brush properly. Dip only the bottom third of the bristles in the paint. Then gently tap the brush on both sides of the can and lift it out without wiping it against the can's edge. This makes cleanup easier too.

Don't try to break up lumps in old paint; you'll just end up brushing the pieces on your job. Instead, strain the paint through window screening into another container.

TACKLING TRIM

When doing the trim, wrap cloth around your ladder tops to avoid marring the newly painted siding. For ladder safety tips, see p.171.

On panel doors, start by outlining each panel edge. Then fill in the panel. Finish by painting the rails and stiles. Start at the top of the door and work downward.

Stile

Rail

Don't forget to do a door's edges. They need to be protected by weather-resistant exterior paint. To reach the bottom edge, you may find it necessary to take the door off its hinges.

To avoid getting trim paint on the siding, keep your brush's bristles pointing toward the edge that you must cut cleanly.

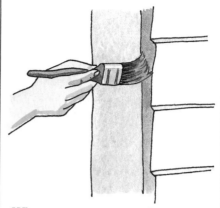

When painting a circular object, such as a drain pipe, you'll get better coverage if you work diagonally around it first and then make long strokes along its length.

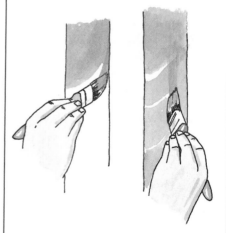

Need to use the stairs while you're painting them? Paint every other step. Let them dry thoroughly before painting the skipped steps.

Make quick work of railings and openwork with a sprayer. Just be sure to put cardboard or some other shield behind them to block the overspray.

Workshop

PLANNING A WORKSHOP

If a workbench requires more space than you have, build a fold-down unit in your garage. Use a solid-core door for the benchtop; fasten it to a wall, using a piano hinge. Legs should also be attached with hinges.

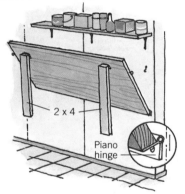

For most people, the ideal height for a workbench is 34 to 36 inches. If you need a shorter or taller surface, choose a height midway between your waist and your hips.

Because concrete is hard on the feet and damages tools that are dropped accidentally, cushion the workshop floor with old sheets of plywood or carpet. Or use unfolded, flattened cardboard boxes.

IMPROVING SAFETY AND EFFICIENCY

When working with any power tool—whether it's large or small, stationary or portable—use only a heavy-duty, grounded (three-prong) extension cord that is 14-gauge or larger.

Short of space in your workshop? A back-of-the-door tool rack with a built-in drawer is ideal for storing small tools and supplies. Mount the rack to a solid-core door, or to the internal cross rails of a hollow-core door.

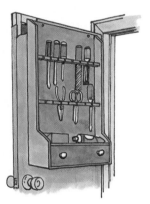

To keep power-tool cords out of the way as you work, hook the slack on a long spring screwed into the ceiling above your workbench.

Store discarded toxic chemicals, such as solvents, in a separate sealed trash container. For the location of an approved disposal site that's nearby, contact your state's department of environmental conservation.

183

A BASIC HOUSEHOLD TOOL KIT

You don't need an arsenal of tools to be prepared for emergency repairs and routine maintenance, but your tools should be the best quality you can afford. Except for doing specialized chores, most householders can get by with the following hand and power tools:

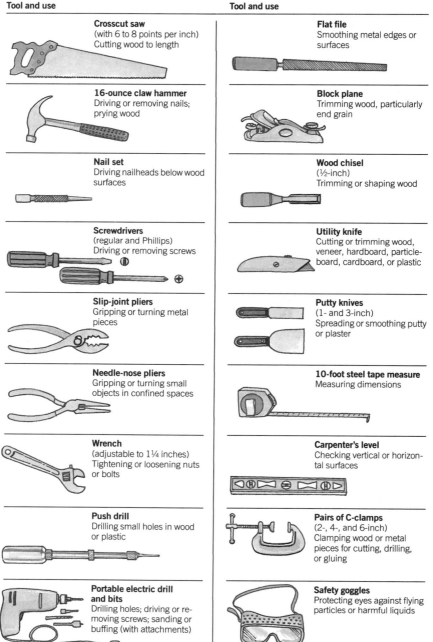

Tool and use

Crosscut saw
(with 6 to 8 points per inch)
Cutting wood to length

16-ounce claw hammer
Driving or removing nails;
prying wood

Nail set
Driving nailheads below wood
surfaces

Screwdrivers
(regular and Phillips)
Driving or removing screws

Slip-joint pliers
Gripping or turning metal
pieces

Needle-nose pliers
Gripping or turning small
objects in confined spaces

Wrench
(adjustable to 1¼ inches)
Tightening or loosening nuts
or bolts

Push drill
Drilling small holes in wood
or plastic

**Portable electric drill
and bits**
Drilling holes; driving or removing screws; sanding or
buffing (with attachments)

Tool and use

Flat file
Smoothing metal edges or
surfaces

Block plane
Trimming wood, particularly
end grain

Wood chisel
(½-inch)
Trimming or shaping wood

Utility knife
Cutting or trimming wood,
veneer, hardboard, particleboard, cardboard, or plastic

Putty knives
(1- and 3-inch)
Spreading or smoothing putty
or plaster

10-foot steel tape measure
Measuring dimensions

Carpenter's level
Checking vertical or horizontal surfaces

Pairs of C-clamps
(2-, 4-, and 6-inch)
Clamping wood or metal
pieces for cutting, drilling,
or gluing

Safety goggles
Protecting eyes against flying
particles or harmful liquids

Because linseed oil is prone to spontaneous combustion, even in cold weather, quickly discard any rag used on linseed oil or a product that contains linseed oil.

STORING TOOLS

To help yourself identify borrowed tools, paint your initials or engrave your name on them.

If you store tools on wall hooks, paint the outline of each tool on the wall to remind you and others where to replace a tool.

If you have small children, store all tools in locked cabinets or drawers. As the children grow up, introduce them gradually to the safe use of hand tools; continue to lock up power tools.

To make a handy rack for screwdrivers and other small tools, drill a series of ½- to 2-inch holes through a 1 x 3. Mount the rack on the wall with angle brackets.

Need a storage receptacle for sharp or pointed tools? Cut a block of plastic foam from the lining material in an appliance carton.

Do your tool drawers slip off their glides and spill their contents? Screw an oblong stop to the inside of the drawer's back panel. Fasten the stop with a pivot, which can be turned to a horizontal position if the drawer needs to be removed.

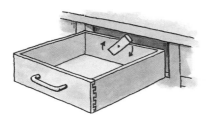

To protect the teeth of a small circular-saw blade, cut an old automobile-tire inner tube and stretch it around the blade. For a handsaw blade, use a slit length of old garden hose.

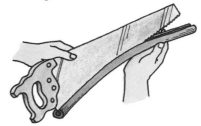

To prevent metal tools from rusting, store them in sealed wooden bins with camphor and sawdust.

STORING SUPPLIES

In a garage, you can store lumber and pipe on exposed ceiling joists. Screw cross members to the bottom edges of joists to support materials you wish to tuck up and out of the way.

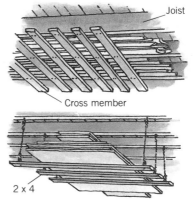

Here's a simple assembly you can make for off-the-floor storage for plywood and other sheet materials. Insert screw eyes into 5-foot lengths of 2 x 4's. Using S-hooks, fasten a heavy chain to each screw eye. Suspend chains from ceiling joists. For adequate support, use three 5-foot lengths.

Looking for convenient, out-of-the-way storage space? Use the unfinished stud spaces of your workshop walls. To make shelves, nail old boards horizontally between the studs.

A good way to organize washers and nuts is to hang them according to size on large safety pins or on wire coat hangers whose necks have been untwisted.

Jars with screw tops are ideal for storing small items, such as nails, screws, nuts, and bolts. You can double your shelf capacity by screwing the lids to the underside of shelves. Place a lock washer under the head of the screw so that the lid won't turn when you unscrew the jar.

If you need a rack to store abrasive discs, cut off one-third to one-half of an aluminum pie plate and fasten it to the wall bottom side out.

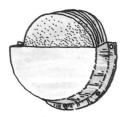

A good way to monitor your supply of paints, glues, and other liquids in opaque containers is to wrap a rubber band around each container at the level of its contents. Remember to adjust the rubber band as the level changes.

MARKING AND MEASURING

Always read a rule straight on, with your eyes directly in front of or above the point being read. If you're off to one side, your reading will be distorted.

For more accurate marking and measuring, hold a ruler on its edge rather than flat against the surface. Mark points at the tip of a V so that they'll be easier to spot.

Here's a quick, easy way to make a long, straight line. Pin two points of a carpenter's chalk line to the surface. Lift the taut line at an intermediate point and allow it to snap back quickly. The result will be a straight chalk line.

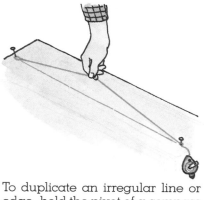

To duplicate an irregular line or edge, hold the pivot of a compass on the line or against the edge to be duplicated and move both points evenly as you scribe.

If you know the span of your hand, you can approximate measurements when you don't have a ruler. With your fingers spread out as widely as possible, measure the distance between the tips of your thumb and your pinky. To measure a distance, "walk" your hand along the surface, counting the "steps"; then multiply by your hand span. For short distances, use a finger segment that approximates 1 inch.

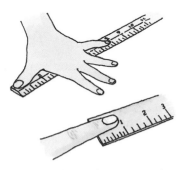

To divide a board into equal sections, lay a rule at an angle across the board. Align the end of the rule with one edge of the board. At the other edge, position an inch mark that is evenly divisible by the number of sections you want. Mark the appropriate intervals along the rule.

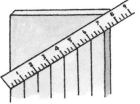

SAWING AND CUTTING

Save elbow grease by using soap. Rub your handsaw blade with a bar of dry soap to reduce friction.

To reduce splintering when crosscutting, place the board so that the growth rings arc downward.

SAWING A BOARD

1. Using a sharp pencil and a combination square, mark the cutting line across the top edge of the board.

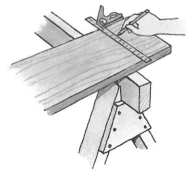

2. Set the board on sawhorses, with the waste section on the outside. Allow several inches of clearance for the saw.

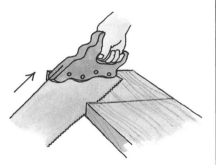

3. Place the end of the blade nearest the handle just outside the pencil line. Begin the cut with a few short pull strokes toward you.

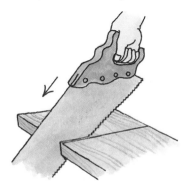

4. Once a groove has been formed, use longer strokes, pressing down on push strokes and relaxing on pull strokes.

Here's a crosscutting guide that keeps a handsaw cutting straight and at the correct angle. Rest the jig on the work and let its face guide your saw blade.

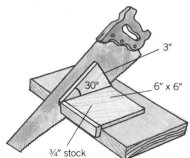

3"

30°

6" x 6"

¾" stock

To hand-saw a thin slice from the end of a board, clamp a longer piece of scrap wood underneath it and cut through both pieces. This will make the task much easier.

If your handsaw begins to bind as you cut with the grain, insert a screwdriver into the end of the kerf (the channel made by the blade) to hold it open.

Here's how to prevent a saber saw blade from breaking when you cut a circle out of plywood. Make straight cuts from the edges of the wood to the circumference. Space the cuts about 30 degrees apart, in alignment with the diameter. The waste will fall off in sections as you cut the circumference, relieving stress on the blade.

Having a hard time starting a hacksaw in metal? Nick the edge of the material with a file.

When using a hole-saw drill attachment, avoid tearing the back surface of the wood. Drill about halfway through the wood, until the tip of the bit pierces the back surface. Then insert the bit into the opening on the reverse side and complete the hole.

To make it easier to cut through knots in wood, rock your saw to change the angle of the stroke.

When using a combination or try square to check that a surface is regular or a corner is right-angled, position the square against the work and hold both up to the light. If light is visible between the square and the work, correct the irregularity by planing or sanding the work's edge.

DRIVING NAILS

To get full advantage of the weight of a hammer's head, hold the handle as far from the head as possible without sacrificing a firm grip. After the nail is started, swing the hammer from your elbow.

In general, nails should be approximately the same length as the combined thickness of the stock that's being fastened.

If a nail is too small to hold with your fingers, use a bobby pin or a pair of needle-nose pliers to hold it in place as you hammer.

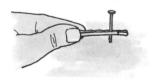

For starting brads or tacks that are shorter than 1 inch, use a magnetized tack hammer.

When starting a nail, hold it between your index and middle fingers with your palm up. If you accidentally miss the head, you'll strike the fleshy part of your fingers, which hurts a lot less than hitting your thumb or fingernail.

An easy way to avoid splitting wood is to blunt the sharp points of nails. Tap them with a hammer.

Here's how to conceal a nailhead. Chisel a shaving parallel to the wood grain, leaving the shaving attached to the surface. Drive in the nail. Glue the shaving back in place over the nailhead.

When fastening moldings with finishing nails, use a strip of pegboard scrap to shield the wood. Drive nails through one of the holes as far as possible, then set the heads with a nail set.

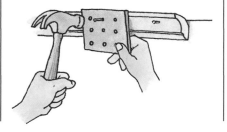

To remove a nail whose head is below the wood surface, place the hammer claw slightly in front of the nail with the tapered ends on the wood. Strike the hammer face with a rubber mallet to drive the claws into the wood surface.

Cutting pliers are ideal for removing nails with narrow or broken heads. Rock the pliers back and forth gently to ease the nail out.

DRILLING HOLES

Although a single-speed, ¼-inch drill is adequate for drilling holes in wood, a variable-speed, ⅜-inch model with reversing capability is more versatile. It will drill holes in masonry, drive and remove screws, and accept attachments for sanding, wire-brushing, and polishing.

To increase precision and reduce bit breakage, hold a drill with your palm high up on the handle, directly behind the chuck. Extend your index finger along the drill's body and use your second or third finger to operate the trigger.

If you lubricate drill bits with silicone spray before using them, they'll break less easily and stay sharp longer.

To prevent a drill bit from wandering as you start a hole, use a nail set to make an indentation where the hole's center will be.

Need more light on the spot you're drilling? Tape a penlight to the casing of your drill.

To make depth stops for your drill bits, drill undersize holes through the center of corks. Each cork should fit its bit snugly so that when you drill a hole to the proper depth, the cork doesn't move up on the bit.

When drilling smooth sheet metal, stick a piece of masking tape where the hole's center will be. This prevents the bit from wandering.

Here's how to avoid splintering the back surface of wood every time the tip of the bit emerges. Place a block of scrap wood under the piece. The bit won't tear the wood as it breaks through.

To prevent splintering when drilling holes with an auger or paddle bit, drill from one side until the bit tip emerges. Then turn the work over and finish the hole from the opposite side.

DRIVING SCREWS

The tip of a screwdriver should match the screw slot's length and width as closely as possible. A tip that's too narrow can damage the slot; one that's too large can mar the surface of the wood.

When working on the surface of wood, use a screwdriver with a winged blade. For work below the surface, the wingless type is better because it won't mar the wood as the screw is tightened.

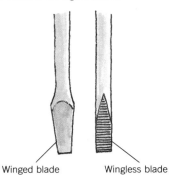

Winged blade   Wingless blade

To start a screw in a hard-to-reach spot, push the screw through a slit strip of masking tape (adhesive side up). Place the screwdriver tip into the screw slot and fold the tape ends to secure the screw to the screwdriver. Remove the tape after the screw has been started.

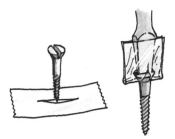

If screws are hard to turn or tighten, try rubbing their threads with soap or paraffin.

Unable to tighten a loose screw? Replace it with one that's larger in diameter, or insert wooden toothpicks to give the threads something to grip. If these fail, insert a plastic plug of the correct size into the screw hole, or squeeze wood filler into the hole and drive the screw while the filler is still wet.

Because a screw can only enter wood at the rate its thread cuts the wood, applying more pressure to a hard-to-turn screw is *not* the answer. What does help is to use a large-handled screwdriver with a blade as wide as the screw's slot.

To increase torque (turning force), use a wrench in conjunction with a large-handled, square-shanked screwdriver.

Want to conceal the head of a screw? First drill a pilot hole. Then drill a countersink hole with a bit that's the same size as the screw head. Insert the screw below the wood's surface. Fill the hole with a plug cut from the same wood or with wood putty.

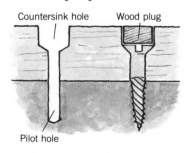

Countersink hole   Wood plug

Pilot hole

GLUING AND CLAMPING

If you're about to spread glue on a joint's surfaces, stop! First do a dry run-through with the clamps you plan to use.

If your C-clamps are too small for a particular job, place the stationary jaws of two clamps against one another to form an S, then tighten the screws onto the work.

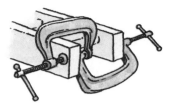

Two C-clamps and a length of braided wire cable can be used to make a clamp of any capacity. Loop the ends of the cable around the stationary jaws of the clamps, then tighten the adjustable screw pads around the work.

If you have any old thread spools, don't throw them away; they can be used to make a clamp. Find a bolt long and narrow enough to fit through two spools and the workpiece. Then insert the bolt through the spool holes, and tighten a wing nut to close the "jaws."

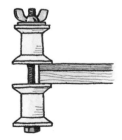

When applying wood glue, keep in mind that less is more. Apply thin, even coats of glue on mating surfaces; then clamp them together tightly for the correct length of time (p. 192).

To prevent glue squeeze-out from staining the area around a joint, apply masking tape to adjacent surfaces. Peel off the tape after the clamps have been removed and the glue has dried.

You'll know that clamps are sufficiently tight when a thin line of glue appears along the entire joint. Avoid overtightening; this can distort the work and weaken the joint by squeezing out too much of the glue.

Wood blocks taped to the jaws of clamps serve two purposes: they protect surfaces of the work from being marred or stained, and they distribute pressure more evenly, resulting in stronger glue joints.

Nothing's worse than finishing a gluing job only to find that the clamps or wood blocks are stuck to the wood. Avoid this by placing sheets of wax paper between surfaces and clamps.

To improvise a benchtop clamp for a large frame or other workpiece, secure stops to a benchtop and use paired wedges to hold work between them.

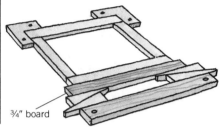

¾″ board

WHICH GLUE FOR THE JOB?

Material	Adhesive type	Instructions	Comments
Wood to wood (indoors)	Polyvinyl acetate (white glue) or aliphatic resin (yellow carpenter's glue)	Ready to use; apply sparingly to both mating surfaces; clamp for 1½ to 4 hours; let dry for 24 hours at 70° F or above	Clamp polyvinyl acetate within 15 minutes of application, aliphatic resin within 5 minutes; dries clear or yellow; non-waterproof; for cleanup, use soap and warm water
Wood to wood (outdoors)	Resorcinol	Mix components in a disposable container; apply to both mating surfaces; let set for 5 minutes; clamp for 16 hours; let dry for 24 hours at 70° F or above	Clamp within 1 hour of application; dries brown; waterproof; for cleanup, use cool water while wet
Laminate, veneer, or fabric to wood or wood products	Contact cement	Ready to use; apply to both mating surfaces and let dry; position material on underlayer, using brown paper to separate glued surfaces; when ready, remove brown paper and burnish top layer to underlayer with roller or wood block; no clamping necessary; let dry for 24 hours at 70° F or above	Join mating surfaces after application has dried on both surfaces; dries amber; water-resistant; for cleanup, see container for appropriate thinner
Metal to metal	Epoxy	Mix components in a disposable container; apply to both mating surfaces; clamp for 8 hours; let dry for 24 hours at 70° F or above	Clamp immediately after application; dries clear, white, or gray; water-resistant; for cleanup, use acetone while wet
Nonporous surfaces (metal, rubber, plastic, ceramic, and glass)	Cyanoacrylate (instant glue)	Ready to use; apply sparingly to one mating surface; press mating surfaces together, exerting pressure for 10 to 30 seconds; no clamping necessary; let dry for 12 hours at 70° F or above	Join mating surfaces immediately after application; dries clear; water-resistant; for cleanup, see container for appropriate thinner

Caution: The fumes from some glues are dangerous; therefore, always use glue in a well-ventilated area and never near an open flame. Cyanoacrylates bond to the skin; wear rubber gloves to prevent contact

ORGANIZING THE GARAGE OR CARPORT

Attach mirrors in the front and rear corners of your garage or carport. Install them at a height at which you can see if your car lights are working as you back out.

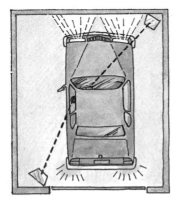

Hang an old worn-out tire from a garage or carport rafter, positioning it so that it rests against the back wall. If you happen to enter the area too fast, or if your brakes don't stop the car in time, the car's nose will hit soft rubber instead of a hard wall.

To make your garage or carport look neater, paint boundary lines on the floor to keep cars, bikes, lawn mowers, and other vehicles in their assigned spots.

Make a permanent hanger for an extension cord by tying rawhide or heavy twine behind the plug. After rolling up the cord, wrap the rawhide or twine around it, tie a bow, and use one of the bow loops to hang up the cord.

KEEPING THE FLOOR CLEAN

Kitty litter does a good job sopping up oil and other auto fluids. When there's a leak, place paper towels under your car until you can have repairs made.

To remove oil from a concrete driveway or garage floor, pour paint thinner over the affected area and cover with kitty litter. Leaving the garage door open, give the litter time to absorb the oil; then sweep up.

Caution: When using paint thinner, make sure that nobody smokes or strikes matches in the vicinity and that the working area is well ventilated.

A push broom makes the best garage-floor sweeper. To keep the handle from loosening, reinforce it by screwing lengths of ⅛-inch-thick wire or a wire hanger between the pole and the broom head.

CLEANING THE WINDSHIELD

Moisten a rag or sponge with rubbing alcohol or mineral spirits to wipe away any windshield spots that resist store-bought window cleaners.

Are your car's windshield wipers smearing the windshield? Clean the windshield *and* the wiper blades with rubbing alcohol. If this doesn't work, scrub the windshield with a low-abrasion scouring powder to remove possible waxy buildup.

Sponge the inside of windows with vinegar to remove haze from plastic fumes in a new car. Rinse with water and wipe them dry.

WASHING AND WAXING

Wash your car with a solution of dishwashing detergent and water. Starting with the roof, wash and rinse in sections so that the soap doesn't dry on the car. Dry with an old bath towel; then for a supershine, finish off with a good-quality chamois.

After a car has been thoroughly washed and waxed, spruce it up every now and then by hosing it down and wiping it dry with clean cloths or a sponge.

Shine up your car with the right kind of product. If your car is new, buy one designed specifically for new cars. If your car is older, however, you'll need a cleaner-polish with a light abrasive; severely weathered cars require an even more abrasive product.

WHEN TO SERVICE YOUR CAR

In addition to the regularly scheduled maintenance services outlined for your car by the manufacturer in the owner's manual, the following recommendations will help you keep your car trouble-free

While driving, be alert to the onset of any of the following; report it to a mechanic as soon as possible:

Slower-than-normal cranking

Vibration

Brake-pedal softness or hardness; brake noise

Steering-wheel pull

Unfamiliar engine noise

Automatic-transmission noise; slipping; erratic or rough shifting

Engine roughness and loss of power

Hard starting

Deterioration in ride and handling

Clutch chatter or slipping

Exhaust-system roar

No horn

Windshield-wiper streaking

Gasoline or other unusual odor

A dashboard warning light that comes on

A gauge that shows an abnormal reading

When filling the fuel tank:

Check engine oil level

Check coolant level

Once a month and before a long drive:

Check tire pressure (including that of the spare); examine tires for cuts and abnormal wear

Once a month (contd.)

Be sure that all lights work

Check ground beneath parked car for fluid leaks

Check automatic-transmission fluid level

Twice yearly (usually spring and fall):

Check power-steering, brake, and manual-transmission fluid levels

Check fluid level of hydraulically operated clutch

Check fluid level in rear axle

Check temperature protection strength of coolant

Inspect drive belts

Check radiator, heater, and air-conditioner hoses

Inspect exhaust-system components for signs of rust-through; retighten clamps

Rotate tires if mileage traveled since last rotation conforms with tire maker's rotation recommendation

Check front-wheel-drive axle boots for cracks and leaks

Examine battery-cable terminals for corrosion

Yearly:

Inspect brake lines for cracks; inspect brake pads and linings for wear (do this twice a year if most of your driving is stop-and-go)

Lubricate lock cylinders, body points, door hinges, hood hinges and latches, trunk hinges and latches, fuel-door hinges; check door weatherstripping

Test ability of parking brake and *Park* position of automatic transmission to hold

Make your whitewall tires sparkling clean. Apply undiluted liquid laundry detergent to wet tires with a scrub brush, then rinse.

ELIMINATING RUST

Apply a thin layer of clear silicone rubber sealant along the tops of body moldings to keep water from getting behind the moldings. Water trapped there can cause rust.

An electric hand grinder with a conical stone removes dime-size rust spots without damaging the surrounding paint. Use it carefully to avoid penetrating the metal. Follow with primer and paint.

Get rid of rust in hard-to-reach corners with a gasket scraper (available at auto parts stores). Brush with a small wire brush, then prime and paint.

CAR PROBLEMS

When a mechanic is working on your drum brakes, make sure he returns the plugs to the inspection holes in the backing plates. If he fails to reinstall these plugs, road grit will enter the brake housing and cause excessive wear.

It is important to check the brake fluid every 20,000 miles to see that it is no more than ½ inch below the top of the reservoir. If it is, have a mechanic check for a leak in the system.

CHANGING AN AIR FILTER

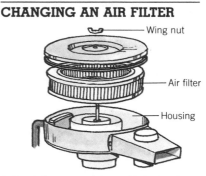

1. The air filter is usually located in the housing at the top of the carburetor. Remove its cover by undoing the wing nut, clips, or nuts holding it in place. Disconnect any hose that's in the way. Lift out the filter.

2. Examine the filter for dirt, tears, or damage. Tap it against a solid surface to dislodge dirt and dust. Hold a light inside the filter as you revolve the filter around it. If you see light and the element is not coated with oil, you need not replace the filter.

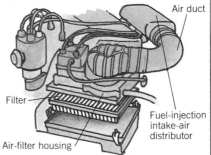

3. In some cars the air filter is hard to find. To locate it, trace the large air duct from the carburetor or from the intake-air distributor to its end. Undo the fasteners and proceed as explained. To reinstall the old filter or install a new one, reverse the procedure and secure the cover.

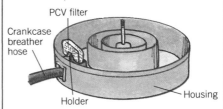

4. If your car has a positive crankcase ventilation (PCV) filter, inspect it as well. With the air-cleaner cover off, simply pull the PCV intake air filter out of its holder. (You needn't remove the clip and the holder or disconnect the hose.) Examine the filter; if it's dirty, clogged, or oil-soaked, replace it.

Spray belt dressing on the fan belt while the engine is running to tell at once if a squeal is caused by the belt. If the noise disappears, replace the fan belt. If it doesn't, look elsewhere for the problem.

If your car surges when you drive with the cruise control engaged, check for a bad speedometer cable or a clogged cruise-control vacuum hose. (Note: Add-on cruise controls don't have vacuum hoses.)

Are you suddenly feeling steering-wheel vibration in your front-wheel-drive car? Put your car on jack stands or have it lifted. Then

squeeze the boot over the inner tie-rod socket on each side of the vehicle as you turn the wheel to the left and right. If parts inside the boot feel loose, replace both sockets to avoid losing your steering.

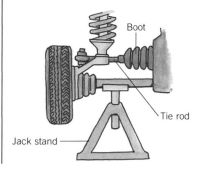
Boot
Tie rod
Jack stand

CHANGING THE OIL AND THE OIL FILTER

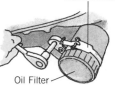
Band wrench
Oil Filter

1. Warm the car's engine; unless there is adequate working space beneath the car, raise and support the front of the car on jack stands or on ramps. (It's unsafe to work under a car supported only by the jack that comes with the car.) Place a pan beneath the drain plug.

2. Loosen the plug with a wrench; then turn by hand. Pull the plug away quickly to avoid hot oil. Drainage is complete when drips are 15 seconds apart. Clean the drain plug and drain hole with a soft rag or paper towel. Replace and tighten the plug by hand; then give it a half-turn with a wrench.

3. Although automobile manufacturers specify a new oil filter every other oil change, ideally, you should change the oil filter every time you change the oil. Move the pan beneath the filter. With a filter wrench, loosen the filter counterclockwise; then unscrew it by hand.

4. Wipe clean the mating surfaces of the filter and the engine. Coat the gasket of the new filter with clean engine oil; thread the filter clockwise onto the mounting stud, hand-tighten until the filter gasket makes light contact with the base; then turn 180 degrees with a filter wrench.

5. Lower the car. Wipe the oil-filler area clean and add the quantity and type of oil your owner's manual calls for. Run the engine for about a minute; then turn it off. Check for leaks at the plug and filter; then, with the dipstick, check the oil level and add more oil if necessary.

6. Pour the old oil into a plastic container with a top and dispose of it properly by taking it to a service station with a used-oil holding tank.

MAINTENANCE MISCELLANY

A thin coating of silicone dielectric grease (sold in hardware stores) or petroleum jelly will help prevent battery-terminal corrosion.

To loosen an oil filter that won't budge, buy a filter wrench or chain-type locking pliers that can grasp the filter close to the base, minimizing the twisting force.

Don't wait for radiator hoses to burst and leave you stranded. At least once a year feel the hoses. If they're spongy, disconnect them; push a rag into each hose, then pull it out. If flakes of rubber come out with the rag, replace the hose—it's starting to deteriorate.

To prevent excess wear on your tires, never turn the steering wheel while the car is standing still.

To see at a glance whether vehicle vibration has caused loosening of the nuts and bolts on wheels, put a dot of paint on each fastener as well as dots on adjacent parts. If side-by-side dots go out of line, you'll know the fastener needs retightening.

FUEL ECONOMY

Unless your owner's manual specifically recommends premium gasoline, don't buy it because you think it will provide greater fuel economy or more power. It doesn't—except in high-performance turbocharged engines. The only reason to switch from regular gasoline to premium is to rid an engine of a ping; but first see if a different brand of regular will do the job.

Don't top off a fuel tank in hot weather. Heat increases the pressure in a tank so that the fuel rises and overflows—an unnecessary waste.

Suspect a fuel leak if your fuel economy drops or you smell gasoline. If no fuel is leaking, try replacing the filter in the base of the evaporative emissions charcoal canister. (If there is no filter, replace the canister.) After 30,000 miles, this part can clog and cause these conditions.

Neither a dawdler nor a racer be. To attain maximum fuel economy when starting a car from a standstill, reach your desired speed quickly and smoothly. *Smoothly* is the key word.

OTHER ECONOMY MEASURES

Instead of replacing a coolant overflow tank that's leaking, insert a heavy-duty plastic freezer bag in the tank to hold the coolant.

Be safe and save money—replace shock absorbers in pairs. If only one shock is leaking or worn out, replace the other shock on the same axle even if the latter is all right; otherwise, vehicle stability will be affected.

ROAD EMERGENCIES

Getting stuck is no fun; it's also dangerous. Warn motorists by doing all of the following: open the hood; turn on the hazard-warning flashers; tie a distress flag to the door handle or to the antenna; and place warning flares 10 and 300 feet to the rear of the car and 100 feet to the front.

If the accelerator jams, tap it lightly; then lift up on it with your toe. If this doesn't free it, quickly shift into *Neutral*, apply the brakes to stop the car, then turn off the ignition.

To stop a car when the brakes fail, try pumping the brakes rapidly and repeatedly. If that doesn't slow the car, shift into low gear and gradually apply the parking brake.

REPLACING SPARK PLUGS

For peak ignition-system performance, inspect your car's spark plugs annually, or at least every 10,000 miles. If they appear worn or fouled, replace them—usually every 2 years or 20,000 miles. Any

major brand of spark plug should perform properly in your engine if you use the part number for your make, model, and engine as listed in the plug manufacturer's catalog and install it correctly.

1. Let the engine cool, and label spark plug cables according to their location before removing them. Twist the boot to free the cable, then blow debris out of the plug port with compressed air. Fit a spark plug socket over the plug and apply pressure counterclockwise with a ratchet wrench to remove the plug. For hard-to-remove plugs, use a ratchet wrench and a U-joint.

2. As you take out each plug, wrap it with masking tape and note its engine location and whether it has deposits, oil, or carbon on its tips so that you can tell a mechanic later.

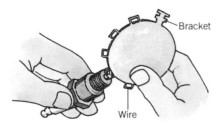

Bracket

Wire

3. Using a spark plug gauge, set the gap on the new plugs according to the specifications printed in the owner's manual or on a sticker under the car's hood. The specified thickness gauge should just slide through the gap between the electrodes (not easily and not with great force). Fit the gauge wire snugly in the gap. Use the gauge's bracket to bend the L-shaped side electrode to adjust the gap. Recheck with the wire.

4. Apply a coat of antiseize compound to the plug threads before installation in an aluminum cylinder head. Insert the plugs and screw them carefully into the engine (don't cross threads) until finger-tight. Using the ratchet wrench, turn the plugs with a gasket a quarter to a half turn; others a sixteenth. Apply silicone dielectric grease to the inside of the rubber nipple before reconnecting the cables to the plugs.

If dashboard lights or an accessory stops working, check for a blown fuse. If there is none, grasp the fuse controlling the device with a fuse puller. Move the fuse in and out. If the accessory works, pull the fuse. With an emery board, sand the contacts of the fuse and the holder to remove corrosion. Reinsert fuse.

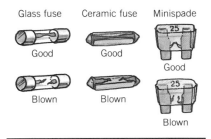

Glass fuse	Ceramic fuse	Minispade
Good	Good	Good
Blown	Blown	Blown

FLAT TIRES

Keep both your hands free for changing a flat tire at night—buy a magnetized battery-operated light or make a flashlight holder using a suction cup and a swivel clamp (available in hardware or photography stores).

If penetrating oil or rust remover isn't available to loosen frozen nuts and bolts, pour cola on them and let it penetrate.

OVERHEATING

If the temperature warning light glows or the temperature gauge nears the overheat mark while you're in traffic, turn the heater and the fan on at high speed until you can stop safely or get to a garage.

CHANGING A TIRE

1. Turn on the hazard warning flashers. Shift an automatic transmission into *Park*, a manual transmission into *Reverse*. Set the parking brake and turn off the ignition.

2. Check that the spare is inflated; if it's not, you'll have to pay for emergency road service. If the spare is adequate, block the tire that's diagonally opposite the flat tire with a chock or a large rock. Pry off the wheel cover and loosen each lug nut with one turn of the wrench.

3. Follow the instructions in the owner's manual or glued in the jack compartment, and jack the car up to raise the tire approximately 3 inches off the ground. (If you've parked the car on a soft surface, place a board under the jack to serve as a firm base.)

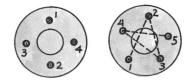

4. Remove the lug nuts, the wheel, and the tire; put on the spare. Reinstall the nuts by hand, tapered end first. Tighten the nuts with a wrench in the crisscross pattern shown. (Improperly tightened, they cause unequal pressure that can distort a wheel.) Lower the car and remove the jack and chock. Wrench-tighten all the nuts again in the correct sequence and tap the wheel cover into place.

To prevent road breakdowns, replace all hoses and belts every 4 years or 50,000 miles.

BATTERY PROBLEMS

If you have to jump-start a battery, make sure that both batteries are of the same voltage. Wear goggles to protect your eyes. Connect cables in the order illustrated below; disconnect them in reverse order.

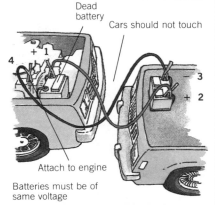

Dead battery

Cars should not touch

Attach to engine

Batteries must be of same voltage

If your battery has to be recharged every few weeks, check your car's interior lights. First push the switch button on the glove compartment to see if the light goes out, then open the hood and the trunk just a crack to see if either light is on. If so, remove the bulb until you can have repairs made.

COLD WEATHER

A car kept in a cold garage during subzero weather will start much more quickly in the morning if you buy a battery warmer, a low-wattage heating element in a blanket of insulation. It even helps a little when not plugged in because the insulation holds in heat.

If you park your car outdoors overnight in cold weather, position it so that the morning sun will hit the hood; if you're parking the car for the whole day, position it for the

A TOOL KIT FOR ROAD EMERGENCIES

Keep the following tools and supplies in your car to handle common emergencies. Wrap metal tools in cloths to prevent rattling. Keep all small items in an old suitcase or duffel bag. (For a winter emergency kit, see p.201.)

General equipment
Flashlight and spare batteries
Light that plugs into the cigarette lighter or clips to the car battery
Emergency flares and distress flag
Work gloves

Supplies
Squeeze-type siphon to pump gas from a fellow motorist's tank to yours
Gallon plastic jug to hold water or gas
Quart of engine oil
Board (2 feet by 1 foot) to serve as a base for a jack
Wheel chock (or use a roadside stone to chock the wheel)
Penetrating oil
Tire sealant-inflator
Jumper cables

Spare fuse kit and fuse puller
Scrap electrical wire for lashing down a sprung trunk lid or hood or for tying up a dropped tail pipe
Duct tape
Spare radiator hose
Spare fan belt
Spare clamp

Tools
Adjustable wrench
Insulated slip-joint, needle-nose, and locking pliers
Insulated screwdrivers: one Phillips head, one standard
Utility knife
Jack
Lug wrench; 2- to 3-foot length of pipe that fits over the end of the wrench

afternoon sun. The warmth from the sun may make the difference between starting and not starting.

If your car keeps stalling after you start it and before it warms up, the thermostatically controlled valve in the air-cleaner housing may be stuck. To check, reach with your hand or a screwdriver into the air-cleaner snorkel while the engine is running (cold). If the plate isn't closed to begin with and doesn't open gradually as the engine warms up, see an auto mechanic.

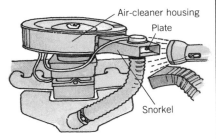

Air-cleaner housing

Plate

Snorkel

On cars that have carburetors, a malfunctioning choke vacuum break (also called a vacuum pull) may cause repeated stalling before the engine warms up in winter. Ask an auto mechanic to test this part.

If, on a mild winter day, you've flooded the engine from excessive pumping of the accelerator (you may smell gas) and your car has a carburetor, push the accelerator to the floor and keep it there for 15 seconds as you crank the engine. If the car still doesn't start, turn off the ignition for about a minute; then repeat the procedure.

DRIVING IN SNOW

Put snow tires on the front wheels of vehicles with front-drive axles and on the rear wheels of those with rear-drive axles.

PREPARING FOR WINTER

To get you and your car safely through the winter, have the following done before the onset of cold weather:

1. Ask a mechanic to test and replace the battery if it doesn't deliver current according to its cold-cranking amperage rating.
2. Tune the ignition and fuel systems. If necessary, install new spark plugs, test spark plug cables, adjust ignition timing, have cylinder performance tested, replace air and fuel filters, adjust slow and fast idle speeds, test the automatic choke, see that the carburetor's thermostatic air cleaner is working properly, inspect for vacuum leaks, inspect the distributor cap and rotor, and check the manifold heat control valve (if your car has one).
3. Drain, flush, and fill the cooling system with a mixture of antifreeze and water, in a concentration of 50 to 70 percent antifreeze. If the solution presently in the cooling system is less than 2 years old, you need only test it with a hydrometer to determine if it provides the necessary protection. If not, add more antifreeze.
4. Mount snow tires; make sure that all the tires (including the spare) are properly inflated and have adequate tread.
5. Test the heater, windshield defroster, and rear-window deicer/defogger.
6. Replace worn windshield wiper-blade squeegees.
7. See that the reservoir is filled with wintertime windshield-washer fluid.
8. Test all lights and flashers.
9. Add a scraper and brush to your emergency tool kit (p.200).
10. If you travel in areas where heavy snows are possible, gather emergency equipment: blankets or sleeping bags, a shovel, bags of sand, candles, matches, canned goods, plastic eating utensils, an empty 2-pound coffee can (to hold water or candles), and plastic bags.

Even in heavy snow country, keep your tires inflated at the pressure recommended by your owner's manual. Lowering the pressure won't give you better traction—it will only cause the outer parts of the tread to wear more rapidly.

For extra traction, place four 50-pound sacks of sand in the trunk of your car. (If necessary, you can spread this sand around the tires to help you out of a snowdrift or off a patch of ice.)

FROZEN LOCKS

If the door or trunk lock freezes, heat its key with a match; then quickly put the key into the cylinder and turn. To prevent burned fingers, wear gloves.

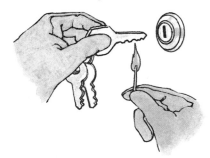

To keep locks from freezing, squirt some graphite lubricant (never oil) into the cylinders; then open and close the lock several times.

RUST PREVENTION

Salt splashed into the wheel wells can cause rust; be sure to hose away salt at the end of winter and at least once before then.

At the beginning of spring, rid the bottom of your car of all rust-causing agents. Park the car over a lawn-soaker hose and turn on the water for at least 20 minutes.

To prevent rust, most car doors have underside drain holes so that water can escape and moisture can dry. These holes eventually get plugged. At least once a year, probe them with a small screwdriver or a wire coat hanger to unclog them.

RAIN AND FOG

After driving through a deep puddle, test the brakes to make sure that they hold. If they're wet and don't hold, drop your speed to about 20 miles an hour and put your left foot lightly on the brake pedal. Driving like this for about a quarter of a mile will generate enough heat to dry the linings.

For maximum visibility in fog, a combination of fog lights and low headlight beams works best. Next best are the low beams by themselves. High beams provide minimum visibility.

If you pull over to the side of the road in fog, remember to turn on your hazard-warning flashers. A steady glow from parking lights may make a driver behind you think that you're driving too—and he may plow right into you.

SUMMERTIME

Before storing snow tires for the summer, spray them with silicone (never a petroleum product) to keep the rubber from drying. Do the same for conventional tires that you store for the winter. Lay stored tires flat, not on edge.

If your car begins to stall or hesitate in summer, switch to a different brand of gasoline. Alcohol blended into some brands can lead to problems in hot weather.

Yard & Garden

PLANNING FOR GARDEN ENJOYMENT

Beautifying your yard is satisfying—and even profitable. Well-placed trees, shrubs, flowering plants, and an attractive lawn can increase your property's value by as much as 10 percent.

Before drawing up a plan, call your municipality's building department. Ask about zoning and building regulations and laws that concern digging for any purpose other than tilling the soil.

Landscaping can make a mobile home look permanent. It may also change its property tax classification and increase the tax rate.

A detailed landscaping plan will help you visualize your future yard and give an idea of how to program the project in stages.

For accuracy, base your landscape plan on the property dimensions given in your deed survey. If you don't have a deed survey, ask the village, town, county, or city clerk where you can get one.

MAKING A PLAN FOR LANDSCAPING YOUR YARD

Tape a sheet of graph paper to a work surface. Then, referring to your deed survey or builder's plan, draw the outlines of such features as the house, garage, shed, driveway, existing trees, shrubs, and rock outcroppings. Mark the locations of drains, sewers, telephone, electric, and gas lines to avoid damage while landscaping. Indicate wind and sun directions to help you decide where to put trees, shrubs, hedges, beds, and fencing. Show areas of poor drainage, which you may want to correct. Identify house windows and all views: those you wish to keep and those you want to camouflage. Tape a sheet of tracing paper over this plan to draft your landscape design. Replace it with another sheet for changes.

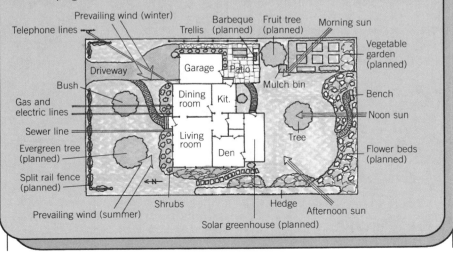

Prevailing wind (winter) · Telephone lines · Trellis · Barbeque (planned) · Fruit tree (planned) · Morning sun · Driveway · Garage · Patio · Vegetable garden (planned) · Bush · Mulch bin · Bench · Gas and electric lines · Dining room · Kit. · Sewer line · Noon sun · Evergreen tree (planned) · Living room · Den · Tree · Flower beds (planned) · Split rail fence (planned) · Shrubs · Hedge · Afternoon sun · Prevailing wind (summer) · Solar greenhouse (planned)

For quick and easy landscape plans, project photo slides of your yard onto large pieces of paper. After you trace the outlines of existing elements, sketch in your changes or additions. You'll see right away how the landscaping will look.

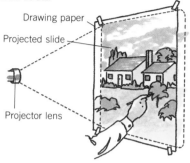

Drawing paper
Projected slide
Projector lens

Two weeks before planting, spray poison ivy and poison oak with glyphosphates on a windless day. Wear heavy-duty cotton gardening gloves when you spray and also when you cut off the dead plants. Double-bag the plants for disposal or for burying.

Keep your goal in mind when planning the placement of shade trees. If you want afternoon shade on a southwest-facing patio, for instance, plant a small tree no more than 15 feet south and west of it. For a tree that will grow to be very large, you must increase these distances accordingly.

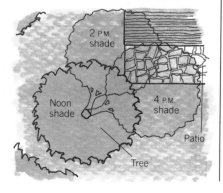

2 P.M. shade
Noon shade
4 P.M. shade
Patio
Tree

Plan your planting for a brilliant fall-foliage display. Ginkgo trees, spice bushes, birches, witch hazels, sugar maples, poplars, and summer sweets provide brilliant yellows; red oaks, tupelos, arrowwoods, and winged euonymuses furnish gorgeous reds.

Avoid planting trees or shrubs over or near drains, waterlines, and septic fields. Their extensive root systems—particularly those of such water-loving species as willows, sweet gums, and ornamental figs—can crack and clog the tile or pipe.

If you find that you have to run a sewer, gas, or drain line under a tree, aiming the trench under the trunk's center may avoid extreme root damage.

Lateral planting beds will make your yard look longer and deeper, if you angle their inside borders toward each other from the front to the rear of the yard.

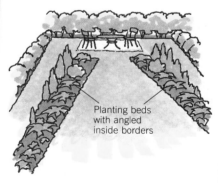

Planting beds with angled inside borders

GARDEN STRUCTURES

If your property's grade must be raised because of construction, protect your valuable trees with a drainage and air circulation system so that they won't suffocate. Consult a landscapist for this task.

Highlight garden features at night with spotlights and floodlights. You can plan the effect of their placement by positioning a high-powered flashlight in various locations. Well-lit paths and entrances promote safety and help discourage burglars.

Spotlight

Floodlight

Creosote-treated lumber greatly prolongs the life of fences and retaining walls, but it can also be toxic to plants. Lumber treated with copper-based preservatives is safer.

To help fence posts shed rain water effectively, saw off their tops at an angle or cover them with sloping metal caps (available at most lumberyards).

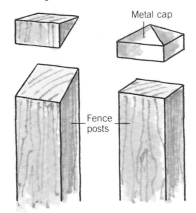

Metal cap

Fence posts

YOUR SOIL'S pH FACTOR

Before you landscape, test your soil's alkalinity and acidity. Do-it-yourself soil-test kits aren't reliable. Your local Cooperative Extension Service can do the job (free, in some states) or advise you. The service is listed in the telephone directory under U.S. government, Department of Agriculture. Dig up a tablespoon of soil from five different parts of your yard. Dry them, then seal them in a plastic bag labeled with your name, address, and telephone number. Wrap the bag and mail it in. The Cooperative Extension Service will get back to you in about a week.

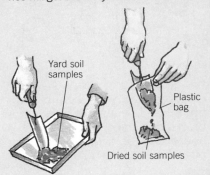

Yard soil samples

Plastic bag

Dried soil samples

Test results will reveal your soil's pH. The pH scale ranges from 1 to 14, indicating whether the soil is sweet (alkaline) or sour (acid). Most plants flourish in neutral soils (pH 6.5 to 8); some, however, require distinctly acid (pH 4 to 6) or alkaline soils (pH 8 or higher). The test results will indicate which trees and plants are right for your yard. If, after testing, you still want to plant species that are not suited to your soil, you'll need to alter the soil.

Acid-favoring trees: Fir, flowering dogwood, hemlock, hickory, oak, pine, spruce, sweet bay.

Acid-favoring shrubs: Andromeda, azalea, cistus, heather, holly, mountain laurel, rhododendron.

Alkaline-favoring trees: Juniper, plane tree, black locust.

Alkaline-favoring shrubs: Bamboo, barberry, butterfly bush, cotoneaster, forsythia, lilac, pyracantha.

TREES AND SHRUBS

Are chilling winds inflating your home heating bill? If so, shield the windy side of your house with a staggered double row of ever-green trees.

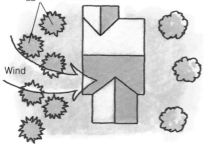

Staggered double row

Wind

Let deciduous trees and shrubs help regulate your home's tem-perature. In summer their sun-blocking leaves help keep the house cool; in winter their bare branches let the sun shine in.

Since lightning often strikes tulip, oak, and maple trees, plant them well away from your house. An additional safety measure: Have a tree-care specialist install light-ning-protection devices on any tall trees near your house.

When shrub branches are split or broken, it's better to prune them back than to try mending them with a splint.

BUYING AND PLANTING

Don't buy a burlapped evergreen that has a cracked, loose soil ball. Its leaves may wilt or curl after you have planted it. Or, after a brief healthy period, its leaves may fall off and it will die.

If you're a bargain hunter, bare-root trees and shrubs may be for you. They're often less than half the price of balled-and-burlapped specimens, and if pruned back properly, they have a very high survival rate.

You can successfully plant many trees in early fall, but some, such as magnolias, birches, and red maples, are better off being plant-ed in the early spring.

When you have to transplant a large shrub, put it on a snow shov-el and slide it across the lawn.

FERTILIZING AND WATERING

Feed tree roots in late fall when the ground is moist; use a fertilizer of medium nitrogen content: 2 pounds per trunk-diameter-inch at breast height. Pour it in evenly spaced holes, 2 feet deep, from the trunk to a few feet beyond the drip line. Or use micropore release packets. Their fertilizer is slowly released over 3 to 8 years.

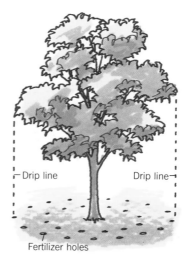

Drip line   Drip line

7
Fertilizer holes

American beech and crab apple trees are especially sensitive to fertilizer. When treating them, re-duce the usual dosage by half.

Foliar-feed your shrubs for quick results. Liquid fertilizer sprayed onto the leaves is absorbed by plant tissues in minutes.

If your shrubs' yellowing leaves result from iron-poor soil, use an iron-mixture spray: 1 teaspoon chelated iron to 1 gallon water.

Water your rhododendrons, laurels, and hollies during midwinter thaws if the soil is dry. Because their broad evergreen leaves give off moisture, they need those extra showers even in winter.

PRUNING

Your maples, elms, dogwoods, birches, and yellowwoods won't "bleed" if you prune them in late summer or early fall.

For cleaner, faster healing cuts, use a bypass (hook-and-blade) pruner on branches.

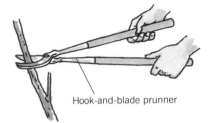

Hook-and-blade prunner

Prune trees in winter when they're dormant. Less trauma for them and no leaf-raking for you.

Prune forsythia and honeysuckle, as well as other spring-flowering shrubs, after they bloom; shrubs that flower in summer (rose of Sharon, for example) should be pruned when they're dormant.

PLANTING A YOUNG TREE

The best time to plant a young tree is on a cool, windless, and overcast day in early spring or early fall. You'll need a shovel, long-nose pliers, a hammer, a garden hose, two 6-foot wooden stakes, two 6- inch rubber buffers (from an old hose), 24 feet of heavy-gauge wire, and soil nutrients (those indicated by a soil test) plus peat moss or compost. Water the tree's root ball well before you begin the task.

Excavated soil

Planting hole

Burlapped root ball

Buffers

Wire

Stakes

"Dish"

1. Dig a hole that's roughly twice the diameter of your tree's root ball and 1½ times as deep. Crumble the soil you've dug up together with the peat moss or compost and the added nutrients. Make your mix 1 part additive, 2 parts soil.

2. Refill the hole until the tree can sit with its crown at the same level as the surrounding ground. Untie the ball's burlap casing. Roll down the casing carefully so that the soil ball remains intact. Finish refilling.

3. Tamp the soil around the tree into a dishlike depression. Fill it with water and let it soak in. Beyond the tree's roots, drive stakes 2 feet into the wet soil. Wrap the wired buffers around the trunk as you anchor the tree to the stakes. Leave some slack.

Avoid collar damage when pruning a damaged limb by stub-cutting it first and then sawing off the stub where the collar ends. This promotes quick healing and lessens the chance of decay.

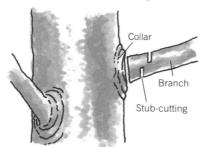

It's better to let tree cuts heal on their own rather than treat them with wound dressing. By keeping the wood damp, wound dressing encourages decay.

Don't give apple trees a heavy trimming in summer. If you cut off a lot of foliage, you expose their delicate bark to the hot sun, which can cause scorching.

PROTECTION FROM WILDLIFE

Protect your shrubs from hungry deer: Suspend nylon stockings stuffed with barbershop clippings, or Ivory soap wrapped in netting, from the shrubs' branches.

Deerproof shrubs or other plants by surrounding them with a trail of lion manure. Zoos give it away. Deer give it a wide berth.

Protect your saplings from rabbits and mice: Wrap their trunks with strips of fiberglass insulation.

CUTTING BACK AND RETRAINING OVERGROWN HEDGES

Some hedge plants, such as privet, yew, and boxwood, react well to drastic pruning. Cut them back to 6-inch stumps and they'll quickly sprout new growth. Forsythia, rugosa roses, and barberry also may regain vigor after you've cut back their old branches to ground level.

Such drastic pruning must be done in early spring and you must give the plants extra fertilizer and regular waterings.

Most hedge plants, however, require more gradual training and should be cut back in stages over a 3-year period. Here's how:

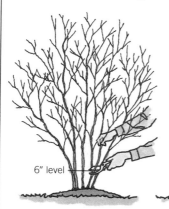

1. In early spring, reach in near the center of the shrub and cut back two or three of the oldest branches to 6-inch stumps.

2. The following spring, when you see new growth sprouting from these stumps, prune the other large branches.

3. During the third spring, cut back the youngest branches to reduce the hedge to the desired height and width.

Have squirrels been harvesting your apples and pears before you've had a chance to do the job? Puncture a hole in a dozen cheap aluminum pie plates; tie them singly with twine to the low branches of your fruit trees. The clanging will frighten the squirrels away.

Aluminum pie plates

LAWN PROBLEMS

If a soil test shows that your soil needs lime, apply it in early fall and thereafter no oftener than every 3 years. If you've already limed too much and your soil suffers from calcium excess, treat it with elemental sulphur: 5 pounds per 1,000 square feet.

If moles are tunneling your lawn, there are grubs in it. Treat the lawn with an insecticide (diazinon or chlorpyrifos) to rid it of grubs, and the moles will depart.

Patches of turf mysteriously torn up overnight? Quite likely the work of insect-seeking raccoons or skunks. A sprinkling of moth crystals may help to persuade them to dine elsewhere.

LAWN MAINTENANCE

Question: With all the different brands of turf fertilizer on the market, how can I choose the one that is best for my lawn?
Answer: Shop by formula, not by brand. The three numbers on the product's label—10-6-4, for example—stand for the percentages of major nutrients it contains—nitrogen, phosphorus, and potassium, in that order. The high nitrogen content of 10-6-4 (10 percent) makes this an ideal spring-feeding formula, one that encourages leaf growth. Switch to 5-10-5 in fall when the high phosphorus content (10 percent) benefits the roots.

Question: My neighbor spreads lime on his lawn every spring. Is that necessary?
Answer: Only if a soil test (p.205) shows that your lawn's pH needs adjusting. Too much lime encourages crabgrass.

Question: How can I tell when my lawn needs watering?
Answer: If your footprints stay on the lawn, it needs water. Well-watered turf springs back; dry grass doesn't.

Question: How often should I water my lawn, and how much water does it need?
Answer: In general, you should water twice a week, ½ inch of water each time; if the soil is sandy, ½ inch three times weekly. To gauge the amount, place measure-marked containers within the sprinkler's range.

Question: How often should I mow?
Answer: A weekly light mowing is good for most lawns. Never cut more than 40 percent of the leaf blades; a "butch haircut" weakens turf and causes browning.

Question: Is there any way to make leaf removal easier?
Answer: Rent an industrial-grade leaf blower. It will make a clean sweep in a short time. Or let gravity work for you: rake leaves down a slope. Bag them for disposal or run them through a shredder for mulch or compost.

Question: My turf fertilizer contains synthetic nitrogen. Is organic better?
Answer: Because organics release their nutrients more slowly, their benefits last longer than those of synthetics.

Moss on your lawn may result from poor drainage and compacted soil. A cheap remedy is gypsum, spread at the rate of 40 pounds per 1,000 square feet.

If your lawn gets heavy traffic, you can increase its resilience by encouraging strong root growth. Apply superphosphate: 10 pounds per 100 square feet annually.

Accumulations of leaves left on the lawn will smother the grass. Rake them away promptly before they form a blanket.

CUTTING THE GRASS

If grass tips turn white after you've mowed, your mower blades probably need to be sharpened. Rotary blades should be honed monthly, reel types annually.

Swiftly turning mower-blade tips can turn sticks and stones into dangerous missiles. Use a rear-mounted grass-collection system to prevent accidents caused by flying objects.

Wear "spiker shoes" (available at most garden centers) when mowing to help loosen and aerate compacted soil. Or if you prefer, aerate later with a rented hand-push or power lawn aerator.

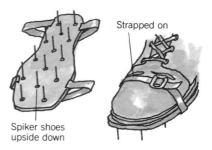

Strapped on

Spiker shoes upside down

GETTING RID OF LAWN WEEDS

Know your enemy well! Accurate identification is the key to weed control; different weed types need different treatments.

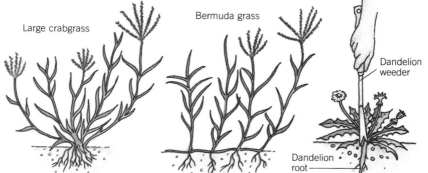

Large crabgrass

Bermuda grass

Dandelion weeder

Dandelion root

Annual weeds. In spring, crabgrass and other annual weed grasses sprout. As they grow, they tend to crowd out the turf grasses. About the time forsythia blossoms, you can eliminate the annual weed grasses with a pre-emergent herbicide such as benefin, bensulide, DCPA, pendimethalin, and siduron. Except for siduron, however, these chemicals also inhibit germination of desirable grasses for about 2 months.

Perennial weeds. Grasses that are heat and drought tolerant, such as zoysia and Bermuda grass, are turf grasses in the South. In the North, where bluegrasses and fescues predominate, they're considered weeds. Preemergents won't control perennial weed grasses. Instead, spray isolated clumps with glyphosphate. For widespread infestations, kill the entire lawn with glyphosphate, then reseed.

Broadleaf weeds. You can uproot some of these perennials (plantain and other fibrous-root species) with a trowel; tap-rooted species must be levered out with a dandelion weeder. Certain weeds with tenacious roots (knotweed, chickweed) are easier to eliminate by treating them with 2,4-D or some other chemical in spring or fall. Check with your local Cooperative Extension Service on such treatments.

Tractor wheels won't compact the soil if you vary your mowing pattern weekly.

When mowing without a grass-catcher, mow inward and counterclockwise from the lawn's outer perimeter. Clippings won't pile up on uncut turf and clog your mower; they'll be blown outward.

Prevent houseflies from breeding in grass clippings matted on mower parts. Wash the clippings off before putting your mower away.

PATCHING OR STARTING A LAWN

Renovate your lawn in late summer-early fall. However, if you live in the Southwest, renovate in early spring-late summer (warm season grasses) and early fall (cool season grasses).

Embarrassed by bare patches on your lawn? Reseed them during late winter thaws. As the soil thaws and refreezes, it crumbles into a ready-made seedbed.

Buy only "certified" grass seed. This label means that the container has been state inspected for purity and quality. Certified grass seed also contains less weed seed than non-certified types.

Be sure to specify "fertile loam" when buying topsoil to supplement existing soil; if you say just "topsoil," you may wind up with a poor, worthless soil.

When spreading seed or fertilizer, ensure even coverage by working in a crisscross pattern. Spread one half moving from north to south; the other half from east to west.

Lightly rake the soil to bury grass seed for germination. Or drag the bottom end of a chain link fence section across the seeded patch.

Salt hay makes an ideal light mulch for newly seeded lawns. Available at most garden centers, it's cheap and free of weed seeds, and it decomposes rapidly.

To keep seed from being washed off a steep slope, peg cheesecloth over it. Grass will grow right through the porous cloth, which can be removed later.

Water a newly sown seedbed daily (twice a day when the weather is sunny or windy). Keep the soil moist but not flooded.

When rototilling for a new lawn, break up clods that are larger than golf balls, but don't reduce the soil to powder—powder eliminates the surface crevices where seeds find shelter from the drying wind and sun.

IMPROVING GARDEN SOIL

Leave healthy topsoil alone. Tilling or spading yearly only destroys soil structure and curbs fertility. If you want to give your soil extra enrichment, use an organic mulch; it not only controls weeds, it breaks down into humus.

Coffee grounds are good for your garden. Sprinkle them around melons and carrots, for instance. As they decompose, they supply the soil with nutrients.

You can still grow flowers and vegetables even if your soil turns out to be infertile, stony, and poorly drained. Solve the problem by building framed raised beds and filling them with enriched soil. See the box on the next page.

A cheap and nutritious mulch for your flower beds? Try autumn leaves. Run your power mower over them to chop them up.

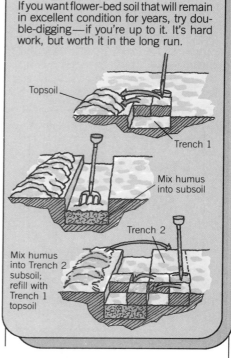

DOUBLE-DIGGING

If you want flower-bed soil that will remain in excellent condition for years, try double-digging—if you're up to it. It's hard work, but worth it in the long run.

Topsoil

Trench 1

Mix humus into subsoil

Trench 2

Mix humus into Trench 2 subsoil; refill with Trench 1 topsoil

COMPOSTING THE EASY WAY

Choose an isolated corner of your yard—a partially shady, sunny, well-drained, slightly sloping spot—for your compost heap. You can build or buy a compost bin of wire mesh or wooden slats (one side removable) or leave your compost pile freestanding. In hot weather, compost may be garden-ready in roughly 6 weeks.

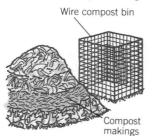

Wire compost bin

Compost makings

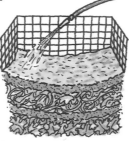

Garden-ready compost

1. Pile compost makings near the bin: dead leaves, grass clippings, weeds, and such kitchen waste as coffee grounds and fruit and vegetable peelings (no cooked foods or fat).

2. Stack the mixture in the bin in concave layers 5 to 10 inches deep. Wet each layer thoroughly, sprinkle the makings with several shovels of 10-10-10 fertilizer or horse manure, and add 2 inches of rich garden soil.

3. Turn the pile with a fork every other week (or be lazy and don't, if you can wait a year for results). Keep the pile wet. When the compost pile becomes crumbly brown, it's garden-ready.

PLANNING AND PLANTING FLOWER BEDS

Keep your flower border to a reasonable width—5 to 6 feet is the best. Arrange to have a narrow path at the back of the bed to make weeding easier.

For a beautiful, stronger display, plant flowers in groups of at least three of the same type and color. Larger groupings or drifts are even more dramatic.

If you have a shady garden, think of it as a challenge instead of a limitation. Many beautiful flowering plants can tolerate shade in partial or full doses: coralbells, meadow rue, goatsbeard, lady's-mantle, and solomon's seal are just a few.

BULBS

Plant bulbs at a depth two and a half times their diameter. A daffodil bulb with a diameter of 3 inches should be planted roughly 7½ inches deep.

If deer are a problem in your area, plant daffodils and forget about tulips. Deer relish tulip flowers but won't touch daffodils.

Fertilize your tulips with a commercial bulb food in early spring before their tips appear. Spread it over the bed, rake it lightly into the soil, and let spring showers take care of the rest.

Do you want your spring bulbs to have bigger, longer-lasting blossoms? Save the potash-rich wood ashes from your stove or fireplace and sprinkle them over the soil at the start of the growing season. Wood ashes increase soil acidity.

BUILDING A RAISED BED

Raised beds provide many advantages, such as warmer planting soil, reduced weeding, and minimal soil erosion; they're attractive looking structures too.

You can build an 8- by 12-foot, two-tier, raised bed in a few days. You'll need 10 used 8-foot railroad ties (two sawn in half), 12 3-foot, ⅜-inch reinforcing bars (rebars), a dozen 12-inch galvanized spikes, a shovel, and a 6-pound mallet. If you want a raised bed higher than 3 feet, check local building codes to see if it's allowed.

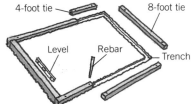

1. Choose a site, then lay the first tier (four 8-footers and two halves) in an 8- by 12-foot rectangle; where the ends meet, leave space for drainage. Mark the tier's outline with a shovel blade; then remove the ties and dig out a level trench 2 inches deep. About 6 inches from the ends of each tie drill a ¾-inch hole.

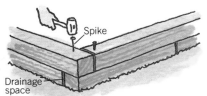

2. Reposition the ties in the trench, check them with a level, then nail them to the ground with the rebars. Position the second-level ties so that they overlap the ends of those beneath; this strengthens the frame. Spike the two levels together.

3. Fill the frame with organic materials, such as crop and kitchen waste, leaves, and wood chips; mix them with topsoil and fresh manure. Cover with black polyethylene sheeting and let the mixture decompose during the winter. Next spring, your raised bed will be ready for planting.

Some gardeners gather ripening bulb foliage into bunches, bend them over, and put a rubber band around each bunch. Then they interplant with annuals, which soon grow and hide the foliage.

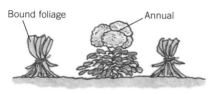

Bound foliage — Annual

Allow bulb foliage on your lawn to die back before you mow. It's a source of nourishment for next year's flowers.

PROPAGATING BULBS

Increasing hyacinths is easy. In early summer, as their leaves die back, dig up the bulbs. Quarter them lengthwise and then dip them in a powdered fungicide

(captan or sulphur). Seal the quartered bulbs in a plastic bag with moist vermiculite. Store the bag in a light but not sunny place at 70° F until the bulbs root (it takes several months). Plant them in potting mixture and then transplant them outdoors in the fall.

If you want more daffodils and grape hyacinths, simply make use of their bulblets. In early summer, when the foliage is brown, excavate the bulbs, pry off the bulblets, and then replant them all. It'll be 1 to 2 years before grape hyacinths produce blooms; 2 to 3 years for daffodils.

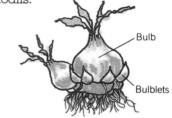

Bulb

Bulblets

TRANSPLANTING SEEDLINGS

Before transplanting seedlings outdoors, ready them for the change: Place their flats in a cold frame for 2 weeks or outside in the sun for 1 week, gradually increasing the daily dose. Transplant them when all danger of frost is past and the soil is warm. Perform this task on a cloudy day or a windless afternoon or evening.

Compost

Cardboard strip

1. With a trowel dig a furrow or individual holes deep enough to accommodate the seedlings at the same level at which they've been growing. Mix compost with the soil at the bottom, or work in 1 teaspoon 5-10-10 fertilizer (per seedling) in the holes or furrow and cover with 2 inches of soil to prevent contact with seedlings' roots. Fill with water and let it soak in.

2. Water the flats well a day before you transplant. Carefully work your trowel into the soil under a row of seedlings; use your hand for added support as you lift them out of the flat. Gently separate the seedlings, keeping the soil-covered roots intact as much as possible.

3. Wrap a 2-inch strip of cardboard or tarpaper around the stem of each vegetable seedling to protect it from cutworms; better still, collar it with a bottomless styrofoam cup. Place seedlings in the furrow or holes; fill in and firm soil around each stem. Half of the collar should be visible. Water generously; keep moist until seedlings are well established and show signs of growth.

When forcing crocus or hyacinth bulbs, add charcoal to the water to avoid unsightly algae growth.

Don't waste time (and garden space) planting bulbs that were forced indoors for winter bloom. They'll never bloom again.

CHOOSING ROSES

For free advice on planning or planting a rose garden, write to the American Rose Society, P.O. Box 30,000, Shreveport LA, 71130. It'll put you in touch with expert rose growers in your area.

Price isn't always a guide to rose quality. No. 1 roses (the finest) usually cost more than Nos. ½ and 2. But tried-and-true classics (more plentiful) are often cheaper than the latest prize winners.

If you want roses that are hardier and longer-lived than common grafted roses, purchase "own-root roses"—bushes grown from cuttings. They're worth the extra cost in terms of strength and longevity.

If you live in the Deep South or Gulf states, hybrid tea roses may not be a good choice for your garden; they have low tolerance for extreme heat and humidity. Instead, plant old-fashioned tea roses, Chinas, and noisettes—living antique types that thrive in sultry weather.

Rugged rugosa roses are an ideal choice for northern or seaside plantings. These attractive shrubs will survive salt spray, prolonged drought, and temperatures as low as -20° F. They grow into dense hedges which, like all hedges, must be controlled periodically by pruning.

Climbing roses make a beautiful ground cover. Just peg their canes to the ground with wire hoops—a good way to beautify banks.

HOW TO CONTROL AND INCREASE YOUR PERENNIALS

Many perennials grow outward, dying at the center. This can give your flower bed or border a ragged, unhealthy appearance. If you have overgrown perennials, rejuvenate them by dividing each one into two or three plants. Water them first, then dig them up and divide them a couple of days later. Although most perennials can be divided in either spring or fall, there are exceptions, such as peonies (fall) and chrysanthemums and shasta daisies (spring).

Spading fork

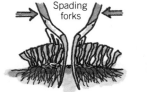

Spading forks

Replanted clump

1. Cut your perennials back to a height of 6 inches so that you can easily choose those that need dividing. After you've selected one, dig out the entire clump, being careful to keep the roots as intact as possible.

2. Take two spading forks and insert them back-to-back into the clump. Press their handles together and pry the plant apart slowly. If it has a dead center, divide the living portion into smaller clumps for replanting.

3. Enrich the soil in the hole with humus and a nitrogen-free fertilizer such as 0-10-10. Replant one clump in the old hole and the others elsewhere in the flower bed or border.

ROSE CLASSES: THEIR CARE AND CHARACTERISTICS

Feed your roses a balanced fertilizer (5-10-5) or prepared rose food in spring when the buds swell; when one blooming period ends (to encourage another); and in mid-to-late August for a fall flowering. Roses should not be fed during the first year after planting.

The majority of roses fall into one of the following classes:

Hybrid tea rose. They bloom continuously from late spring until frost and display large, bright, double flowers (usually one per stem) with conical centers. If you live in the North, cut their canes back in the early spring—12 to 14 inches; 18 to 24 inches in the South. Elegant-stemmed, they make ideal cut roses.

Old garden rose. This broad class includes such southern types as the China, tea, and noisette roses; northern, winter-hardy types such as hybrid perpetuals, bourbons, and gallicas, and any rose introduced before the hybrid tea's first appearance (1864). The southern types require relatively little pruning or spraying. Northern types benefit from spring pruning of no more than one third of each cane and another similar pruning after the first flush of flowers.

Floribunda. They bloom heavily throughout the growing season, displaying clusters of saucer-shaped flowers. Although hardier and more disease resistant than hybrid teas, they require the same treatment. They make an excellent flowering hedge.

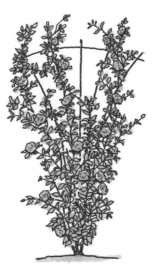

Grandiflora. These tall, stately bushes bloom much like floribundas, combining that class's free-flowering, hardy habits with the blossoms of the hybrid tea. They require the same care as the hybrid tea.

Climber. This catchall class includes ever-bloomers and once-blooming roses. Carefully prune everblooming varieties in early spring: Remove dead and diseased matter; retain new canes. When blossoms fade, encourage new flower growth by cutting back the side branches ¼ inch above the second set of five-leaflet leaves. Prune ramblers and other once-blooming types after flowering; remove dead canes.

MAINTAINING ROSES

When pruning roses, start by removing the three D's: dead, damaged, and diseased wood. Finish by getting rid of all crossing and weak branches.

If your roses' leaves develop sooty spots and fall off prematurely, the bush is probably suffering from black spot, a fungus disease. Spray with dodine or mancozeb, following label directions.

Would you like your hybrid tea roses to bear larger flowers? With your fingertips, carefully nip off the tiny side buds below the central terminal bud.

VEGETABLES AND FRUITS

Lick weed problems before starting a new garden: Plant buckwheat in the spring. Thick growing, it smothers weeds and adds humus to the soil. Be sure to turn this crop under before it sets seed.

Radishes can serve several purposes when you sow them along with slow starters such as carrots. Quick sprouters, they make good row markers; they also loosen the soil as they push up and as you harvest them.

If you're saddled with a space problem in your yard, consider planting dwarf fruit trees. Many bear fruit earlier than standard varieties, and you'll never need a ladder to prune, spray, or harvest.

INCREASING CROPS

Make the most of your garden space by planting lettuce seedlings between slow-maturing vegetables (broccoli, cabbage).

You can increase the productivity of a small garden by planting fruits and vegetables among flowers. Strawberries, parsley, and chives make neat borders; carrot and asparagus fronds are attractive among perennials.

PLANTING BARE-ROOT ROSES

You can order bare-root roses by mail or buy them from a local nursery. You should plant them only in early spring or late fall, depending on your climate zone. Reliable suppliers will schedule their delivery to arrive at the correct planting time in your area.

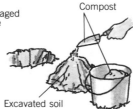

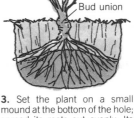

Damaged cane

Pruning shears

Compost

Excavated soil

Bud union

1. Unpack bare-root plants as soon as they arrive and immerse them — roots and stems — in a pail of water for 24 hours. Cut back broken roots and damaged canes before planting.

2. Dig a hole that will accommodate the roots without crowding. Add compost, peat moss, or well-rotted manure to the excavated soil, increasing the soil's volume one third.

3. Set the plant on a small mound at the bottom of the hole; spread its roots out evenly. Its bud union should be level with the surrounding bed. Fill the hole three-quarters full. Tamp the soil, then fill with water. After it drains, finish filling the hole.

217

Reap several harvests from your spinach, lettuce, and chard: Cut them back to 2 inches instead of uprooting the plant. They'll grow back again and again.

Harvest several cabbages from one plant. When spring-planted cabbages are somewhat larger than baseballs, cut them off, but leave four outer leaves on each stalk. In autumn, there'll be a small, delicious cabbage for each outer leaf.

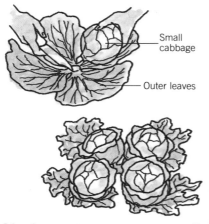

Small cabbage

Outer leaves

After harvesting your peas, cut off the plants for your compost heap and leave the roots in the ground; they're a rich source of nitrogen. Plant green beans several inches away from these roots so that they can benefit from them. Leave green bean roots in the ground after harvest; they're nitrogen-rich too. You can plant other crops in this area next season without using a nitrogen fertilizer.

ENCOURAGING GROWTH

Want a two-week head start on melons? Bottomless plastic milk jugs set over the seedlings make effective miniature greenhouses. On sunny days, remove the caps for ventilation.

Did you know that 6 to 7 pounds of human hair contain as much nitrogen as 200 pounds of manure? Get clippings from a local barbershop to enrich your compost heap.

MULCHES

Make your newspapers do double duty: use them for mulch after you've read them. A layer, several sheets thick and anchored with rocks, makes a cheap, water-conserving, biodegradable mulch. Avoid pages with colored ink; they may contain lead.

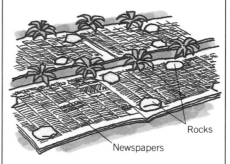

Rocks

Newspapers

Get earlier, heftier tomato crops by mulching with black plastic. An efficient solar collector, this material warms the soil and increases yields. To achieve even greater growth, set bottomless, 22-ounce containers (large soda pop or milk shake) around tomato transplants. These waxed cardboard chimneys vent the plastic's heat up around the plants.

While your watermelons grow, their vines can act as a living mulch around root crops such as onions, carrots, and beets. Plant root crops in rows 8 feet apart, with hills of watermelons running down the center.

When preparing your strawberry garden for winter, apply mulch only after the ground freezes. If you do it before, the mulch might stimulate root growth and jeopardize the plants when sub-zero temperatures do arrive.

CHOOSING MULCHES

Mulches protect and improve the soil they cover by conserving moisture, keeping soil temperature uniform, and reducing weed problems. Many kinds of materials, each with advantages and drawbacks, make good mulches.

Organic mulches. These include such materials as buckwheat, ground corncobs, cocoa-bean hulls, grass clippings, old hay, shredded leaves, pine needles, and shredded or chipped bark. Because many are agricultural by-products, they may be quite inexpensive locally. Organic mulches add humus and nutrients to the soil as they decompose. They also serve as insulation, keeping the soil cool in hot weather. Apply a 2- to 4-inch layer in midspring; turn over with a spading fork in late fall to evict over-wintering insects and rodents.

Inert mulches. Asphalt paper, crushed stone, pebbles, gravel chips, fiberglass insulation, black plastic film, and plastic fabric (spun-bonded polypropylene) are among the inert mulches. Because they don't decompose, they last longer than the organics but lack their soil-building qualities. Plastic mulches are especially effective at curbing weed growth and warming the soil to speed the growth of heat-loving crops such as peppers, tomatoes, and eggplant. Roll up and store plastic mulches during winter. None of the inert-mulch materials harbor insect and animal pests.

Double your yields of squash, cucumbers, and corn by using sheets of aluminum-foil mulch. The reflected light repels insects while enhancing plant growth.

Not all leaves are suitable for mulch. Acacia, walnut, eucalyptus, California bay, juniper, camphor, cypress, and pittosporum leaves release chemicals toxic to plants as they decompose. Oak leaves decompose very slowly.

Looking for cheap or free mulch sources? Check out what's available locally: spent mushroom compost, seaweed, and tobacco stems are all good.

DEALING WITH PESTS

Garlic is said to ward off aphids, snails, and caterpillars. Toss 3 garlic heads and 6 tablespoons mineral oil into a blender and mix until smooth. Let the mixture stand at room temperature for 48 hours; then add it to a solution of 1 pint hot water and 1 tablespoon oil-base soap. Pour into screw-top jars and refrigerate. Gardeners who concoct this brew claim that 2 tablespoons added to 4 pints of water makes a potent spray.

If you're tired of dealing with garden pests and disease-prone vegetables, plant a crop of kohlrabi. It's virtually pest- and disease-free, and if you plant this hardy vegetable in late summer, you can harvest even past frost.

Planting marigolds among your beans, spinach, tomatoes, and celery may help protect these vegetables from root nematodes and other insects. The roots of marigolds produce a chemical in the soil that kills nematodes.

Drape old sheer curtains over your fruit vines and berry bushes to frustrate hungry birds and other animals. The material won't harm plants or animals.

Are earwigs the cause of your young plants dying or vanishing overnight? Dampen newspaper, roll it into a tight cylinder, then place it near the scene of the crime. It should be full of earwigs the next morning when you unroll it. Burn it up or bag it well. Continue doing this until the morning the newspaper is empty.

Dampened newspaper

Earwig

Take careful note of signal words on the labels of pesticide containers; someone's life may depend on it. "Danger—Poison" means that even a taste may be a lethal dose; "Warning" tells you that as little as 1 teaspoon can be fatal; "Caution" indicates that 2 tablespoons is too much. Use only pesticides that have such labels.

Store all pesticides and pesticide equipment in a separate, well-ventilated, locked cabinet marked "Danger — Pesticides." This cabinet should be kept in an area that's free from excessive cold, moisture, and heat.

GARDEN TOOLS AND FURNITURE: CARE AND STORAGE

Use a reel-on-wheels to keep your garden hose unsnarled and transportable. Store it in the garage or shed. Vinyl hoses, in particular, should be sheltered from the sun's ultraviolet rays, which cause vinyl to deteriorate.

Is your hose leaking—spouting water from pin-sized holes? Seal them carefully with the glowing point of a heated ice pick.

Ice pick

If you have a sink in your potting shed, mount a hose reel on the wall next to it for ready connection. Run the hose from the door or window into the garden.

Be sure to sharpen your hoe on the right side—the inside edge—so that you can pull it through the ground with considerable ease.

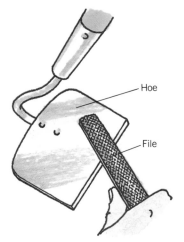

Hoe

File

RUST PREVENTION

Clean and lubricate your digging tools in a sand–motor oil mixture. Keep a tub of it (1 quart old motor oil to 40 pounds sand) in your tool shed. Just plunge the blades into the mix several times after use.

Protect the moving parts of gardening machinery, such as mower blades, and keep your tools rust- and corrosion-free with moisture-displacing spray lubricants such as WD-40, LPS-1, and CRC.

Stubborn rust on your tools? Rub them with a soap-filled steel wool pad dipped in kerosene or turpentine. Finish them off with a brisk rub on wadded aluminum foil.

STORAGE SOLUTIONS

Time to put away lightweight, fold-up patio furniture and your basement is cluttered? Make use of the joists. Equip them with ¾-inch dowels inserted and glued in predrilled holes. Hang your furniture on the dowels.

Need more space for tool storage? Hang them on the exterior walls of your shed if there's an overhanging roof. Protect your tools' metal parts with taped plastic sheeting.

Store your long-handled gardening tools on hooks on the wall instead of leaning them against the wall. They'll take less space, be easier to select, and you won't trip over them.

Garage rafter space shouldn't be overlooked. It's ideal for storing tools and outdoor furniture.

A hinged deck bench is a convenient place to store gardening and cleaning supplies and tools or outdoor furniture cushions.

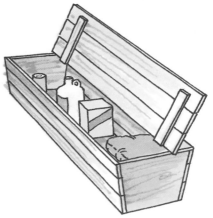

CLEANING JOBS

Are the aluminum parts of your patio furniture looking worn and dingy? Spruce them up with a detergent-and-water scrub. Wipe dry with a soft absorbent cloth, then weatherproof the parts with a coat of car wax.

Scrub mildew from your wooden patio furniture with a solution made of 1 cup ammonia, ½ cup vinegar, ¼ cup baking soda, and 1 gallon water. Wipe it off with an absorbent cloth. When the furniture is completely dry, coat each piece with mildew-resistant paint, available at hardware stores. If the wood is unpainted, coat it with a latex primer. Make sure it dries thoroughly before you treat it with mildew-resistant paint.

Index

225

Acknowledgments

Acropolis Books Ltd. PARENT TRICKS-OF-THE-TRADE by Kathleen Touw and illustrated by Loel Barr, copyright © 1981 by Acropolis Books Ltd. COLOR ME BEAUTIFUL by Carole Jackson, copyright © 1980 by Acropolis Books Ltd. Reprinted by permission. *Addison-Wesley Publishing Company* TAKE CARE OF YOURSELF by D.M. Vickery & J.F. Fries, copyright © 1985 Addison-Wesley Publishing Company. Reprinted by permission. *American Apparel Manufacturers Association* CONSUMER CARE GUIDE FOR APPAREL. Reprinted by permission. *Arbor House Publishing Co.* HINTS FROM HELOISE, copyright © 1980 by King Features Syndicate, Inc. HELOISE'S BEAUTY BOOK, copyright © 1985 by King Features Syndicate, Inc. Reprinted by permission. *Atheneum Publishers, Inc.* FEAST WITHOUT FUSS by Pamela Harlech, copyright © 1977 by Pamela Harlech. Reprinted by permission. *Avon Books* SEW SUCCESSFUL by Claire B. Shaeffer, copyright © 1984 by Claire B. Shaeffer. Reprinted by permission of Dominick Abel Literary Agency. *Charles C. Thomas, Publisher* SUBURBAN BURGLARY by George Rengart & John Wasilchick, copyright © 1985 by Charles C. Thomas, Publisher. Reprinted by permission. *Chronicle Books* CUTTING-UP IN THE KITCHEN by Merle Ellis, copyright © 1975 by Merle Ellis. Reprinted by permission. *Church & Dwight Co., Inc.* ARM & HAMMER BAKING SODA GREAT IDEAS CLINIC. ARM & HAMMER is a trademark of Church & Dwight Co., Inc. Reprinted by permission. *Coats & Clark Inc.* BUTTONS, SNAPS, HOOKS AND EYES, copyright © 1983 by Coats & Clark Inc. MENDING, copyright © 1978 by Coats & Clark Inc. Reprinted by permission. *The Countryman Press* HOMEOWNER'S GUIDE TO LANDSCAPE DESIGN by Timothy Michel, copyright © 1983 by The Countryman Press. Reprinted by permission. *Crown Publishers, Inc.* CRIME STOPPERS by Wesley Cox, copyright © 1983 by Wesley Cox. Reprinted by permission. *Dell Publishing Co., Inc.* SMART SHOPPING WITH COUPONS & REFUNDS by Bonnie Storch Kupris, copyright © 1980 by Bonnie Storch Kupris. CATS: BREEDS, CARE, AND BEHAVIOR by Shirlee A. Kalstone, copyright © 1983 by Shirlee A. Kalstone, Dell Publishing Co., Inc. and Sanford Greenburger Associates Inc. TIPS FOR TODDLERS by Brooke McKamy Beebe, copyright © 1983 by Brooke McKamy Beebe. Reprinted by permission. *Dodd, Mead & Company, Inc.* EVERYTHING YOU WANTED TO KNOW ABOUT COSMETICS by Toni Stabile, copyright © 1984 by Toni Stabile. Reprinted by permission of Dodd, Mead & Company, Inc., and Toni Stabile. *Dorling Kindersley Ltd.* COLOR RIGHT DRESS RIGHT by Liz E. London and Anne H. Adams, copyright © 1985 by Dorling Kindersley Ltd, London, text copyright © 1985 by Liz E. London and Anne H. Adams. Reprinted by permission of Liz E. London and Anne H. Adams. *Doubleday & Co., Inc.* TRAINING YOU TO TRAIN YOUR DOG by Blanche Saunders, copyright © 1946 by United Specialists, Inc. MARY ELLEN PINKHAM'S 1000 NEW HELPFUL HINTS, copyright © 1983 by Mary Ellen Pinkham. SYLVIA PORTER'S NEW MONEY BOOK FOR THE 80's, copyright © 1975, 1979 by Sylvia Porter. THE AMY VANDERBILT COMPLETE BOOK OF ETIQUETTE: A GUIDE TO CONTEMPORARY LIVING. Revised and expanded by Letitia Baldridge, copyright © 1978 by Curtis B. Kellar and Lincoln G. Clark, Executors of the Estate of Amy Vanderbilt Kellar and Doubleday & Company, Inc. THE FURNITURE DOCTOR by George Grotz, copyright © 1962 by George Grotz. THE INDOOR CAT by Patricia Curtis, copyright © 1981 by Patricia Curtis. Reprinted by permission. *E.P. Dutton Company, Inc.* TIME MANAGEMENT MADE EASY by Peter A. Turla and Kathleen L. Hawkins, copyright © 1984 by Peter A. Turla and Kathleen L. Hawkins. Reprinted by permission. *The East Woods Press* INTERIOR FINISH AND CARPENTRY: SOME TRICKS OF THE TRADE, by Bob Syvanen, copyright © 1982 by Bob Syvanen. Reprinted by permission. *Encyclopaedia Britannica, Inc.* 1980 MEDICAL AND HEALTH ANNUAL, copyright © 1979 by Encyclopaedia Britannica, Inc. Reprinted by permission. *Facts on File Publications* HELPFUL HINTS FOR BETTER LIVING by Hap Hatton and Laura Torber, copyright © 1984 by Hap Hatton and Laura Torber. Reprinted by permission. *Gaines Foods, Inc.* FEEDING YOUR DOG RIGHT, copyright © 1982 by General Foods Corporation. Reprinted by permission. *Globe Mini Mag* SEWING TRICKS, copyright © 1984 by Globe Mini Mag. Reprinted by permission of Globe Mini Mag and Deutsch, Levy & Engel. *Harcourt Brace Jovanovich, Inc.* THE I HATE TO HOUSEKEEP BOOK by Peg Bracken, copyright © 1962 by Peg Bracken. Reprinted by permission. *Harper & Row, Publishers, Inc.* THE AIDA GREY BEAUTY BOOK by Aida Grey and Kathie Gordon, copyright © 1979 by Aida Grey and Kathie Gordon. Reprinted by permission. *Henry Holt and Company, Inc.* KITCHEN WISDOM by Frieda Arkin, copyright © 1977 by Frieda Arkin. Reprinted by permission of Henry Holt and Company, and Severn House Publishers Ltd. MORE KITCHEN WISDOM, by Frieda Arkin, copyright © 1982 by Frieda Arkin. Reprinted by permission of Henry Holt and Company. *Holt, Rinehart and Winston* PERSONAL & FAMILY SAFETY & CRIME PREVENTION by Nancy Z. Olson, copyright © 1980 by Preventive Medicine Institute/Strang Clinic. Reprinted by permission. *Home Magazine Ltd.*, May, 1983 issue. Reprinted by permission. *Houghton Mifflin Company* TAYLOR'S ENCYCLOPEDIA OF GARDENING, copyright © 1961 by Norman Taylor. Reprinted by permission. *Jonathan David Publishers, Inc.* THE HOUSEHOLD BOOK OF HINTS AND TIPS by Diane Raintree, copyright © 1979 by Jonathan David Publishers, Inc. Reprinted by permission. *Little, Brown and Company* MARSHALL LOEB'S 1986 MONEY GUIDE, copyright © 1985 by Marshall Loeb Enterprises, Inc. FAST AND LOW by Joan Stillman, copyright © 1985 by Joan Stillman. Reprinted by permission. *Macmillan Publishing Company* THE PRUNING MANUAL, Based on THE PRUNING MANUAL by L.H. Bailey by E.P. Christopher, copyright © 1954, 1982 by E.P. Christopher. TREES FOR AMERICAN GARDENS by Donald Wyman, copyright © 1965 by Donald Wyman. SHRUBS AND VINES FOR AMERICAN GARDENS, copyright © 1949 by Donald Wyman. THE GOOD DOG BOOK by Mordecai Seigal, copyright © 1977 by Mordecai Siegal. HOWARD HILLMAN'S KITCHEN SECRETS by Howard Hillman, copyright © 1985 by Howard Hillman. Reprinted by permission. UPHOLSTERING by James E. Brumbough, copyright © 1986 by Macmillan Publishing Co. *The Maytag Company* MAYTAG GAS COOKING APPLIANCE SERVICE MANUAL, MAYTAG ELECTRIC COOKING PRODUCTS SERVICE MANUAL, copyright © 1982 by The Maytag Company. MAYTAG ENCYCLOPEDIA OF HOME LAUNDRY, copyright © 1973 by The Maytag Company. Reprinted by permission. *McGraw-Hill Book Company* THE MEAT BOARD MEAT BOOK by Barbara Bloch, copyright © 1977 by National Live Stock & Meat Board and The Benjamin Company, Inc. Reprinted by permission of The Benjamin Company, Inc. HOW TO RESTORE AND REPAIR PRACTICALLY EVERYTHING by Lorraine Johnson, copyright © 1984 by Lorraine Johnson. Reprinted by permission. *William Morrow & Company, Inc.* 20001 HINTS FOR WORKING MOTHERS by Gloria Gilbert Mayer, copyright © 1983 by Gloria Gilbert Mayer. Reprinted by permission. *Necessary Trading Company.* NECESSARY CATALOGUE, Volume 3, copyright © 1983 by Necessary Trading Company. Reprinted by permission. *Nitty Gritty Productions* HOUSEHOLD HINTS by Anna Cope, copyright © 1980 by Nitty Gritty Productions. Reprinted by permission. *101 Productions* WORKING FAMILY'S GUIDE by Sheila Kennedy and Susan Seidman, copyright © 1980 by Sheila Kennedy and Susan Seidman. Reprinted by permission. *Orbis Book Publishing Corporation Ltd.* THE CAT CARE QUESTION AND ANSWER BOOK, copyright © 1981 by Orbis Publishing Corporation Ltd. *Oxmoor House* HOME PAINT BOOK by Richard V. Nunn, copyright © 1975 by Oxmoor House ®. Reproduced by permission. *Penguin Books Ltd.* THE NATIONAL TRUST MANUAL OF HOUSEKEEPING by Hermione Sandwith and Sheila Stainton (Allen Lane in association with the National Trust, 1984), copyright © 1984 by The National Trust. *Prentice-Hall, Inc.* BUILT-INS, STORAGE AND SPACEMAKING by Allen D. Bragdon, copyright © 1983 by Allen D. Bragdon. CARING FOR YOUR AGING PARENTS by Robert R. Cadmus, M.D., copyright © 1984 by Prentice-Hall, Inc. SUPER HANDYMAN'S ENCYCLOPEDIA OF HOME REPAIR HINTS by Al Carrell, copyright © 1971 by King Features Syndicate, Inc. LOOKING AFTER YOUR DOG by John and Mary Holmes, copyright © 1981 by John and Mary Holmes. SPEED SEWING by Janice S. Saunders, copyright © 1982 by Van Nostrand Reinhold Company, Inc. Reprinted by permission. *The Putnam Publishing Group* A BASIC GUIDE TO DOG TRAINING AND OBEDIENCE by Margaret English, copyright © 1979 by Margaret English. ABOUT FACE by Jeffery Bruce & Sherry Suib Cohen, copyright © 1984 by Jeffrey Bruce and Sherry Suib Cohen. ALWAYS BEAUTIFUL by Kaylan Pickford, copyright © 1985 by Kaylan Pickford. ADRIENNE ARPEL'S 851 FAST BEAUTY FIXES AND FACTS by Adrienne Arpel with Ronnie Sue Ebenstein, copyright © 1985 by Adrienne Newman and